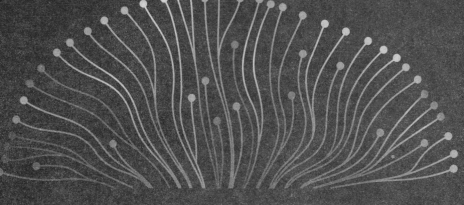

FIRE UP YOUR WRITING BRAIN

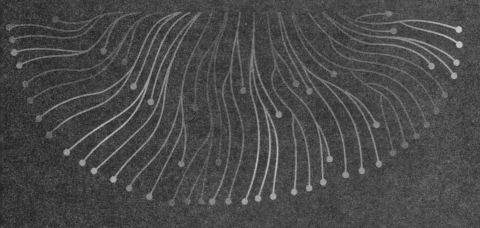

WRITER'S DIGEST
BOOKS

WritersDigest.com
Cincinnati, Ohio

For more resources for writers, visit www.writersdigest.com.

19 18 17 16   5 4 3

Distributed in Canada by Fraser Direct
100 Armstrong Avenue
Georgetown, Ontario, Canada L7G 5S4
Tel: (905) 877-4411

Distributed in the U.K. and Europe by F+W Media International
Brunel House, Newton Abbot, Devon, TQ12 4PU, England
Tel: (+44) 1626-323200, Fax: (+44) 1626-323319
E-mail: postmaster@davidandcharles.co.uk

Distributed in Australia by Capricorn Link
P.O. Box 704, Windsor, NSW 2756 Australia
Tel: (02) 4577-3555, Fax: (02) 4577-5288
E-mail: books@capricornlink.com.au

ISBN-13: 978-1-59963-914-7

Edited by Cris Freese
Designed by Alexis Brown
Production coordinated by Debbie Thomas

DEDICATION

I dedicate this book, as I do every book I write, to my children, Brooke and Brett Aved, because they are my *raison d étre* and the inspiration for me expending vast amounts of energy and focus on writing—and they taught me a lot about life, passion, commitment, and growth. Thank you, my beloveds!

ACKNOWLEDGMENTS

My eternal gratitude goes to Paula Munier, who has also been an inspiration and a dear friend for more than thirty years. Thank you to *Writer's Digest* publisher Phil Sexton and his team, particularly Cris Freese who helped shape the work as my editor, but also to everyone behind the scenes, from the interior design, cover design, and sales—our mutual pursuit of originality, creativity, and practicality made the book what it is—and I *appreciate* what you do. Thanks to my online scribe tribe—Indi Zeleny, John K. Waters, Mardeene Mitchell, Meera Lester, and Paula Munier—whose input is priceless, and also to my editing clients who entrust me with their work. I also thank my brothers, Jim and Roy Reynolds, my sister Rozanne Reynolds, and all my nieces and nephews who have long shared my personal journey and continue to inspire me. A huge thanks to Teresa Aubele-Futch, the brilliant neuroscientist who co-authored *Train Your Brain to Get Happy* and *Train Your Brain to Get Rich* with me, and offered her expertise on this book, as well. And, last, but never least, thank you Jan Berry-Kadrie, for opening my eyes to possibility and encouraging me to claim my talent, my ambition, and my passion for writing.

ABOUT THE AUTHOR

Susan Reynolds has authored or edited more than forty-five nonfiction and fiction books. Recently, she co-authored *Train Your Brain to Get Happy*, *Train Your Brain to Get Rich*, *Healthiest You Ever*, and *Meditation for Moms*. She has also authored *Everything Enneagram*, and was the creator and editor of Adams Media's My Hero series, which includes *My Teacher Is My Hero* (2008), *My Mom Is My Hero* (2009), *My Dad Is My Hero* (2009), and *My Dog Is My Hero* (2010). She also edited *Woodstock Revisited, 50 far out, groovy, peace-inducing, flashback-inducing stories from those who were there* (2009). Ms. Reynolds has a B.A. in Psychology and has often written about psychological concepts, including a blog for Psychologytoday.com. In pursuit of her own happiness, Ms. Reynolds uprooted her life and spent a year in Paris, reinventing herself and her career trajectory. Upon return, she founded Literary Cottage, a literary consulting firm based in Boston, through which she edits and coaches other writers in pursuit of happiness through publishing. She is also currently editor of *GRAND Magazine*, and serves as a judge for *Writer's Digest*'s annual writing contests.

INTRODUCTION

At this very moment, some forty thousand neuroscientists around the world are focused on understanding the miraculous functions our brain performs—one of which is the ability to achieve writing genius. In the last decade, these scientists confirmed that our brains continue to evolve, grow, and change throughout our lifetimes—provided we offer stimulation, specialized training, and rewards to motivate it.

Neuroscientists call this ability to change "plasticity" and the ability to generate, regenerate, and reassign existing neurons "neurogenesis." The way that our brains perform is literally mind-boggling: You have the world's greatest supercomputer, with over 20 *billion* brain cells (neurons) and the possibility of forming 100 *trillion* synapses (neuronal connections) at your disposal. And here's the kicker: In many cases, the types of connections that form are *up to you*—they are guided by your experiences, your decisions, and your desires. If you program your brain mindfully and support it in its quest to fulfill your chosen pursuit, your brain will happily aid you in becoming more creative, more productive, and more successful—in whatever form of writing you pursue.

In *Fire Up Your Writing Brain*, we will begin by discussing aspects of neuroscience related to creativity and writing, designed to bring your full consciousness—and appreciation—to the vast possibility your brain offers. We move briskly through these basics, and then spend the next eleven chapters discussing specific ways you can protect, nurture, stimulate, program, and reward your brain to generate and maximize its inherent writing genius.

You'll learn:

- how to identify, reinforce, and maximize what attracted your brain to writing

- if you're a "top brain" or "bottom brain" writer, and why it matters
- how to prepare, program, and tap into your brain's "vast neuronal forest" to achieve writing genius
- how to fire up a lagging brain and propel it into overdrive when you need it
- how to build cognitive templates that accelerate your learning curve
- specific, step-by-step strategies for brainstorming brilliant story, character, and plot ideas—from beginning to end
- how to use *metacognition* and *global ignition* to boost creativity and perfect your craft
- how to hardwire your brain for endurance and increased productivity—even while you're sleeping
- how to conquer cognitive inertia and train your brain to "go with the flow"
- how to conceive, create, and craft your work for maximum success

Throughout the book, each chapter includes specific ways to *fire up your writing brain*, as well as a Train Your Writing Brain exercise (specific writing, cognitive, and creative exercises) designed to expand your creativity, and program and support your brain in becoming a fantastic storyteller. Although most references are to novel writing, the same principles apply for all storytelling—whether it's a memoir, play, screenplay, poem, or song.

To accommodate your writing process, we address "the beginning," "the middle," and "the end" stages of writing and crafting your story, in a way that mirrors the natural structure and progression of storytelling—*which your brain will appreciate!*

Throughout, you'll learn concrete and applicable strategies for engaging your brain's writing genius in conceiving, creating, and crafting written work that will boost your creativity, productivity, and success. So, let's get this journey underway—your talented and receptive brain stands ready to do your bidding.

CHAPTER 1

WHAT YOUR WRITING BRAIN CAN DO FOR YOU

"A writer is someone who can make a riddle out of an answer."

—KARL KRAUS

In case you hadn't noticed, the field of neuroscience is *everything* these days. Not only is the study of the human brain the fastest moving, most complex frontier in physical science, there are amazing leaps forward in understanding how the human brain does what it does so well—and where and why wires get crossed—occurring across the world. International scientists are currently focused on figuring out how the brain's massive networking system works—from mapping a single connection between two neurons (a synapse) to mapping brain regions trillions of times larger.

The brain is, after all, the most complex piece of organized matter in our entire known universe, consisting of 86 billion (some still say 100 billion) neurons (and ten to fifty times more "helper" cells, known as *glia*). All neurons have a central body, or nucleus, where cellular metabolism takes place, but they also have incredibly long, stretched-out "arms" (known as axons) and thousands of smaller "arms" (known as dendrites). Tiny electrical currents undulate along the neuron's surface. When a stimulus occurs (inside or outside the human body), or the need to send a message arises, neurotransmitters are released to help the neuron translate the jolt of electric current, or spike, into a message that can pass across a synapse and into another neuron, where another spike begins. Each neuron forms as many as 15,000 synapses, giving your brain the potential to form some 100 trillion synapses.

IT'S ALL IN THE WIRING

If the brain's complexity sounds infinite, take heart in knowing that it often feels that way to neuroscientists, many of whom are focusing on how all those "wires"—linking and interconnecting neurons and neuronal structures in one region of the brain to neuronal structures in other regions of the brain—work their miracles. The brain is a unique organ in that it has a great number of structurally distinct, heterogeneous, yet interconnected components, which depend on the activity and coactivity of large populations of neurons, in distributed networks, that are subject to rapid changes. This circuitry forms as a result of our preprogrammed development and our individual life experiences; the neural activity that courses through and alters the brain generates our thoughts, our behavior, our memories, and so on; neural circuits tell activity how to propagate, and neural activity tells circuits how to change.

Thanks to the invention of imaging systems that show the brain in action, neuroscientists have only recently confirmed that this massive, complex neuronal linkage system, also known as a connection matrix (first defined as the "human connectome" by scientist Olaf Sporns in 2005), determines how cognitive function emerges from the human brain's neuronal structure and dynamics. Scientists are now actively seeking an understanding of the following:

- how the many millions of neurons associated with a perception, thought, decision, or movement are dynamically linked within circuits and networks
- how even the simplest perceptual task involves the activity of millions of neurons distributed across many brain regions
- how simple percepts arise from patterned neural activity and how the resulting percepts are linked to emotion, motivation, and action

All of which means the neuroscientists, and researchers in the many new fields arising as a result of breakthroughs in neuroscience, have a lot of work ahead.

RESPECT YOUR NEURONAL WEALTH

Even the simplest brains are extraordinarily complex—in structure and function. The specialized brain cells, or neurons, located in your cerebral cortex, the outermost layer of the brain, play a key role in perception, attention, memory, and thought. The cerebral (thinking) cortex of a rat might have 15 to 20 million neurons; a cat, 300 million; and a chimpanzee, 5 to 6 billion. For a human, the figure is around 20 billion. The human brain has approximately 86 billion neurons in total. Appreciate the neuronal wealth at your disposal—and take responsibility for shaping the way your brain processes writing.

MAPPING THE HUMAN CONNECTOME

H. Sebastian Seung, Professor of Computational Neuroscience, MIT Investigator, and "rock-star" author of *Connectome: How the Brain's Wiring Makes Us Who We Are*, believes that understanding how our brains are wired holds the key to finally understanding who we are and how we function in the world—on a microscopic level. "You are not your genes, you are your connectomes," Dr. Seung states, while also noting that human brains "have one million times more connections than your genomes have letters." He believes that all the things that define a human being emerge from the way the brain cells and various brain regions are connected, and how well the individual's connectome functions.

As such, he (along with others) has dedicated himself to mapping the human connectome, one cell at a time, slicing and dicing microscopic slivers to re-create three-dimensional representations. With a team already at work, they've learned that it takes about fifty hours to map one neuron's dendritic tree, and his ultimate goal is to create three-dimensional maps of all 86 billion (give or take) neurons, tracking each connection, which can be as high as ten thousand connections per neuron. Dr. Seung predicts the mapping will require at least a decade of work, and that it may not be achievable. Still, his passion for the quest is infectious and has created an online community of participants.

It's been suggested that mapping brain activity will produce nearly as much data as the seventeen-mile-long Large Hadron Collider, one of the most advanced astronomical observatories, yet the most challenging aspect will be managing the sheer volume of information neuroscientists collect.

FIRE UP YOUR SUPERCOMPUTER

Some estimate that digitally mapping the human brain's connectome at the level of an electron microscope would require a zettabyte of computer space. How much is a zettabyte? It's a newly-created computational number (because advances in computer capacity are throttling forward), somewhat equivalent to a trillion gigabytes or, as one computational genius suggested, around 75 billion 16-gigabyte iPads. Try thinking of that capability when you need to fire up your writing brain.

WHAT YOUR BRAIN CAN DO FOR YOU

In recent decades, neuroscientists have discovered many surprising facts about our brains, some of which nullify what we once thought (that brains stop growing at an early age) and others which offer immeasurable hope (a healthy person can train her brain to do pretty much whatever she wants). When it comes to your writing brain, you can construct a network of neuronal connections that will launch a new level of writing, helping you become the writer you've always longed to be—working at a more imaginative, more meaningful, and more productive level. But, before we dig into specifics, let's begin by listing some of the primary things your writer's brain can do for you:

- add new neurons, even when you're eighty
- create neuronal highways that speed up processing
- create new synapses; renew old synapses; discard unwanted synapses
- wire together, what you want to fire together (Wire whatever emotional happiness you experience while writing with your neuronal connections specific to writing, for example; or link the same neuronal connections related to rewards with what you experience when successfully achieving aspirational word counts. Further explanation follows later in this chapter.)
- maximize or minimize habitual behaviors (gaining control over disruptive emotions; mining productive emotions)
- monitor, experience, remember, and re-create events, as if they are reoccurring
- record and remember stimuli; link new stimuli to existing stimuli
- juggle multiple short-term memories while writing or brainstorming; link them to long-term memory
- warehouse and convert short-term memories to long-term memory (your personal storehouse of ideas)
- get fired up; stay extra alert; fire on all pistons
- create and sustain focus; dial down distractions
- generate empathy and identification; mirror yourself in others
- quiet itself when emotions or stimuli overwhelm it
- program and reprogram neuronal structures to perform better
- surprise you and rise to the occasion
- perform abstract thinking, creatively linking new and existing ideas, in new combinations
- indulge in self-reflection; maintaining a separate sense of self

Whoa, you say, that's a long list! Yes, it is—and it's not everything your brain can do—but you aren't required to remember a single thing on the list. We'll be discussing and reinforcing your knowledge of these capabilities as we go forward. This is, however, a helpful list to flip back to if you find yourself doubting your abilities. You have a magnificent brain—one that is capable of growing and changing, primarily at your bidding. So pause to feel really good about (and recognize) your magnificent brain before we move on.

CONSTRUCT A NEURAL HIGHWAY

In 2012, a team at Massachusetts General Hospital mapped a portion of the brain and discovered that our brain "wiring" is not a jumble, but is, in fact, a remarkable, multi-layered "grid" of neural "highways." It looks very much like a woven rug, with parallel and perpendicular fibers crossing over and under each other in an orderly fashion. So what does that mean for writers? In plain words, it means that our brains contain connective pathways, which are knit into a three-dimensional and multilayered geometric pattern of cross-hatched neural highways; and within that grid, individual nerve fibers are interwoven in consistent patterns. Basically the brain's structural networks are hardware for many interconnected functional networks, also known as software. It's up to you to develop your software and program in as much information regarding writing as possible, particularly information relevant to whatever you're writing about.

NEUROPLASTICITY AND NEUROGENESIS

Neurogenesis literally means the "birth of neurons" and, when scientists verified that the human brain is capable of generating, regenerating, re-assigning, and discarding neurons, the term "neuroplasticity" was coined to reflect the brain's flexibility. It does not mean that you can untangle your brain and stretch it, like one might with warm taffy, across a room. The *plasticity* in neuroscience is a term used to indicate that your brain has the capacity to grow and change throughout your life—a fairly recent discovery that created a major breakthrough in neuroscience.

Scientists had long thought that the number and capacity of neurons were pretty much set at birth, with some neurogenesis occurring during adolescence and into early adulthood. Obviously they knew all humans had the capacity to learn, and they knew that you could lose neurons; they just didn't know that you could generate and regenerate neurons. It's only in the last two decades or so that neuroscientists discovered that the human brain has the *plasticity* that's necessary to do the following things:

- change its physical structure
- repair damaged regions inflicted by strokes, concussions, or other injuries
- re-assign the tasks of a damaged region to a healthy one
- grow new neurons and discard neurons not in use
- rewire existing neuronal connections
- create complex neuronal networks to master new skills

It all boils down to this: What you choose to do—think, read, study, practice—affects how your brain either grows or shrinks, expands or contracts, learns or stagnates. Our brains are amazing thinking, dreaming, imagining, and producing machines, reliant upon their masters to program, nurture, guide, and direct them. What you do— or don't do—to stimulate, guide, and fire up your writing brain has everything to do with whether you will maximize your own genius.

GETTING DOWN TO BRAIN FACTS

So let's begin by discussing certain facts you need to know in order to maximize your brain's potential. We'll be discussing these functions throughout the book in sidebars and at the end of each chapter, we'll offer a "Train Your Writing Brain" exercise designed to bolster your neuronal networks related to writing. Some will be specific to working on a novel, memoir, or other fiction, but all will reinforce the way your brain thinks about writing.

Neural Networks Are Always Forming

Even before you were born, your neurons began linking and forming increasingly complex, neuronal networks at an astronomical rate, and they'll continue forming networks until you die. How many form, where they're formed, how they interconnect, and how strong and active your neuronal networks connected to writing become depends on how much you study, learn, and practice writing—and all the various skills you'll need to become a far better writer, such as the ability to recognize patterns, formulate templates, generate ideas, experiment, think outside the box, foster persistence, improve focus, reward productivity, develop empathy, and strengthen social networks.

FOSTER CURIOSITY

We all know that it's easier to learn when you are interested in what you're studying, but it seems that curiosity itself may bolster learning and memory in general. Scientists who study curiosity (and few do, which seems curious) say that being in a curious state of mind seems to place a stamp of importance on pieces of information, even if they seemingly fly by when skimming material. Your brain more easily stores these bits of information away for safekeeping than when you are not curious, which means synapses to existing information can be formed. This link between curiosity and memory may even extend beyond the topics that people find fascinating to any material processed while in a curious state of mind.

Experiences Form and Shape Your Neuronal Structures

What you're exposed to from birth, what you study, and what you spend your time doing or focusing on matters. Unless you were born a writing genius—which may be true for a few lucky souls—the more time and attention you spend developing and practicing the craft of writing, the better writer you'll become.

Your Brain Cells Can Be Reprogrammed

Neurons and neuronal circuits can be repurposed should the need arise (due to strokes or accidental brain damage). We've recently seen how people who suffer massive brain damage (such as former Senator

Gabrielle Giffords, who was shot in the head, leading to brain damage) are able to reprogram brain areas, not previously involved in speech, to speak. It's a long and laborious process, but possible.

Neural Circuits Not Used Will Be Pruned

We've all heard the cliché "use it, or lose it," which has become cliché because, well, we've all been there or witnessed it happening to others. If you want to become a better writer, it's important to write as often as possible and to push yourself to further develop your craft. This capability also means that you can prune behavior that isn't serving you and replace it with healthier, more productive behavior and writing habits. If you're bogged down by self-doubt, you can change that!

BEWARE SYNAPTIC PRUNING

Synaptic pruning occurs when your brain discards neuronal connections and neurons that aren't being used. While this happens massively in early childhood, as a way to form and shape the ideal brain for each individual, it also occurs in adulthood, though at a much slower pace. Basically, if you are not engaging the brain cells related to your ability to conceive, create, and craft fiction (or nonfiction, poetry, lyrics), your brain will assume that these activities aren't essential to your well-being—and synapses will weaken and eventually be pruned. If you're spending too much time in front of the mind-numbing television or not working at your craft regularly, brain cells needed to create original work may begin fading with each hour spent vegetating.

Your Brain Can Reactivate Long-Dormant Circuitry

Once you've mastered a skill, you can spur your brain to reactivate the ability. If you haven't written for a long time, you can send out a clarion call to the neuronal networks you established in the past, regroup them, and proceed to rebuild, strengthen, and add to them by employing dedicated, focused practice.

Your Brain Can Quiet Aberrant Circuits

Circuits connected to depression, post-traumatic stress disorder (PTSD), obsessive-compulsive disorder (OCD), phobias, and so on, don't have to wreak havoc in your life. If your brain is drowning in cortisol (a stress hormone) and short of dopamine (a feel-good neurotransmitter), you have the power to alter your brain's dysfunctional circuits and better control disruptive emotions. You can harness all the genius that arises out of emotion without suffering for your art.

Your Brain Can Yield to Your Wishes

Some parts of your brain can exert control over other parts and change how much they affect your mood, decision-making faculties, and thought processes. You have the power within your brain to tamp down fear and divert all those pesky, nonproductive thoughts that sometimes subvert your attempts to write. Your brain is under your command, and all you have to do is learn how to maximize its creativity, energy, and productivity.

VISUALIZE YOUR BRAIN

The average adult brain weighs about 3 pounds and is about 5.9 inches long. To get a sense of its size, put your two palms together and ball your hands into fists. It may appear remarkably small, but within that small area, the multitude of squished wrinkles and folds house millions upon millions of neurons whose proximity facilitates the process of making new neuronal connections. If you compare the size of your brain to that of a microchip, you'll have a better appreciation for your brain's massive potential to process and retain new information.

HOW IT AFFECTS YOUR WRITING

All human brains are similar in some basic ways. For example, all human brains rely on the occipital lobe at the back of the brain to analyze and process visual information. Also, many parts of the brain are preprogrammed to perform certain actions, such as hearing, seeing, smelling, and involuntary breathing. However, studies are confirming that some of these preprogrammed functions can be refined, with a little extra effort.

Although the human brain had the highly complex capacity to learn a language much earlier—spoken language likely developed some 250,000 years ago, around the same time our ancestors began crafting tools—the ability to read and write is not, in fact, that old in terms of human development. Prehistoric cave drawings, simple carvings, and line drawings have been dated back approximately 35,000 years. They were used as symbolic representations of events and depictions of physical objects that began to give man a way to reflect on his past, share knowledge, and plan for his future. These communication tools evolved into petroglyphs, which evolved into hieroglyphics, which eventually evolved into alphabets. Approximately 6,000 years ago, merchants used cuneiform signs (wedge-shaped cones) to mark their goods, and papyrus scrolls first appeared some 5,000 years ago. Chinese and Phoenician alphabets (which evolved into Hebrew) date back 4,000 years; and a thousand years later, Greek and Latin alphabets emerged.

While our alphabet uses twenty-six letters and the Chinese alphabet uses thousands of abstract symbols, both written languages require specialized brain activity and complex communication among various areas of the brain.

To learn to read and write, humans must learn to recognize a series of symbols and then "teach" the areas of the mind dedicated to language to associate those written symbols with spoken sounds—and a sequence of sounds to words. It's important to note that those who are deaf and use sign languages use the same part of the brain that non-deaf persons use for speech in order to communicate—thus "speech" and "listening" areas of the brain are actually "producing language" and "receiving language" parts of the brain.

Learning the meanings of the words comes with extensive teaching and practice, which begins in early childhood and, like learning to walk, rapidly advances. Most language acquisition occurs as a result of focused instruction or mirroring on the part of parents. How you learn to read and write relies on how the brain is structured (at birth your brain has the capacity to learn language and speech, but not to read or write), but how, when, and why you learn any new skill depends on how much energy you put into it.

As a writer, you likely loved language and had an affinity for connecting symbols with letters, sounds with letters, letters and sounds with words, and eventually words with sentences. The learning during childhood is massive, but throughout your life, you have the ability to decide how much further you wish to advance your linguistic skills. You also have the ability to determine how you see the world and control how you think about the world and yourself in it.

HOW YOUR BRAIN WRITES

Most of our predominant language centers are in the left hemisphere of our brains; however, the right hemisphere processes and transfers signatures and other "graphic images or pictures" to the left hemisphere. To write, the two hemispheres have to communicate— we picture what we want to say in the right hemisphere, but the left translates those visual images into words. Even writing a simple note is a complex, voluntary procedure (that eventually becomes automatic) that engages all the lobes of your cerebral cortex to communicate with other parts of your brain—the limbic (emotional) system, the hippocampus (engaging your memory), the brain stem, and the cerebellum—and the spinal cord. Here's a simplified perspective on how the brain prepares to write:

- The cingulate cortex (central control in the frontal lobes) heeds your desire to use writing as a way to communicate something.
- The limbic system interjects emotional subtext related to what you're writing.
- The visual cortex looks for the paper (or keyboard) you'll write on and begins to internally visualize how the writing should look on the page.
- The left angular gyrus (a part of the parietal lobe) converts the visual perception of letters into the comprehension of words.
- The Broca's and Wernicke's brain areas may assist with processing and make contributions related to the expression and comprehension of spoken language.
- The corpus callosum (which connects the cerebral cortex's left and right hemispheres) combines the pictorial/holistic right-brain procedures with their sequential/linguistic left-brain counterparts.
- The parietal lobe coordinates all these signals and sends them to the motor cortex, which sends the motor signal to the arm, hand, and fingers.

The signal then travels along the pyramidal track (controls voluntary fine movements) to the fingers. Along the way, it passes through the limbic system (where emotions are processed), through the hippocampus (where memory occurs and offers input/perspective), and through the basal ganglia (which manages fine motor control). On its journey, the signal also passes through the brainstem (where primitive impulses or unconscious desires might interfere); and, before the signal exits, the cerebellum records the whole process and helps your brain integrate it so you are able to perform it as an automatic habit. Like speech, handwriting is learned through interaction with other people and is influenced by social and environmental variables, as well as by an individual's brain capabilities.

EMBRACE CURSIVE

Schools are downplaying—and even eliminating—the need to learn to write cursive, despite its necessity to engage highly complex cognitive processes and achieve mastery of a precise motor coordination. (It takes children years to master handwriting and some stroke victims relearn language by tracing letters with their fingers.) Writing in cursive also increases a sense of harmony and balance, and writing on paper provides creative options: to manipulate the medium in multidimensional, innovative, or expressive ways (such as cutting, folding, pasting, ripping, or coloring the paper). Also, when you write in longhand on paper and then edit, there'll be a visual and tactile record of your creative process for you and others to study. Learning to write (and writing) in cursive, on paper, fosters creativity and should not be surrendered.

THE ROLE HANDWRITING PLAYS

Handwriting starts out as a chain of isolated motor movements, which we struggle to learn; until, eventually, with a lot of practice, the process congeals into a sort of kinetic melody that our brains can orchestrate without having to pause to remember how each letter should look or to think through how to make each pen stroke or how it should feel scratching across the paper. Handwriting is one of the most advanced human capabilities, because it combines all the complexities of language in concert with intricate psychomotor activity. It gives physical form to our thoughts and emotions, which is why some of us fall completely in love with the act of writing and spend hours searching for the perfect notebook for brainstorming ideas, journaling, or writing.

Handwriting Helps with Comprehension and Thinking

Multiple studies have found that students using longhand to record notes were better able to answer questions on the lecture than those using a laptop. The scientists noted that those working on paper, in longhand, rephrased information as they took notes, which required them to carry out a preliminary process of summarizing and comprehension; in contrast, those working on a keyboard tended to take a lot of notes, sometimes even making a literal transcript, but avoided what is known as "desirable difficulty." Psychologist Robert Bjork coined this term, which suggests that making the learning process a little harder at the beginning (perhaps by requiring handwritten notes or asking people to wrestle with and explain new concepts early in the process) reaps dividends at the end, with better retention and comprehension of the material.

Handwriting Helps You More Fully Express Emotions

"With handwriting we come closer to the intimacy of the author," psychiatrist Roland Jouvent explained. "That's why we are more powerfully moved by the handwritten manuscript of a poem by Verlaine than by the same work simply printed in a book. Each person's hand is different: The gesture is charged with emotion, lending it a special charm." Cursive, in particular, adds an element of dancing, instilling "a melody" in the message.

WRITE TO GIVE YOUR BRAIN A RUSH

Fifteen to twenty minutes of expressive writing, three to five times a week has been shown to have positive health benefits, including long-term improvements in mood, stress levels, and depressive symptoms. Those who experienced stressful or traumatic events and wrote about it had fewer illnesses, lower blood pressure, and spent less time in the hospital. A 2013 study showed that patients who had biopsies and wrote about their experience (twenty minutes a day, three days in a row, two weeks before the biopsy) healed faster. Asthma patients who write have fewer attacks; AIDS patients who write have higher T-cell counts; and cancer patients who write report more optimistic perspectives and improved quality of life. Writing in a journal and blogging results in the release of enough dopamine to create positive effects similar to the effect running or listening to music produces. Moral: *Write a blog and give your brain a rush.*

THE ROLE COGNITION PLAYS

Cognition is the act of thinking—what your brain does—and human beings are unique in our ability to understand how we think. As far as we know, humans are the only species that has the capacity to self-reflect. It's how you use these fantastic cognitive skills that matters.

- The more you fire up certain neurons, the more active they remain. The more sustained and focused effort you put into writing a novel (or a screenplay, etc.), the better your brain will do what you want (and need) it to do, which is become a more creative, productive, and successful writer. We'll talk about global excitation, focus, concentration, and more in upcoming chapters.
- The more you use your brain, the more blood flows freely to the neurons being used, providing glucose and oxygen to keep your brain performing at maximum capacity. Whatever improves blood flow improves your brain. That means that exercise, or at least plenty of moving around, has to be part of your routine.
- What you "wire together" will "fire together," meaning whatever synapses occur while you are writing link to writing. If, for example, you make writing a pleasant activity, the neurons fired up to experience and record pleasure will wire to the writing neurons; and the more they occur in tandem, the stronger the synapses (connections) become. The more you link writing with happiness, accomplishment, and fulfillment, the more those "thoughts" will be connected and will trigger the types of motivational feelings that will keep you writing.
- New neurons in your hippocampus provide more room for new memories and new learning. Your brain is always capable of learning new skills—even at advanced ages. It may simply take a little longer.

- You can tap into memories that have been stored in your hippocampus for decades and re-create the feelings that accompanied the memories, which is helpful when you need to incorporate sound, taste, touch, smell, hear, and sight into scenes.
- The more you ask your brain to do, the more space it sets up to accommodate your desires. If you ask it to help you write a novel, it will make space for a new neuronal network dedicated to the task, and it will begin linking existing neuronal networks to whatever new ones will be generated. The more gray matter you assign to writing, the larger that neuronal network will grow.

That's a pretty impressive list, right? With such a magnificent organ at your disposal, don't you think you should take the best care possible to keep it in prime working condition?

WEAVE A TIGHT WEB

Stanislas Dehaene, author of *Consciousness and the Brain: Deciphering How the Brain Codes Our Thoughts*, calls the part of the brain that allows us to think "a vast neuronal forest of the cortex," where a tight web of oscillating neurons—millions upon millions—are discharging at random. When a stimulant occurs, receptive neurons incite neighboring, excitatory neurons to broadcast the message, joining what amounts to a "shouting match" for your full, conscious attention. For something to become coded in your brain (a conscious realization or memory that can be retrieved), neuronal "conversations" have to travel long distances, top to bottom, over the wide expanse of the neuronal web. How tightly your brain web has been woven and how well neurons travel determine what you excel at doing and what you haven't yet developed. To strengthen your ability to think well while writing, consistently fire up the neurons related to writing. The more you stimulate them, the tighter the web grows.

THE ROLE CONCEPTUAL NETWORKS PLAY

Many psychologists and neuroscientists posit that human learning and memory takes place within what are called "conceptual networks" of linked ideas. For instance, if you were to think of the word *sleep*, you would probably think about the act of sleeping and also about things that are linked to sleep: pillows, a bed, your bedroom, and so on. Thus you're not really thinking of just "sleep"; you're thinking of the sum of all of the ideas surrounding the concept of "sleep." Something similar happens when you think about writing: You have a series of ideas all linked together, forming conceptual memory networks related to all aspects of writing and storytelling—maybe you think of your favorite pen, your latest story idea, specific research you need to do to flush out the idea, what you already know about creating memorable characters or how to structure a novel, and so on. Having all of these ideas linked together generates a valuable neural architecture for writing that you can add to the groundwork that's already there. Once you link the ideas, your brain will begin to work its magic. After all, each of those linked ideas represents linked neurons in your brain.

All new stimuli can be filtered through your existing conceptual network, matching new information with existing "patterns" and integrating the knowledge, making it available for new constructs. This process bolsters your higher thinking via executive functions of the prefrontal cortex. When you need a solution to a problem or a fresh idea, your brain summons your prefrontal cortex to ask the hippocampus for memories related to the current situation, and the broader your base knowledge, the better your prefrontal cortex can offer pertinent responses—because you have more ideas and concepts already in your network. The greater the links and cross-connections among networks of stored information, the greater your access to original thoughts and solutions. Thus, the more input you provide to this conceptual framework—how to fire up your writing brain, how to create memorable characters and maximize plot, grammar dos and don'ts, knowledge on topics specific to your work in progress, how other authors have portrayed a similar story, spinoff ideas, etc.—the more connections your brain will make.

Here's how it works: When certain memory networks are regularly and repeatedly used, they form extensive synapses that recognize patterns. When you need to write a scene, your prefrontal cortex will access the networks formed when you wrote previous scenes, bringing to mind everything you've learned up to this point in time—and it can make new and sometimes startling connections, which is where originality begins. Your brain is processing everything you've fed it and all those synapses are "talking" to each other. The facts, procedures, and observations you've gathered are processed symbolically in the writing process—giving the memory another storage modality and truly illuminating the patterns for the brain to follow as it adds new learning to existing concept networks. The more extensive your brain's collection of memory networks (links and cross-connections), the more successful it will be in activating the best prior knowledge to predict the best responses, answers, and choices for any new situation.

THE PERILS OF MULTITASKING

Many believe—even brag—that they can successfully multitask, but recent studies have shown that your brain can't do two activities that require cognitive attention simultaneously. (You can eat and read at the same time because eating doesn't require cognitive attention.) When two activities simultaneously engage your prefrontal cortex (thinking brain), it has to shift from one task to the other, even if you think you're doing both at once. Multitasking can also mean shifting attention from your computer to your smartphone, from writing to e-mail.

Basically, when you focus on a cognitive task, the anterior part of your prefrontal cortex communicates your desire to perform the task to the posterior part of your prefrontal cortex, and together they execute the task. However, when you add a second cognitive task, the brain has to split or shift from one region to another, assigning either the right or the left side of the brain to the new task, dividing the resources in two. If you add a third cognitive task, studies have shown that you're likely to lose your train of thought and make three times as many errors. These results were discussed in a 2010 French study that also revealed that the two areas of the brain are, in fact, competing with each other and not working together, which equates to putting yourself at odds with yourself.

Other studies have shown that multitasking on three or more tasks at once (particularly if they are cognitive tasks, such as reading, writing, or responding to emails) can have the equivalent effect of smoking marijuana or staying up all night, and can reduce adult cognitive capacity to that of an eight-year-old. Over time, multitaskers, particularly those who jump from one electronic device to the next, become more susceptible to distractions, have trouble keeping tasks separate in their minds, and lose density in the anterior cingulate cortex, which is responsible for emotional intelligence—again, making you more like that eight-year-old.

It's best to marshal all your brain resources on one task at a time. You can, however, listen to music while you work, and some low-level ambient noise (such as being in a coffee shop) is also okay, because your brain doesn't have to downshift and may even focus a little better in those circumstances. However, the volume level must remain constant, as your brain will eventually ignore neutral stimuli that don't change.

WRITE WHEN TIRED

When you're tired your brain isn't as good at filtering out distractions or focusing, which is why ideas sometimes "pop in" when you've stopped concentrating on a task. Studies have shown that your brain is more apt to be more open to new ideas and new ways of thinking about things— and a broader way of thinking about things—when you're physically tired. So mine those opportunities, particularly if you're feeling stuck and need a fresh way of looking at something. However, your brain still requires adequate sleep, so don't stay up all night!

TAKE CARE OF YOUR BRAIN'S HEALTH

Since we'll soon be leaping into specifics about how your brain can help you conceive, create, and craft stories, we'll conclude this chapter with a list of five things you can do for your brain today—and, hopefully, you'll proceed to do them every day. Treat your brain well, and it will deliver the goods when you most need them. To nurture the greatest writing computer you'll ever own, do the following:

1. **EAT FOOD THAT'S GOOD FOR BODY AND BRAIN.** Your brain makes up only about 2 percent of your body mass but consumes over 20 percent of the oxygen and nutrients you feed your body each day. Be sure to select foods that will nourish both body and brain, and steer clear of anything that will clog your arteries, heart, and brain. Basically you should avoid all processed (boxed, prepared) food and choose lean protein, whole grains, tons of fresh vegetables, fruits (particularly berries), and some nuts (particularly walnuts, almonds, and hazelnuts) over supplements.

2. **MOVE YOUR BODY EVERY DAY.** Exercise increases blood flow and oxygen throughout your body, including to your brain. The more you move, the sharper your brain will be; the less you move, the duller your brain will be. Aerobic exercise, getting your heart rate elevated for a period of twenty minutes or so (a walk will do it), spurs neurogenesis, the birth of new neurons and neuronal synapses. It also fosters brain plasticity (the ability to grow and change) and a greater capacity for memory, attention span, and cognitive efficiency.

3. **STIMULATE YOUR BRAIN.** Give your brain something to conquer. Your brain loves—and will rise to meet—a challenge and will grow only *if* you give it reasons to learn new skills. Plus, if you aren't reinforcing new skills (in our case, writing skills), your brain assumes those skills aren't important to you and will pare back how much energy (and storage) it puts toward writing. Think of your brain as a warrior who needs a fresh battle each day.

4. **REDUCE STRESS.** Stress not only reduces your brain's ability to focus, ongoing stress thwarts neuroplasticity, your brain's ability to grow, change, make new—and often surprising—associations and think new thoughts. While exercise (physical and mental) bolsters the birth of neurons, stress destroys neurons and can lead to short- and long-term decreased functioning, including memory. Meditation and exercise are great stress reducers. Do something to expend pent up energy and if you find yourself constantly worrying, consider cognitive-based behavior therapy to break that negative cycle.

5. **GET PLENTY OF SLEEP.** Sleep is the time when your brain processes everything it's been exposed to throughout the day—either in dreams or not. All those synapses have to settle in or separate out, filing away what your brain recognizes as your priorities and connecting the thoughts that spun through your gray matter while awake. REM (Rapid Eye Movement) sleep is essential to brain health and rejuvenation. Countless studies have shown that quality sleep is paramount not only to your health, but to your brain. Do whatever it takes to get eight solid hours of sleep at night.

Always remember that your brain health really matters, in the short- and long-term. If you want your brilliant brain to function at its peak capacity, treat it with respect; if you want it to stay agile well into old age, keep it stimulated and well nourished (nutritious food plus vigorous exercise). Your brain is a supercomputer, and you're the sole person responsible for programming and maintenance.

Now that you have the basic knowledge you need, we'll launch into how you can use what's known about brains to bolster your writing skills. That discussion begins by first assessing what may have already programmed your brain to become a writer, in the hope it will light the way to conceiving, creating, and crafting stories that sell. But first, take a few minutes to complete your first assignment, which we'll call Train Your Writing Brain. It's designed to help you bolster your brain, fire up those writing neurons, and get some serious writing done.

TRAIN YOUR WRITING BRAIN: CHECK YOUR LEARNING RETENTION

You've just read more than 3,000 words about your brain. To test your memory and retention skills, see if you can answer the following questions without looking back:

1. How many neurons does your brain have?
2. How many of these cells are neurons?
3. How many synapses is the brain capable of forming?
4. Your brain's ability to change is called what?
5. Author Stanislas Dehaene called the part of the brain that allows us to think "a vast neuronal forest." Can you remember what scientists now call the vast network of neurons in your brain?
6. We discussed many things that your brain can do to help you become a better writer. Can you list five?

If your memory retention was good, pat yourself on the back. If it wasn't good, you may want to pay closer attention when you read/research, pausing occasionally to let thoughts penetrate, or writing down important information, as both of these actions foster more synaptic connections and alert your brain that you want the information committed to long-term memory.

Answers found on the next page.

ANSWERS

1. 86 billion
2. 20 billion, the rest are helper cells
3. 100 trillion synapses
4. neuroplasticity
5. the connectome
6. ways your brain can help you write:

   a. add new neurons, even when you're eighty-years-old
   b. create neuronal highways that speed up processing
   c. create new synapses; renew old synapses; discard unwanted synapses
   d. wire together what you want to fire together (emotional happiness with writing, for example)
   e. maximize or minimize habitual behaviors (gain control over disruptive emotions; mine productive emotions)
   f. monitor, experience, remember, and re-create events, as if they are occurring again
   g. record and remember stimuli; link new stimuli to existing stimuli
   h. retain and access short-term memories while writing; link them to long-term memory
   i. warehouse long-term memory (your personal storehouse of ideas)
   j. get fired up; stay extra alert; fire on all pistons
   k. create and sustain focus; dial down distractions
   l. generate empathy and identification; mirror yourself in others
   m. quiet itself when emotions or stimuli overwhelm it
   n. program and reprogram neuronal structures to perform better
   o. surprise you and rise to the occasion
   p. engage in abstract thinking, creatively link new and existing ideas in new combinations
   q. self-reflect; maintain a separate sense of self

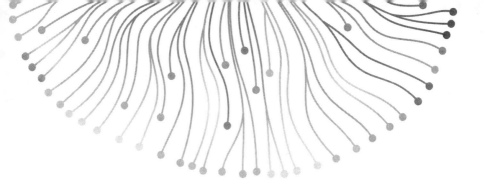

PREPPING YOUR WRITING BRAIN

"When I was six or seven, I used to read a thesaurus searching for the words that meant exactly what I felt. And I could never find them. I could see shades of meaning in the different ways something could be said; I could appreciate the difference, say, between the verbs 'fall' and 'catapult.' But when I had a feeling like sadness, I couldn't find a word that meant everything that I felt inside of me. I always felt that words were inadequate, that I'd never been able to express myself—ever. Even now, it's so hard to express what I think and feel, the totality of what I've seen."

—**AMY TAN**

CHAPTER 2

AWAKEN YOUR WRITING BRAIN

Create the Mindset to Write

"The story—from Rumplestiltskin to *War and Peace*—is one of the basic tools invented by the human mind for the purpose of understanding. There have been great societies that did not use the wheel, but there have been no societies that did not tell stories."

—URSULA LE GUIN

Whether you're already a writer, earning money as a writer—novelist, poet, nonfiction author, screenwriter, scriptwriter; newspaper, magazine, or online content writer; and so on—or whether you are someone who longs to write but has never put pen to paper, you likely already possess certain qualities and affinities that make you good at what you do, or that, together, contribute to the appeal of writing. Many writers feel a calling to become a writer, and many, many writers come to writing from a passion for reading, or for researching and reporting the truth, or from mining situations, characters, and emotions in an attempt to understand the human condition.

In my experience, most novelists, screenwriters, poets, and playwrights fell in love with reading, storytelling, movies, plays, and words at an early age. Most seemed to be more affected than usual by the experiences that reading conjured, often reporting that they fell under a spell when reading books they loved—they even remembered the most moving passages decades later. Most read extensively throughout their childhood and into adulthood. For others, hearing stories as a child left indelible impressions of the mannerisms, follies, bravery, and cowardice of certain characters. Overhearing adult conversations left them feeling mesmerized by the unique ways people expressed themselves, and they experienced an unquenchable desire for hearing—reading, and then writing—stories themselves.

EMBRACE YOUR IMAGINATION

Margaret Atwood, author of more than twenty-five works of poetry, nonfiction, and fiction, including *The Handmaid's Tale*, *Cat's Eye*, and *The Blind Assassin*, noted in her book *Negotiating with the Dead, A Writer on Writing* that many people believe that people who write experienced something in their childhood that made them become writers. She couldn't identify a common thread, except perhaps that many writers mention a love for books and solitude in their childhoods. Atwood credited the genesis of her own writing to "the inability to distinguish between the real and the imagined, or rather the attitude that what we consider real is also imagined: every life is also an inner life, a life created."

Many writers had difficult or exceptional childhoods and feel that somehow they were "born" to write the story of what happened in their family or the story of what their parents did—or didn't do—that made their childhoods unique and unforgettable. A lot of writers harbor hurt feelings and learn to use writing as a means to express those feelings and find some way to move past them, or at least to learn from them; that is, writing is often transformative.

SCULPT YOUR WRITING BRAIN

If you've ever been around a litter of newborn puppies or kittens, you've likely observed that some are feisty and adventurous, some greedily suckle, some cower while others show dominance, and so on. Studies have found that such personality differences will still appear, even when animals are cloned (meaning that they are genetically identical).

In 2013, a researcher cloned a group of genetically identical mice and released them into a large enclosure that provided opportunities for exploration and play. Within a few months, the mouse clones that had explored the most actively sprouted new nerve cells throughout their brains, especially in the hippocampus, a region crucial for memory and spatial navigation; less-adventurous clones showed less brain development.

We may not know why some personality differences exist from birth, but this study suggests that individual experiences sculpt individual brains and personalities, too, even if those brains are genetically identical. Moral: *What are you doing to sculpt your brain for writing?*

IT REQUIRES DEVOTION

We've all met people who profess a strong desire to become a writer and then sheepishly—or not—confess that they don't read, that they haven't read a novel in years, and they don't devour magazine articles, historical tomes, or nonfiction books. They just want *to be* writers. Often these people are dilettantes who imagine that being a writer is fun. And it is … sometimes. Mostly, however, writing requires massive dedication, a whole lot of time spent alone, way too much sitting, countless hours spent *thinking hard*, and unending, and occasionally painful, dedication to forming ideas and laboring over the production of sentences, paragraphs, scenes, dialogue, punctuation, and all the elements that go into writing a novel, a play, a screenplay, or a poem. When we're not writing, we're thinking, plotting, imagining, or editing, which can be far more tedious than cranking out first drafts.

GET YOUR GENES IN LINE

The science of epigenetics (*epi* means *outside*) has determined that your lifestyle can override your genes; that is, if your familial DNA falls short of the qualities you need to become a best-selling writer, those limitations can be conquered. Just as early childhood experiences mold and shape the brain, the life you lead, what you eat, what you read or watch, how deeply you think, how you spend time, what you focus on, how you regularly exercise your body, and so, on can counteract any limiting genetic issues. To become the writer you've always longed to be, bolster those areas of brainpower where real or imagined shortcomings exist and keep working at it until it becomes second nature—your brain's new reality.

IT BEGINS WITH A LOVE FOR LANGUAGE

For me, and this is likely true for most aspiring writers, words and language become worlds unto themselves. Writers seem to simply love words, and they experience a visceral feeling of passion and excitement when reading stories and poems. Writers may also have an affinity for remembering lots of words, unusual words, or words with complicated, nuanced meanings. Likely more than most, they also remember certain stories, certain characters, certain images that arose fully formed from a book they read thirty years ago, and writers whose style of writing mesmerized them then—and mesmerize them now. Early in life, those who go on to become creative writers likely recognize those feelings as passion, and, for many, storytelling and writing become a source of immense pleasure, titillating challenge, and refuge—one arena in which they feel most fully like themselves. Many writers recognize themselves in the characters and recognize that the person who created those characters and wrote the scenes that drew them so deeply into the story were *their people*, the tribe they'd been seeking from an early age. While other children relish activity, particularly outdoors, future writers usually enjoy being inside, reading nonfiction books, a novel, a short story or poem. Reading brings future writers physical and mental pleasures, in ways it may not do so for other children.

IF YOU'RE SMART, YOU'RE SMART

A 1983 book by author Howard Gardner developed a "multiple intelligence theory" that identified eight types of intelligence:

- Kinesthetic: body smart
- Logical: math smart
- Linguistic: language smart
- Interpersonal: people smart
- Intrapersonal: self smart
- Auditory: musical smart
- Visual/spatial: picture smart
- Naturalistic: nature smart

Neuroscientists now know that intelligence is a general property that stems from a part of the brain called the frontal cortices, and that we apply this general intelligence to different tasks such as music, language, and logic; that is, *brains do not have specific, multiple intelligences.* In spite of what Gardner proposed, you have the capacity to master whatever you choose to practice. In other words, if you're smart, you're smart.

DO YOU HAVE AN AFFINITY FOR WRITING?

If you feel a burning desire to write, it's highly likely that you already possess certain mental and emotional qualities that can serve you well. Before launching into your next writing project, boldly embrace your strengths and shine a light on the skills you need to develop. These qualities include:

- verbal acuity, usually from an early age
- love for and a unique "ear" for words, language, rhythm, imagery, and story
- vivid imagination and creativity
- strong visual, auditory, and sensate memory

- astute observer who employs all five (or six) senses when witnessing and remembering events
- very conscious of feelings; empathetic, passionate
- inquisitive, curious, open to new thoughts and interpretations
- visionary, see larger picture and envision beginning, middle, and end of stories
- patient, able to delay gratification, allow the telling to unfold
- comfortable being alone for long periods of time
- like to live in your head; daydreamer
- actually *like* to think
- able to focus, capable of occasionally achieving a one-track mind
- detail oriented without being obsessive or an excessive worrier
- affinity for understanding and conveying multiple points of view

Every writer's brain is uniquely "designed" and few possess all of the qualities on the list. What matters most is that you notice the qualities you have and identify how they help—or hinder—your writing. View your affinities in a positive manner and reinforce your use of them to craft works of art by thinking and speaking positive thoughts about your process—it's been scientifically proven that an optimistic brain is a happy and productive brain. It's far too easy to fall into a mindset that writing is hard, arduous, demanding work that requires you to sacrifice a normal life for one filled with deadlines, anxiety, and stress. What's more desirable is to create a mindset that recognizes, utilizes, and celebrates the qualities that brought you to writing and inspires you to write even when it becomes a physical, mental, or emotional challenge. Reaffirming and employing the qualities that accompany your desire to write is more likely to lead to success and pleasure.

LIMIT GOOGLING

Did you know your brain is designed to find the easy way out? Psychologists Susan Fiske and Shelley Taylor coined the term "cognitive miser" to characterize the way our brains seek to conserve energy (by providing limited attention whenever possible) and to keep it simple (by utilizing mental shortcuts). Google and other search engines are a modern convenience we all welcome, but studies revealed that *Googling* relieves your brain of its duty to pose a hard question (which, in itself, is highly valuable) and, more importantly, it frees your brain of the necessity to search deep into its database for the neuronal connections that will eventually lead to the answer. Instead of firing up your brain, your brain barely has to think at all.

Mine Your Affinities for Affirmations

It's helpful to use your affinity list as affirmations to bolster positive thoughts about yourself as a writer: "I am imaginative, creative, and compassionate. I am open to new ways of thinking and fresh ways of seeing certain issues in life. I am able to focus on what I want this particular work to reflect. I love to think, plan, dream, originate. I have a magnificent, energized brain that loves to write." ... And so on.

Also, identifying qualities that aren't yet developed offers you the opportunity to focus on developing those skills. It's quite possible that the innate qualities are there but you simply haven't recognized them or called upon them when writing. Shining a light on them will help your brain focus on what you most appreciate and what you need it to do.

Writing Excellence Can Be Learned

We do know that brain development is dependent upon experience. The more a brain region is used, the bigger it tends to become. This means that some people may become smarter by simply exercising their brains more throughout life. It's been suggested that the genes involved in intelligence work by making people want to learn, and that the act of learning then enlarges the brain.

One thing that is a certainty: Writing is a craft that can be acquired, practiced, and mastered. Just as artists learn about oil and watercolor paints, the delicacy of brushes, the variations of brushstrokes, and the various styles that can imitated, writers learn about imagery, dialogue, narrative, scene building, and other aspects of the craft that they can focus upon and improve with practice. The art emerges as the craft is mastered, as writers learn how to conceive, create, craft, rewrite, reshape, refine, and perfect storytelling.

WORK ON YOUR VERBS

Writing teachers insist that verbs matter. Action-specific, uniquely apt, or surprising verbs are encouraged, and there may be some benefit to using them beyond exciting the reader. Researchers at Michigan State University created a "noun-verb" test to see if they could predict how the brain comes up with unusually creative ideas. MSU neuroscientist Jeremy Gray wanted to prove that the brain works hard to form creative ideas. "Nobody learns their ABCs in kindergarten and suddenly writes a great novel or poem," he says.

Study subjects were given a series of nouns and instructed to respond creatively with a verb for each. They were then measured for creativity through a series of more in-depth methods, including story writing, drawing, and on their creative achievements in real life. Those who came up with creative verbs were those also identified as the most creative in the second part of the test, as measured by the more in-depth methods. So when you need fresh ideas, to fire up your neurons, spend fifteen minutes focused solely on creating new and different action verbs.

WHY WRITERS WRITE

Ask writers why they write, and you're likely to hear that they don't feel complete unless they're writing, or some variation of that explanation. Having a "natural talent" is often attributed, but whether that refers to a talent for language, for storytelling, for researching and reporting facts, for dramatizing, or for being facile with free-form witticisms, who knows? I've often said that I write because I seem to possess an affinity for composition, for expressing my thoughts and feelings, and for writing about characters and situations. Like many, I write journal entries (most never published, by choice) because writing is a process that helps me hone my thoughts and burrow down to the most important feelings, revealing insights that don't come as easily any other way. Mostly, those who choose to write fiction do so because they love reading (or film or stage plays) and always have, and they have a few stories they long to contribute to the world. They hope their stories will be well received and meaningful for years to come, maybe capturing a point in time or aspects of life during their time that will offer something to knowledge one hundred years from now—about their country, about being a man or woman, about being a son or daughter, a father or mother, and so on. Writers love telling stories and feel an urge to create them, and the good news is that by developing your affinities, your perceptions, and your craft each step along the way you can definitely fire up your writing brain to become a better storyteller.

NARROW IT DOWN TO TWO JOBS

The first job of a writer is to notice—to see, hear, smell, taste, touch, feel, and *intuit*—what's important and then to use those stored memories to produce work that can be grasped at once, in prose that is strong and clean, not muddled. The writer's second job is to discover and develop his or her unique voice. Voice equates to your distinctive and exact way of viewing things, combined with a manner of expressing what you see and think in a natural, straightforward, and emotionally truthful way. The words, sentences, tone, and execution of craft should reflect who you are. Narrowing down your responsibility to just two things keeps your brain from feeling overwhelmed. Basically what you need to remember, especially at the beginning of any new work, is not to overcomplicate what's simple.

WHY WRITERS CREATE IN A CERTAIN MEDIUM

Why you write novels, poems, or self-help books may be another question that seems simplistic, but even if you've always been a memoirist or you've always been a journalist, it can be helpful to revisit the whys and wherefores. Did you consciously choose a medium or fall into it somewhat haphazardly? Do you feel that you have certain affinities or certain abilities you feel compelled to use or find easy to maximize and that, therefore, determine which medium you choose: dialogue (scriptwriters), action (anything from comic books to action films), characterization (novels), high drama (plays), feelings (poetry), and so on? Do you feel you've found your niche, or is a large part of your struggle to write (or perhaps even your resistance to write) based on perceived weaknesses that you feel you have to conquer?

Let's discuss various mediums and the affinities or motivations that may reinforce your decision.

- **NONFICTION:** You have the expertise and/or you like working with an expert to educate people on science, art, music, or anything, really. You possess an analytical brain that likes to burrow into topics that fascinate you, and you are adept at then explaining them to others. You have a fresh perspective on a subject that needs exploring.
- **HISTORICAL:** You want to record events as they happened or to revive stories that have been forgotten. You're inspired to capture the essence of people who have greatly affected the world; or you lived through something monumental (like being a soldier in a war) and have a unique contribution to offer.
- **NOVELS:** You long to capture essential knowledge about people and situations. You enjoy inspiring and entertaining others via storytelling. You want to create a work of art that is at once unique and memorable. You want to write stories that help individuals and society come to realizations about what was working, what wasn't working, and what might be needed. You want to shine a light on travesties or to inspire others to create a better world.

- **MEMOIR:** You lived through something that will offer others a way to navigate dangerous waters or that will inspire others to rise to new heights. People are wildly curious about you (for whatever reason). You want to make sense of what happened, find a silver lining in tragedy, and finally appreciate or release past events.
- **COMEDY:** When you talk, people laugh. You have a unique perspective and a razor-sharp, wickedly fast wit. Your lighthearted perspective needs expressing. You feel most alive when making people laugh. The world needs to lighten up. Humor is a healthy coping method.
- **POETRY/LYRICIST:** You enjoy mining your inner thoughts and feelings. You're passionate about the gracefulness of language and the use of metaphor to communicate deep thoughts and resounding notes of spiritual ascendancy or decline. You're deep and intense and have something remarkable to express.
- **NATURE WRITING:** You love bringing the beauty of the world to the forefront. You want to honor the beauty around us all and to help others see with new eyes, understand with fresh knowledge, and respect all the darlings of our universe. Everything in nature is a marvel to you.
- **SCIENCE WRITING:** You want to bring new knowledge to the forefront and to defend or uproot practices that hold the potential to foster life or lead to death. You'll do whatever it takes to promote science.

You get the idea ... choosing your medium is a reflection of personality, affinities, perspective, philosophy, and opportunity—and ideally it should be something you consciously consider. Recognizing your strengths should inform your choices but not necessarily restrict them. Maybe you've been a successful poet but you now long to write a novel (or vice versa). Noting the affinities you already possess that would support experimentation could inspire you to new heights.

UNDERSTANDING THE GENDER COMPONENT

Though some still cling to the idea that men's slightly larger brains give them an edge in high-level cognitive processing—such as writing—it's just not true. It is true, however, that women tend to best men in scholastic achievement. So what are the differences, and do they play a significant role in writing?

Some studies have shown that men have stronger connections between the front and back of their brain (something that helps with connecting what you see with what you do, and seeing and responding quickly), while women have more wiring between the left and right hemispheres of the brain, in an area called the corpus callosum (something that helps with quickly connecting ideas and empathy). The only region where men had more connections between the left and right sides of the brain was in the cerebellum, which plays a vital role in motor control.

All of which means males tend to be better at spatial processing, capable of rotating an object in their minds, something recently documented in infants as young as three months old. They also seem better at judging angle orientation and navigating by cardinal direction. Women, on the other hand, tend to have more verbal fluency and a greater memory for objects and faces—women are better at remembering where things are and who they've seen before. They are also more likely to navigate by using landmarks than cardinal direction.

Thus, as you can see, whatever small differences exist have little to do with intelligence, or anyone's superior cognitive functioning, which means that gender does not play a role in whether someone has an affinity for writing or has real potential to be better at writing. Men's brains are larger because they have larger skulls and higher body mass. Period.

UNDERSTANDING THE EMOTIONAL COMPONENT

Obviously the reasons we've discussed may help you clarify the type of writing you wish to do, but the reasons to *actually* write are often emotional:

- to pummel or even eviscerate an enemy (Not usually a good idea.)
- to spew out feelings that you were unable to expel any other way (Could go badly or could be healing, depending on whether you chose a target or accept responsibility and use the process to better understand and forgive yourself.)
- to express a self-righteous attitude (Dogma is usually shortsighted at best.)
- to spread the message of love or to encourage love (Usually a worthwhile idea, if it's not too saccharin or delusional.)
- to spin a fascinating tale and be seen as clever (Go for it, but strive for genuine, original cleverness.)
- to share a story that dominates your thoughts and keeps asking to be told (Give it a whirl!)
- to accomplish the goal of creating a work of art (Polish your craft and rewrite and rewrite until it truly is unique and meaningful.)
- to make sense of the world around you
- to find your place in the history of literature, science, comedy, or ... (Do your homework so you have something groundbreaking to say or do.)
- to give voice to those who felt dispossessed and unable to fight their own battles
- to use the talents bestowed upon you (Maybe you're just not good at anything else.)
- to expose what is wrong or define what is right with the world
- to capture life in all its complexity

These are all examples of what may be motivating you to write, and while you don't have to bring these motivations to light, in working to identify what compels you to write, you are giving your brain an assignment to use its full capacity to help you fulfill your goal and achieve your desires. This can be helpful when your writing sags and you begin to wonder if it's all worth the effort. If you've provided your brain with the reasons why you are writing your work in progress (or waiting for its time), your brain will bring those ideas back to consciousness when you most need them.

HONOR THE VALUE IN FICTION

Storytelling began as a way for humans to relay information, from where to find food sources to the benefits of familial bonding. Raymond A. Mar, Ph.D. theorizes that fictional stories were the easiest way to memorize and communicate a complex set of information. "You can think of all narrative as just taking this to another level, where people are creating the sort of longer-term fictional stories that have been used with a certain amount of information embedded in them," Mar explained. "It's easier to remember the content of these stories, and they're also a very compelling way to communicate this information." In fact, psychologists and neuroscientists have found that we remember information best when it is delivered in the form of a plot—this is called *semantic memory*. Stories still serve a definitive purpose and the stronger the purpose, the clearer the story—so, *what's your purpose?*

WHY DO YOU WRITE?

It seems like such a simplistic question, yet the answer plays a crucial role in motivating your brain. As we've discussed, writing is not easy—though it may flow for some—and it requires dedication and persistence and a lot of intensive thinking. I know few writers that have the luxury of time and many writers who constantly struggle with self-doubt or feeling discouraged, often questioning why they put themselves through the hoops.

We'll talk more in the next chapter about the values of identifying which type of writer you are, but first, your Train Your Writing

Brain assignment (we'll have one at the end of each chapter, designed to help you fire up your writing brain).

TRAIN YOUR WRITING BRAIN: LIST YOUR RESOURCES AND YOUR MOTIVATIONS

To solidify and validate the characteristics (affinities) you have in your writing arsenal, make a list—include even the seemingly unimportant qualities. If you keep a journal, dedicate at least one page to it; if you don't keep a journal, use good writing paper and a pen—which helps you connect to your brain—and list the attributes that contribute to your ability to write well. Take time to ponder and be as generous and honest as possible—noting strengths, and areas that may need more work. Once your list is complete, use it to state your natural proclivities as an affirmation before you next write.

Keep doing this over time, thereby reinforcing your ownership. Soon doing so may become part of the ritual leading up to writing sessions, effectively evoking the kind of positive mindset that will make your writing sessions more productive—and more satisfying.

Once that list is complete, create another list that details your motivations for working on whatever you're currently working on. Again, be as specific and personal as possible, digging beneath the surface to get really clear on why you are choosing to write about whatever it is you're currently working on, and why completing this work has deep, personal meaning for you.

What you're doing is feeding body, soul, mind, and brain the nourishment all will need to persist and do the best work possible. Your brain is your greatest writing asset, so engage it from the beginning, layering in complexity and encouraging focus, and you will be fostering the kind of writing mindset that reinforces your efforts and leads to successful completion.

WRITERS ON CRAFT

"There's no hole inside of me to fill or anything like that, but once I started doing it, I couldn't imagine wanting to do anything else for a living. I noticed very quickly that writing was the only way to lose track of time."

—MICHAEL LEWIS

"I've never worked a day in my life. The joy of writing has propelled me from day to day and year to year. I want you to envy me my joy. Get out of here tonight and say: 'Am I being joyful?'"

—RAY BRADBURY

"If you are interested in something, no matter what it is, go at it at full speed ahead. Embrace it with both arms, hug it, love it and above all become passionate about it. Lukewarm is no good. Hot is no good either. White hot and passionate is the only thing to be."

—ROALD DAHL

"One day I was at my job as a consulting programmer for Mobil Oil. I was tired of writing programs, so I wrote this sentence: 'On hot sticky days in southern Louisiana, the fire ants swarmed.' I'd never been to Louisiana, and I'd never seen a fire ant, but I thought 'this sounds like the first line of a novel,' so I wrote my first book."

—WALTER MOSLEY

"I would write even if I couldn't make a living at it, because I can't not write. I am amazed and delighted and still in a state of shock about the success of *Water for Elephants*, but that's not why I write. I do it for love. The rest is gravy."

—SARA GRUEN

IDENTIFY YOUR WRITING BRAIN
What Kind of Writer Are You?

"The writer must be four people:
The nut; [that is] the obsédé [the obsessed]
The moron
The stylist and
The critic.
(1) Supplies the material; (2) lets it come out; (3) is taste; (4) is intelligence. A great writer has all four—but you can still be a good writer with only 1 and 2; they're most important."

—SUSAN SONTAG

We remember through stories. Most of the elements of our lives—our experiences, knowledge, dreams, hopes, and wishes—all create and thrive on story. It's clearly how our distant ancestors learned, how countless parents, mentors, and teachers conveyed knowledge and wisdom through the ages, by first focusing on what their offspring needed to know to survive, and later as a way to strengthen familial and community bonds, bring people together, and enjoy each other's company. Story is so deeply ingrained in what it means to be human that our brains have likely adapted to the prominent role story maintains. We have developed what Daniel Pink, author of *A Whole New Mind*, calls "story grammar," which creates a way for humans to understand how the world works and how to connect with others.

Storytelling is so ingrained that we often unwittingly create a structure—Joseph Campbell's *The Hero's Journey*, for example—in stories we tell others and ourselves. Stories help us make sense of the world and our place in it. They also give us a way to think about—dream about, cope with, and learn from—our lives, relationships, choices, past, present, and future, as well imagine new scenarios. Stories posit ideas that our minds can process, including conceptually *thinking about thinking*, which neuroscientists call "metacognition."

Just as our brains have evolved, stories have evolved, becoming more complex, more multidimensional, and more original. Most modern-day humans have far more time to ruminate, to delve deeper into whatever interests them, to access massive amounts of knowledge within seconds, and to know far more about the world they live in—all of which translates into innovation and complexity in storytelling. It's a good time to be a professional storyteller, no matter your venue.

WHAT'S YOUR CHOICE METHOD OF STORYTELLING?

Not everyone is a writer, but all writers are storytellers. Whether they are crafting novels, memoirs, commercials, songs, or poems, they are telling stories. As such, those attracted to writing as an art form or as a profession—or as a passionate expression—likely have an affinity for language and storytelling. The various forms an affinity for writing can take, and defining the qualities that may attract individuals to a certain form of expression, would mostly be guesswork (and inconclusive because there's also a lot of overlap). However, some predilections—assuming all professional writers love writing and have an affinity for words—could be assumed, for example:

- **JOURNALISTS** tend to be extroverted, curious, methodical, organized, inquisitive, persistent, ambitious, and love to investigate or dig deeper into events. They are fascinated by the "news of the day" and want to reveal the truth to change the world.
- **NOVELISTS** are often introverted, contemplative, expansive, and see beneath the surface of what people do and how relationships and society work. They're drawn to original thinking, often adept at seeing something in a revealing way. They want to enlighten or entertain the world, or at least express their unique perspective.

- **MEMOIRISTS** are often introverted, introspective, hypersensitive, nostalgic, transfixed observers, invested in truth, understanding, closure, and justice. They've experienced something that they feel needs to be discussed and ultimately seek more understanding and compassion for themselves—and others.
- **SONGWRITERS** are likely closest to lyrical poets and tend to think melodically and rhythmically; they are typically verbally expressive and have an appreciation for a tightened story arc. They are seduced and mesmerized by the power of music and want to share joy and passion, or they want to use music as a means to motivate others to change society.
- **POETS** are often introverted, introspective, sensitive, passionate, internally driven, and very focused on the beauty and meaning of each word, each expression. They want to capture the complexity of a moment that really matters and might go unnoticed if they don't draw eyes and ears to it.
- **PLAYWRIGHTS** usually have a sophisticated ear for dialogue, love the cadence of speech, know how to hype drama and elevate humor. They prefer one-on-one interactions in stories but are open to collaboration when producing their work. They love the magic, or catastrophe, that occurs when individuals collide.
- **SCREENWRITERS** tend to also be adept at dialogue. They are visual storytellers who "see" the story in their minds, right down to the setting details. They're also collaborative, action oriented, and seek stimulation. They want to show the world what they see—and why it matters.

These are, of course, oversimplifications, but if you're struggling with which medium might be best suited for your proclivities and heart's desire, formulate a list of your own, exploring the personality and affinities that may draw you to a certain form of expression or offer you the best possibility of excelling in one form over another. This kind of list also may help you hone in on unique ways to use the particular talents you have—and to identify which ones you might want to bolster.

Paula Munier, author of *Plot Perfect*, and one of my closest writer friends says that she's an extrovert and thus shouldn't be as attracted as she is to being a novelist; and I joke that I'm an introvert who forced herself to become a journalist—what we mean is that our personalities weren't the "norm" and may have made our initial forays into those forms of writing more challenging. Working as a journalist forced me to become more extroverted, more competitive, and perhaps even more ambitious—and it taught me the basics (who, what, when, where, why, and how), and how to delve deeper into stories. It also taught me how to fire up my writing brain, focus, and get words on paper when a deadline loomed.

Remember: You can create writing templates for your brain and sculpt your brain to improve certain skills related to becoming a more creative, more productive, and more successful writer.

MAKE WRITING YOUR THING

It seems we can all learn a lesson from the 1960s, when youth committed to "doing their thing," pursuing whatever "turned them on." In all the scientific efforts to find magic pills for fighting off dementia and Alzheimer's disease, only regular, aerobic exercise and active mental engagement show any measurable results. Rather than splurging for "brain games," you may be better off to pursue your writing as your "thing." Scientists have found that doing what holds deep, personal meaning to you, thereby exciting your brain, is more effective in keeping your brain supple than any magic pills or games. If your passion is writing, then actively writing—or engaging in activities related to writing—could be exceptionally good for your long-term brain health.

ARE YOU THIS WAY OR THAT WAY?

While this may primarily apply to fiction writing, the notion that only two broad types of writers exist is fairly common. Here are a few comparisons from a host of writers (and reviewers):

THIS WAY	THAT WAY
Those who write what they know	Those who write in order to know
Those who are talented (facile at conveying)	Those who are gifted (transcendent translators)
Those who write the truth	Those who don't write the truth
Those who write to fulfill their artistic vision	Those who write primarily to sell
Those who are inner directed, use themselves as subjects or inspiration	Those who look outward and focus on others as subjects or inspirations
Those who make you think	Those who make you wonder
Those who are in love with words	Those who are in love with imagery
Those who want language transparent, easily shared	Those who want to invent their own obscure language
Those who make you think, "Yes, that's the way it is"	Those who make you think, "I never imagined it could be that way"
Those who self-consciously construct literary meaning	Those whose work is unconscious in origin
Those who are "A" writers (gifted storytellers)	Those who are "B" writers (facile users of language)
Recently published	Unpublished authors (which also includes long-ago published authors)

While many of the above thoughts are amusing, it is worthwhile to ponder what kind of writer you want to be, as doing so, once again, solidifies for your brain what is most important to you—as a writer—and how you want your brain to contribute to the process.

AVOID DELUSION

When writing about the brain, Hollywood screenplays have run the spectrum from mostly wrong to completely inaccurate. For instance, the ability to store memories but subsequently lose them on a selective, timed basis exists only in the screenwriter's imagination.

SOMEWHAT ACCURATE	COMPLETELY INACCURATE
Memento	Total Recall
Finding Nemo	50 First Dates
A Beautiful Mind	Men in Black

Awakenings	The Long Kiss Goodnight
Still Alice	Murder by Night

It's also not true that psychological trauma or a whack in the head or the sight of something familiar will reawaken memory.

WHAT'S YOUR PREFERRED GENRE?

It doesn't take a genius to realize that each of us has a genre—or two or five—we love. The beauty of writing is that you can choose what you want to write about and how you want to write it. To help you think about where you'd like to go, here's a short list of personality/brain traits that might influence which genre you favor:

GENRE	QUALITIES
Literary Fiction	intelligent, hyperobservant, contemplative, original thinker
Nonfiction	prideful about being logical, linear, factual, teacher, aspiring genius
Historical	detail oriented, factual, immersive, nostalgic, values accuracy and truth
Science Fiction	super detail oriented, fantastical, imaginative, visionary, original
Women's Fiction	modern, values relationship/feelings, seeks integration, feminist
Thriller	excitable, fast paced, action oriented, needs lots of stimulation
Mystery	loves puzzles, inquisitive, focuses on details, loves to research
Romance	focuses on relationships and feelings, craves and savors connection
Western	nostalgic, individualistic, feels safer living in the past

Once you identify the genre most suited to your personality—and your brain—the easier it should be to get the words flowing. It's important to keep in mind, however, that authors who ingeniously combine two (or more) genres in a fresh way increase their chances of generating a breakthrough novel, and it's always good to change your mind and experiment.

Recent examples of blended genres that did exceptionally well would be: *Outlander*, which combined time travel, romance, and action adventure; *Pride and Prejudice and Zombies*, which combined classic literature and horror; and *Glory O'Brien's History of the Future*, which blended young adult with romance, science fiction, feminism, and magic realism.

By those titles alone, it's obvious how much fun the authors had thinking outside the limited box of their original genre. Consider your current work in progress and ask yourself what would happen if you added horror elements to your western or blended science fiction with historical elements. It's as easy as loosening strictures, allowing your brain to play, and being appreciative when it comes up with some surprising ideas.

LIMIT TEXTING

In today's modern world, many prefer texting or messaging on social media to speaking with others. While efficient, clipped electronic communication lacks visual and auditory cues, language and vocabulary choices, the sound and cadence of normal conversation, and discernment of emotional context—all of which help writers create realistic, unique characters, situations, and dialogue, and infuse scenes with physicality and emotional subtext—while texting, quite simply, does not.

Next, we move on to the conceptual game of defining your writing brain (or, more correctly, writing habits) as either this or that. Clearly brains are not so strictly categorized, but when it comes to the art of writing, a preponderance of people do lean one direction or the other. Let's begin with Ezra Pound, who put some thought into capturing the differences.

ARE YOU AN INVENTOR, A MASTER, OR A DILUTER?

In describing what he called "pure elements in literature," Ezra Pound, the American expatriate poet and critic who was a major figure in the modernist movement of the 1900s, theorized that literature had been created by what he called "classes of people" consisting of the following (he uses *men* to represent both male and female members of the human race):

1. **INVENTORS.** "Men who found a new process, or whose extant work gives us the first known example of a process."
2. **MASTERS.** "Men who combined a number of such processes, and who used them as well as, or better, than the inventors."
3. **DILUTERS.** "Men who came after the first two kinds of writer and couldn't do the job quite as well."
4. **GOOD WRITERS WITHOUT SALIENT QUALITIES.** "Men who are fortunate enough to be born when the literature of a given country is in good working order, or when some particular branch of writing is 'healthy.' For example, men who wrote sonnets in Dante's time, men who wrote short lyrics in Shakespeare's time, or for several decades thereafter, or who wrote French novels and stories after Flaubert had shown them how."
5. **WRITERS OF BELLES-LETTRES.** "That is, men who didn't really invent anything, but who specialized in some particular part of writing, who couldn't be considered as 'great men' or as authors who were trying to give a complete presentation of life, or of their epoch." One presumes he meant those who write more for entertainment, whose work would have been pleasurable or aesthetically pleasing to read, but not particularly literary.
6. **THE STARTERS OF CRAZES.** (Pound didn't seem to think this category needed definition.)

Pound wanted to encourage readers to be more selective in their choices of literature. He told them they wouldn't be able to distinguish differences or establish value in the writing itself until they familiarized themselves with inventors and masters—something that is also true for novice writers. So let's talk about styles of writing and how you might approach and practice your craft to become one of Ezra Pound's preferred "classes" of writers.

WRITE WITH A SLOW HAND

According to Nobel Prizewinner (for his work on the psychology of judgment and decision making) Daniel Kahneman, author of *Thinking, Fast and Slow*, the brain operates under two systems: System 1 (fast thinking) and System 2 (slow thinking). Fast thinking happens automatically, with little effort or voluntary control, while slow thinking involves reasoning and careful consideration (*metacognition* or *thinking about thinking*, for example). One of the tasks slow thinking handles is overcoming the impulses that arise from fast thinking. Slow thinking is in charge of self-control. There are definite advantages to occasionally writing with a slow hand, to tamping down the rush of automatic thinking in favor of deliberately refining how you craft your story. To slow your thinking, try working with paper and pen, in cursive, employing the swirls and flourishes of yesteryear's penmanship.

ARE YOU A FOX OR A HEDGEHOG?

In 1953, philosopher Isaiah Berlin wrote a collection of essays, *The Hedgehog and the Fox*, in which he classified writers as hedgehogs or foxes. The original line is credited to Greek poet Archilochus (c. 680 B.C.–c. 645 B.C.) who wrote: "The fox knows many things, but the hedgehog knows one big thing." Some believe that Archilochus ingeniously defined the deepest divide writers and thinkers experience, but Berlin says that he'd written the essay "as a kind of enjoyable intellectual game."

Berlin's hedgehogs view the world through the lens of a single defining idea (Plato, Dante, Pascal, Hegel, Dostoevsky, Nietzsche, Ibsen, and Proust, as examples) while foxes draw on a wide variety of experiences and refuse to boil the world down to a single idea (Herodotus, Aristotle, Erasmus, Shakespeare, Montaigne, Molière, Goethe, Pushkin, Balzac, and Joyce, as examples). Berlin says hedgehogs adhere to one unshakeable conceptual and stylistic unity, clinging to a single, universal, organizing principle that he or she fervently believes; whereas foxes adapt his or her strategy to the circumstances, seizing the essence of a vast variety of experiences and objects, seeking to fit them into—or exclude them from—an unchanging, sometimes fanatical unitary inner vision.

Hedgehogs are tenaciously consistent, no matter what they write—both in terms of style and vision. Foxes change their methods and field of reference from book to book, because they don't like to do the same thing again.

So which are you: hedgehog or fox? And which one holds the greatest appeal? It may be time for you to get a little foxy.

NO RIGHT BRAINER

Dating back to the 1970s, someone postulated, and many latched onto the idea, that you were either dominated by your *left brain* (analytical) hemisphere or *right brain* (creative) hemisphere. Despite its popularity, neuroscientists have repeatedly debunked the notion. Your brain does have distinct regions, and we all use both sides of our brains almost all the time. The role played by any given brain area is different depending on the state of the network of which it is currently a part, and how activity unfolds over time often matters more than where it is in the brain. Processing within each relies on a rich, dense network of connections, which then flow through a midline fiber tract known as your corpus callosum. Any natural tendencies you have for writing are not *right brain* but evidence that your hemispheres communicate very well indeed.

ARE YOU A TOP OR A BOTTOM BRAIN?

According to psychologist and neuroscientist Stephen Kosslyn, author of *Top Brain, Bottom Brain*, humans tend to be top-brain or bottom-brain centric, and my interpretation of his theory in relation to determining what kind of writer you tend to be is outlined here:

- Those who strongly favor the **TOP-BRAIN** system collect information about their environment and their emotions to create and adhere to a strategic vision, using future input to make course corrections—they would tend to think their way through writing a book.
- Those who strongly rely on the **BOTTOM-BRAIN** system organize signals from their senses and compare them to what's stored in memory, and their emotions to interpret its significance and then figure out what the plan is—they would tend to feel their way through writing a book.

Let's say you have a book to write: If you primarily rely on your top-brain, you would generate a detailed outline to forge ahead, and risk being so focused on your plan that you forfeit flexibility based on feelings about whether it was working or not working; if you primarily rely on your bottom brain, you might have an idea and simply forge ahead, happy to see where your intuition, filtered by past experiences, takes you, and risk getting lost in unfocused thoughts.

Kosslyn identifies four cognitive modes, which he calls "default modes in thinking," but for the purposes of planning and writing a book (or movie or play), the analogy of a top and bottom brain offers the kind of comparison that could help you contemplate whether you're playing to your strengths when conceiving, creating, and crafting your book, or if you might be too rigidly one way or another. We'll have a quiz at the end of this chapter to see if you're strongly top, strongly bottom, or tend to lean toward the top or bottom modes of thinking.

What matters most, of course, is that interplay occurs between the top and bottom brain. Ideally, you want both hemispheres to communicate and work in tandem—to come up with an idea, create a plan, employ intuition, factor in feelings and prior experience, anticipate consequences, and adapt the plan as needed. What you most need to figure out is if you're stuck in one mode over the distinct advantage of being bidirectional and inclusive.

CREATE A BIDIRECTIONAL CONVERSATION

Many of the neurons in the frontal lobe move in a bidirectional manner, from top to bottom, and vice versa. When something attracts your brain, the information typically travels from the bottom up, but when a conscious event is taking place (during mindfulness, for example), a massive increase in bidirectional causality (an interactive conversation between regions) occurs. Neurons keep on "talking." If stimuli are not registering (for lack of interest or importance), the frontal lobe seems to send messenger neurons down (asking if anything is important right now), but bottom up responses dwindle, which may be why some events never register. When writing, or researching, to keep the "bidirectional conversation" going, be sure to pay closer attention to what you're doing.

ARE YOU A PLOTTER OR A PANTSER?

Some in publishing narrow the way writers work down to two possibilities—plotters or pantsers:

- **PLOTTERS**, of course, are those who wouldn't sit down to write a novel (or screenplay) until they'd come up with and pondered an idea; considered their protagonist's and antagonist's character arcs; conducted fairly extensive research; considered theme, setting, and tone; plotted the story from beginning to end; and created a complex biographical sketch for each of their characters.
- **PANTSERS**, on the other hand, still believe in muses, that inspiration will strike and their task will be to plant themselves in a chair, face a blank page, and dive right in. Even if they feel somewhat tortured by the process, they trust that their subconscious will deliver up a fascinating story idea, unforgettable characters, and take them, and their characters, on a delightfully surprising journey.

Some writers don't begin writing until they have a fairly clear picture of what they're going to write from beginning to end and seem to function best when organized. Others comfortably begin with a vague idea of story and characters, and seem to be comfortable unleashing their unconscious and letting the story unfold as they type. Most writers, however, fall somewhere in the middle, searching for an optimum way to come up with a fabulous and original idea, a way to tell the story that will capture attention and honor their craft, and a way to write it that allows them to get as many words written—as fast as possible—all without sacrificing craft.

BE A PRACTICING AMBI

There's long been a debate about who are the most productive thinkers: those who rely on rational methods or those who rely on intuition. According to Wilma Koutstaal, Ph.D., author of *The Agile Mind*, highly effective problem solvers move rapidly and flexibly from intuitive to rational, and back again; and from specific to abstract thinking, and back again, regardless of what type of problem is addressed. "Mental agility is best promoted by equally valuing intuition and analysis—along with attention to detail and the big picture," she explained. A nimble, ambidextrous mind, dealing effectively with thinking, emotion, and action, employs the conscious, rational style of problem solving *and* the unconscious, intuitive style of problem solving.

ARE YOU A BASHER OR A SWOOPER?

In an interview published in *Timequake* in 1997, novelist and provocateur Kurt Vonnegut described two types of storytellers, saying, "Tellers of stories with ink on paper, not that they matter anymore, have been either swoopers or bashers."

According to Vonnegut, swoopers write a story quickly, which in his description is: "higgledy-piggledy, crinkum-crankum, any which way. Then they go over it again painstakingly, fixing everything that is just plain awful or doesn't work; [while] bashers go one sentence at a time, getting it exactly right before they go on to the next one. When they're done they're done."

Vonnegut considered himself a basher, and considered most men bashers, and most women swoopers. "Writers who are swoopers, it seems to me, find it wonderful that people are funny or tragic or whatever, worth reporting, without wondering why or how people are alive in the first place. Bashers, while ostensibly making sentence after sentence as efficient as possible, may actually be breaking down seeming doors and fences, cutting their ways through seeming barbed-wire entanglements, under fire and in an atmosphere of mustard gas, in search of answers to these eternal questions: 'What in heck should we be doing? What in heck is really going on?'"

Though you may find Mr. Vonnegut's gender-specific attitudes a tad outdated, his descriptions are humorous and do describe a variation in approach that many writers either hate or love, adopt or discard. He offers *pause for thought*, which is what any writer should be doing, as well as evaluating how his or her writing process is working.

ARE YOU A MACRO OR A MICRO?

Novelist Zadie Smith—author of *White Teeth, NW,* and *Changing My Mind*—identified what she saw as two "breeds of novelists." In *Changing My Mind*, Smith described Macro Planners as "novelists who make notes, organize material, configure a plot, and create a structure—all before she writes the title page." Macros are more likely to start anywhere and to switch things around midway through the process, including characters, setting, chapters, and endings.

Smith calls this kind of "radical surgery" unthinkable for her, as she's the other type, the Micro Manager. "I start at the first sentence of a novel and I finish at the last," Smith says. "It would never occur to me to choose among three different endings because I haven't the slightest idea of the ending until I get to it, a fact that will surprise no one who reads my novels."

Smith says it's easy to identify Micro Managers, as the first twenty pages of their manuscript would be an "opening pileup of too-careful, obsessively worried-over sentences, a block of stilted verbiage that only loosens and relaxes after the twenty-page mark is passed." Smith says she typically feels the type of "existential angst" that Kierkegaard believed powers, rather than hinders, creative work. "When I finally settled on a tone, the rest of the book was finished in five months. Worrying over the first twenty pages is a way of working on the whole novel, a way of finding its structure, its plot, its character—all of which, for a Micro Manager, are contained in the sensibility of a sentence. Once the tone is there, all else follows."

WHAT KIND OF WRITING BRAIN DO YOU HAVE?

As we've been discussing, writers usually adopt a manner of writing that works for them—that's if they pursue their craft on a regular basis and actually complete works. Here's a quiz you can take to assist in contemplating how you have been asking your writing brain to work behind the scenes. Hopefully the classifications will offer a window into your writing process—and what adjustments could be made that might make the entire process more suited to how *your* writing brain works.

How My Writing Brain Works
Choose the answer that is closest to the truth:

>   a) I never start writing a novel until I know the beginning, the ending, the characters, and I have a detailed outline.
>   b) I never start writing a novel until I've pinned down what I want to write about, know who I want the characters to be, and have a list of specific plot points.
>   c) I start writing a novel when a topic or character excites me and I'm super juiced about it.
>   d) I start writing a novel when the muse alights upon my shoulder.

>   a) I am obsessed with knowing exactly what's going to happen.
>   b) I never start until I've thought pretty hard about the plotline and characters.

c) I like coming up with an idea and then seeing where it leads me.

d) I like to be surprised by ideas that pop into my head.

a) I use a software program that helps me think about all the various aspects of my story.

b) I have a system I use to create all the major and minor plot points.

c) I think about the broad strokes, but plotting makes me lose my juice.

d) I just sit down and let it flow.

a) I write biographies for every character, even the minor ones.

b) I get to know each of my main characters before I write.

c) I never write biographies, I make it up as I go along.

d) I wait for my characters to surprise me.

a) I read every book on writing I can find and spend weeks poring over them.

b) I read other writers' work to figure out how they handle plotting, characterization, dialogue, etc.

c) I find books that have the same elements (point of view, unstructured plotlines) as the novel I want to write so I can figure out what I want to do.

d) I trust my muse and just write until I get it right.

a) I always write from chapter one through to the end.

b) I work my way through progressively from the beginning to the end, but if I'm having trouble with a particular chapter, I'll skip it and go back to it later.

c) I write where there's heat, skipping around often.

d) I write all the easy scenes first.

a) I have hours I set aside for writing every day, even on the weekends.
b) I write for a few hours every day, except on weekends.
c) I write in a white heat, working every day until I drop.
d) I write when the spirit moves me.

a) I make an outline and never stray from it.
b) I outline my story in broad strokes, but expect it to evolve as I write.
c) I figure out my main plot points, but wing it from there.
d) I haven't outlined anything since essays in college.

a) I only read books in my preferred genres.
b) I read mostly books in my genre and a few outside just for fun.
c) I read books similar to what I want to write, but I also read broadly.
d) I read all sorts of books on all sorts of subjects.

a) I prefer to sign up for a tour with a predetermined itinerary when I travel.
b) I plan my own vacation, down to the last detail.
c) I make hotel reservations and wing it from there.
d) I get on a plane and go.

Now tally up your answers.

IF YOU HAVE MOSTLY A'S, YOU ARE A RATIONAL/TOP BRAIN WRITER. You are more reliant on your cortex and "thinking." This means that you rely on the biggest, most modern part of your brain to think and write. You value intellect above everything else, and you are confident in your own intellectual abilities. You may spend so much time researching and thinking and planning your story that you never write a word. Think your way through your story—from structure and plot to character and craft—but don't forget to engage your feelings as well. Your "top brain" does not contain your emotional structures, and if you're not careful, your story won't either. All plot and no heart is not good storytelling.

IF YOU HAVE MOSTLY B'S, YOU ARE A TOP HEAVY BI-BRAIN WRITER. This means that while you can harness both parts of your brain, you still rely more heavily on intellect than feeling. You have an organized approach to writing; you tend to plot out your stories in advance, in broad strokes rather than beat by beat. Be sure to trust your intuition in your writing process and allow yourself to go where it takes you.

IF YOU HAVE MOSTLY C'S, YOU ARE A BOTTOM HEAVY BI-BRAIN WRITER. The means that you, too, can harness both parts of your brain, but you are more in touch with your feelings. Emotion drives your writing, and while this can help you connect with readers, you need to make sure that you ground those feelings in a solid foundation. Concentrate on building a plot that will support the emotional impact you want to make on readers.

IF YOU HAVE MOSTLY D'S, YOU ARE AN EMOTIONAL/BOTTOM BRAIN WRITER. You are more reliant on your limbic system and "feelings and intuition." Your work may be awash with emotion—but where's the story? You need to harness your feeling to the engine of plot. Winging it may only take you so far; you have to think your way through your plot. You love creating but may resist mastering craft. You may find it difficult to finish your work; you need to adopt a disciplined attitude toward your work.

TRAIN YOUR WRITING BRAIN: DO THE OPPOSITE OF WHAT YOU NORMALLY DO

One of the best pieces of advice I ever got, unrelated to writing, was to break out of ruts by doing the exact opposite of what I'd normally do. If I always turned left when leaving my house, turn right. If I always worked in the early morning hours, only work in the late evening hours. Knowing what kind of writer you prefer to be and what works for you as a writer obviously makes it easier to establish productive writing habits, in which case, you should do more of what you're already doing—but it's good to experiment on occasion. If you're stuck in a rut and your writing sessions have stalled, you might find it effective to do the opposite of what you normally do.

STEP 1: For fun, write a short story (750–1,000 words) completely on the fly, without thinking at all before you sit down to write; and then write another short story only after you've spent at least one full hour thinking about the characters and the plot, and jotting down a detailed outline of what will happen.

STEP 2: Repeat the exercise, but amp up the challenge: Write a longer story or chapter of your novel in progress (3,000–4,000 words). Remember that the first attempt is to be written on the fly, without thinking or planning what you'll write; and the second attempt is only to be written after you've spent at least three hours creating an outline, determining the setting, the plot, which characters will be in the scenes, what will be said, what each will do, and what the outcome will be. Remember to plan the inciting incident and to identify the sources of rising tension, the climactic scenes, and resolution for each (which may be continued conflict).

STEP 3: Record your observations about your writing process. Have you identified the traits, habits, and preferences that most benefit your productivity and artistic expression? Have you realized that you could improve productivity, creativity, and artistic expression, if you came up with techniques that better fit your personality? Have you identified personality traits or habits that are sabotaging your best efforts? Whatever writing methods work for you are fine, but you may well find that your brain has strong preferences and that catering to them will foster greater creativity and make your writing sessions go smoother.

EXTRA CREDIT: Print a short story or chapter you've recently written and use highlighters (yellow for emotion and green for intellect) and highlight the two elements throughout. Are you seeing a pattern? Do your characters rely heavily on intellect to negotiate the world, or do they mostly rely on intuition and emotions? When rewriting, consider ways you can incorporate both rational thinking and emotional feeling in your writing process and in your characters.

WRITERS ON CRAFT

"I write to dream, to connect with other human beings, to record, to clarify, to visit the dead. I have a kind of primitive need to leave a mark on the world. Also, I have a need for money."

—MARY KARR

"Wanting to be a writer is a huge percentage of what makes you be one. You have to want to do it really badly. You have to feel that's what you're supposed to be doing. A lot of my friends who thought about being writers ended up going into law or advertising or PR. They still dreamed about writing, but they couldn't give up their good jobs. Fortunately, I never had a good job to give up."

—SUSAN ORLEAN

"People like me didn't become writers, and probably I would not be a writer today had not a college instructor said to me, 'Why are you premed? You should do something with words.' He then called up his editor at Doubleday and said, 'I've got this student. You should give her a job.'"

—GISH JEN

"The refusal to rest content, the willingness to risk excess on behalf of one's obsessions, is what distinguishes artists from entertainers, and what makes some artists adventurers on behalf of us all."

—JOHN UPDIKE

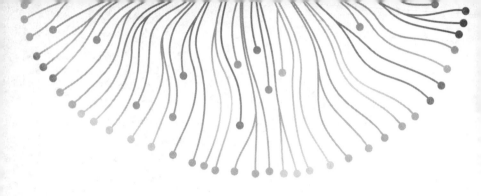

PHASE TWO

YOUR IDEA-GENERATING BRAIN

"We live by stories. It's the principle by which we organize our experience and thus derive our sense of who we are. We're in an unceasing flow of time and events and people, and to make sense of what goes past, we put a beginning and an end to a certain thing, and we leave things out and we heighten other things, and in that way we break the unbroken flow into stories, because that's the only way we can give it significance."

—TOBIAS WOLFF

REINFORCE YOUR WRITING BRAIN

Get Ready to Write

"Most beginning writers—and I was the same—are like chefs trying to cook great dishes that they've never tasted themselves. How can you make a great—or even an adequate—bouillabaisse if you've never had any? If you don't really understand why people read mysteries—or romances or literary novels or thrillers or whatever—then there's no way in the world you're going to write one that anyone wants to publish. This is the meaning of the well-known expression, *Write what you know*."

—DANIEL QUINN

Prepping to write is crucial, particularly if you're new to writing, or if you've not yet formulated a clear picture of what you want the work to be and need inspiration and ideas ... and especially *if* you want your writing brain fired up and ready to go. If you—like the vast majority of writers—have difficulty getting out of the gate, there are lots of things you can do to bolster your inspiration and confidence—and get those synapses firing, sparking a boatload of new ideas.

READ THINGS SIMILAR TO WHAT YOU WANT TO WRITE

It's imperative that you read a lot of books that are similar to what you want to write, particularly if you're a "new" writer. Even if you haven't made a final decision or have a clear understanding of what you will be writing, read what attracts you and you'll likely discover at least the style in which you wish to work.

It Provides Ideas

Reading books similar to what you want to write not only offers ideas, it indoctrinates your brain with the sort of material you want to produce. This does not equate to mimicking ideas, as that's never desirable, but it is always instructive to know what's out there and what's already been written about extensively so you can figure out a way to make your work unique, or at least different from what's available. Depending on the type of work, you may want to take notes. For nonfiction, for example, it's important to make sure you're saying something new, or at least saying something in a new way, with a new slant, so keeping track of what you've read will help as you craft the book. With fiction, it's good to know what types of plots may be oversaturating the market.

PRACTICE DUE DILIGENCE

It's your duty (for your brain) to find novels, songs, poems, or nonfiction books that are similar to what you want to achieve, right down to the minute elements that you most admire (or strongly dislike). It goes back to the long-standing precept that "you have to know the rules to break the rules." You need to lay the groundwork—your conceptual framework—before you can pave new roads. You may fall into the trap of over-emulating other writers' styles in the beginning, but your brain will soon sort this out and begin offering ideas to make what you write your own. This preparatory work primes your brain for the task ahead. It's like programming a computer to do what you want it to do—feed your brain as much relevant input (and some surprising input) as reasonably possible—and reap the rewards when it begins to forge new, surprising connections.

It Bolsters Originality

You'd also be surprised that simply knowing how others have handled subject matters can infuse your work with originality—because you take time to *think harder* and *alert your brain* as to how you can tell a unique story. If you're worried that reading too much may result in poaching storylines, give your brain a rest between the time you read and the time you start to write. If you're still fearful that what you've read might bleed into what you write, jot down the plotlines, characterizations, settings, and so on that left an impression. You can refer back to that list to make sure you're not transgressing or taking advantage of someone else's originality.

It Helps You Get a Feel for Genre

If you're writing in a particular genre, it is an excellent idea to read a number of works so you can get a natural feel for how to introduce the essential elements and how to stand out from the pack. What you are doing is uploading information to your brain about what really appeals to you, how to write the kinds of characters, scenes, and plotlines you love to read, what you think you can do, and what would be a stretch. As you read, your brain will not only be absorbing and filing away words, it will be observing the rhythms of writing: words, language, narrative, dialogue, pacing, setting, scenes, and so on. You are feeding your brain data that it needs to figure out what you're attempting to do (to recognize specific patterns) and how you can maximize your neuronal resources. Give your neocortex a road map, and it will serve you well.

CRYSTALLIZE YOUR INTELLIGENCE

Fluid intelligence (nonspecific, overall cognitive functioning) is hard to effectively change (although daily aerobic exercise helps), but you can change what scientists call your "crystallized intelligence," which effectively means your knowledge and skills in one particular practice (as in the skills involved in writing). Anything you do to become a better writer—studying, analyzing, reading, practicing, experimenting, learning new things, and completing projects—contributes to increasing your crystallized intelligence; that is, your brain's ability to conceive, create, and craft *superior* stories.

READ THINGS THE OPPOSITE
OF WHAT YOU WANT TO WRITE

A good way to mentally shake things up is to read something that is entirely different from what you're writing. This is particularly true if you're a genre writer who has been working at her craft for some time, as your brain likely has the elements down pat and literally has neuronal pathways that leap into action the minute you sit down to work.

It Loosens Up Your Sensibilities

Reading works that are very different from what you want to write is a great way to spark ideas and to shake up a tendency to be too rote, traditional, or predictable. If you write historical novels, for example, reading science fiction could loosen up your tendency to be a little rigid when it comes to style, or maybe it will spur ideas for setting or characterization. If you write mystery novels, reading narrative nonfiction about crimes could spark ideas for really digging into the psychology of criminals. If you write romance novels, reading mystery novels could spark ideas for more complex plots that sustain suspense or create mystery. The point is to loosen up strictures and think outside whatever genre box you may be used to thinking within.

It Leads to Conceptual Blending

Reading (or writing) something very different from your usual preference or style—exposing your brain to something it rarely sees, reads, or writes—is called "conceptual blending." In doing so, you may find that your brain starts popping with fresh ideas or a unique way to tell a story. You've added something new to your framework, and your brain is going to try to find a way to make it fit with what you already know. Even if you're not fully conscious that it's happening, your brain is making new connections to what it already "thinks" storytelling involves, and those new connections may lead to a breakthrough idea, a fresh way to tell a story within your chosen genre; or you may discover that you love westerns.

TAMP DOWN NEURAL NOISE

Studies reveal that children who grow up in poverty hear far fewer words by age five than children who get more one-on-one stimulation in those formative years. This lack of stimulation significantly slows development of language and vocabulary. Worse yet, in the absence of verbal stimulation, a desperate nervous system creates random background activity, which scientists call "neural noise," similar to "static" you'd hear on a radio. The ability to process sound requires microsecond precision in the brain, and children who aren't verbally engaged in the formative years miss the nuances. Individual sounds seem "blurry" to their brains. Musical training appears to strengthen the brain's ability to capture the depth and richness of speech sounds—the fog lifts and consonants and vowels become clearer. If neural noise is making your brain fuzzy, make sure your brain gets the kinds of fine-tuned auditory stimulation it needs to hear the subtle nuances of language—or, better yet, learn to play a musical instrument.

PRACTICE DIVERGENT THINKING

One way to spur creativity is to practice Janusian thinking, a form of divergent thinking that counteracts black-and-white, either/or thinking. Proposed by Albert Rothenberg in the late 1970s (and named after the Roman God Janus, whose two faces each looked in an opposite direction), Janusian thinking actively—and simultaneously—conceives of multiple opposites or antitheses to the central line of thought. Rothenberg studied Nobel Prize winners, creative scientists, and artists and deduced that geniuses, such as Einstein, Mozart, Picasso, and others, had employed this type of divergent thinking in their work. He also identified four phases that they likely experienced over a period of time (consciously or unconsciously):

1. **A UNIQUE MOTIVATION TO CREATE:** The artist is seeking a new way to think about something.
2. **DEVIATION OR SEPARATION FROM WHAT PRECEDED IT:** The artist seeks a fresh approach, not what others have done in similar situations.
3. **THE ABILITY TO EXPERIENCE SIMULTANEOUS OPPOSITION:** The artist can conceive or experience being or not being at the same time.
4. **THE CONSTRUCTION OF THE THEORY, DISCOVERY, OR EXPERIMENTAL WORK:** The artist creates a new idea that arose out of the thinking that preceded the constellation of ideas into a theory or product.

Rothenberg believed that the breakthroughs resulted from seeking the opposite of a certain style, idea, or theory, which helped the artist find a way to travel beyond current thinking (or style).

It Requires Discovery, Experimentation, and Evolution

Typically divergent thinking involves a process of discovery, experimentation, and evolution of work over time (experiment, learn, grow). At some point, the artist (or writer or scientist) would experience the dichotomy of two ideas existing at the same time—a work that is modern and historical, absurd and serious, static and rapidly changing. This is the point at which something new arises, some innovation, some new way to think about and perform your art—once you find the fresh perspective, creativity blossoms. The construction phase would be the actual writing, the implementation of everything you have learned during the Janusian or divergent thought process.

It Requires Breaking Free

All the scientists Rothenberg interviewed talked about the necessity of a fresh approach, which means avoiding existing ideas, especially those ideas that are biases or limitations. Rothenberg thought this phase of breaking free of current ideas was paramount to the sort of critical thinking that leads to true creativity. One way scientists (and artists) came up with something new was to use what he called "distant analogies" to detach from existing knowledge, and that these "distant analogies" were gradually replaced, through experimentation and learning, with analogies specific to the project (experiment, work).

Basically it's not about choosing one idea over another, it's about sustaining the creative tension that can exist between the ideas, and how you find a way to transcend them and create a new idea. Talk about giving your creative brain a workout!

READ POEMS

In an article published in the *Journal of Consciousness Studies*, researchers reported finding activity in a "reading network" of brain areas that were activated in response to any written material. In addition, more emotionally charged writing aroused several regions in the brain (primarily on the right side) that respond to music. In a specific comparison between reading poetry and prose, researchers found evidence that poetry activates the posterior cingulate cortex and medial temporal lobes, parts of the brain linked to introspection. When volunteers read their favorite poems, areas of the brain associated with memory were stimulated more strongly than "reading areas," indicating that reading poems you love is the kind of recollection that evokes strong emotions—and strong emotions are always good for creative writing.

READ BOOKS THAT MAKE YOU THINK ABOUT WRITING

One way to "program" your brain for writing is to read books that critique writers and/or provide a thoughtful discussion about the underlying themes or multiple undercurrents the author appears to be weaving into the work. In reading books that focus on how authors create the "fictive dream," you can learn a lot about how other writers crafted plots, characters, setting, dialogue, pacing, and virtually all of the elements involved in writing fiction (novels, screenplays, plays, short stories, and so on).

Some critics are particularly incisive and will challenge your brain's reach if you struggle to understand what he is saying about the work in question. As critiques and discussions are cerebral in nature, your brain will appreciate the challenge.

The well-known critic Harold Bloom edited a series of books entitled *Bloom's BioCritiques*, which features a variety of his fellow critics discussing an author's body of work. Authors discussed in the series include: Maya Angelou, Jane Austen, The Brontë sisters, Anton Chekhov, Emily Dickinson, William Faulkner, F. Scott Fitzgerald, Robert Frost, Ernest Hemingway, Langston Hughes, Arthur Miller, Toni Morrison, Walt Whitman, Alice Walker, Tennessee Williams, and more.

Bloom also wrote *Shakespeare: The Invention of Human*; *Genius: A Mosaic of One Hundred Exemplary Creative Minds*; *How to Read and Why*; *The Anatomy of Influence: Literature as a Way of Life*; and others. Another resource is Donald Hall's *Literary and Cultural Theory: From Basic Principles to Advanced Applications*.

The important thing with these books, however, is to read (or leaf through) them and forget them. Once you begin to write, you don't want to overthink. These books are to be resourced during the programming phase, when you're inputting as much material as possible for your brilliant brain to file away, adding possibilities for a multitude of new neuronal connections to spark when the real writing begins.

TONI MORRISON ON READING

"I think we erroneously give pride of place to the act of writing rather than the act of reading. I have such reverence for that kind of sensitive reading—it is not just absorbing things and identifying what's wrong, but a much deeper thing that I can see would be perfectly satisfying. Anyway, this separation is fairly recent: not long ago the great readers were the great writers, the great critics were the great novelists, and the great poets were the great translators. People didn't make these big distinctions about which one was more thrilling than the other. Writing for me is just a very sustained process of reading. The only difference is that writing a book might take three or four years, and I'm doing it. I never wrote a line until after I became an editor, and only then because I wanted to read something that I couldn't find. That was the first book I wrote."

—TONI MORRISON

READ A NOVEL TO STIMULATE BRAIN CONNECTIVITY

In a recent study, published in the journal *Brain Connectivity*, researchers asked participants to read the novel *Pompeii* by Robert Harris over the course of nineteen days, during which they scanned the readers' brains to monitor their resting state (what your brain is doing when it doesn't appear to doing anything in particular). After reading sessions, they found "heightened connectivity," similar to muscle memory, in the left temporal cortex, the area of the brain associated with receptivity to language. These significant increases in connectivity were centered on hubs in the left angular/supramarginal gyri and right posterior temporal gyri that correspond to regions previously associated with perspective taking and story comprehension. The brain is actively engaged in processing what it's reading, and this effect lasts after you stop reading.

It Creates Embodied Semantics that Last Five Days

Although those changes seemed to diminish shortly after completing the novel, the researchers also discovered greater activity in the somatosensory cortex, the area responsible for the sense of touch and embodiment, suggesting a potential mechanism for "embodied semantics"—that is, the reader putting themselves (figuratively) in the story in a way that lasted. The changes persisted for *five days* after participants finished reading the novel. That's a great return on reading a novel, particularly when you observe the techniques the writer used to engage the brain. Once you know what will get your brain fired up and still processing five days after the story has been read, you will have a remarkable tool for creating stories that sell.

It Transports You into the Life of the Protagonist

Gregory Burns, lead author of the study, concluded that the neural changes associated with physical sensation and movement systems suggest that reading a novel can transport you into the body of the protagonist. "We already knew that good stories can put you in someone else's shoes in a figurative sense," he explained. "Now we're seeing that something may also be happening biologically."

Basically, reading stories strengthens language processing and leaves a sensory impression, as if the reader had been transported into the experience being dramatized. Obviously this is a skill you want to replicate for your readers!

READ LITERARY FICTION

Understanding others' mental states is a crucial skill that enables the complex social relationships that characterize human societies—and that makes a writer excellent at creating multilayered characters and situations. Not much research has been conducted on the Theory of Mind (our ability to realize that our minds are different than other people's minds and that their emotions are different from ours) that fosters this skill, but recent experiments revealed that reading *literary* fiction led to better performance on tests of *affective* Theory of Mind (understanding others' emotions) and *cognitive* Theory of Mind (understanding others' thinking and state of being), compared with reading nonfiction, popular fiction, or nothing at all. Specifically these results showed that reading literary fiction temporarily enhances Theory of Mind, and, more broadly, that Theory of Mind may be influenced greater by engagement with true works of art. In other words, literary fiction provokes thought, contemplation, expansion, and integration (things going on cognitively beyond the brain functions related to reading, say, magazine articles, interviews, or most nonfiction reporting).

DEVELOP YOUR CRAFT

There's little question that the fastest way to become a published writer is to intently and purposefully work hard at developing your craft. Writer Malcolm Gladwell, author of *Outliers: The Story of Success,* famously proposed that successful people generally spend ten years, or ten thousand hours, perfecting their craft. This has since been contested, but no one can dispute that a combination of intensely studying and practicing your craft—over a period of time—is the best way to shorten the distance between being an amateur and becoming an accomplished, successful professional. Unless you're the kind of genius whose prose simply flows fully formed onto the page, you will have to learn how to create memorable characters; establish and interweave many elements, including setting, tone, style, mood, and theme; and create a plot filled with rising tension and a character-driven, deeply satisfying resolution.

Incredible Resources are a Click Away

The good news is, of course, that there are literally hundreds upon hundreds of books on the craft of writing (any kind of writing, any phase of writing or marketing) that you can read, study, and refer to when writing. It's best to go to a bookstore to pick out ones that "speak" to you, and writers are known to keep and refer back to their dog-eared favorites for decades—because they truly, passionately love them. However, because there are fewer bookstores to browse in these days, an extended list of suggestions (for inspiration, craft, specialized approaches, and all sorts of imaginative resources) is provided in the Appendix located in the back of the book. Buy some and study them, and you'll trim years off the time it would take to learn how to write by experimentation alone.

PRACTICE DEEP READING

Recent research revealed that "deep reading"—defined as reading that is slow, immersive, rich in sensory detail and emotional and moral complexity—is distinctive from light reading—little more than the decoding of words. Deep reading occurs when the language is rich in detail, allusion, and metaphor, and taps into the same brain regions that would activate if the reader were experiencing the event. Deep reading is great exercise for the brain and has been shown to increase empathy, as the reader dives deeper and adds reflection, analysis, and personal subtext to what is being read. It also offers writers a way to appreciate all the qualities that make novels fascinating and meaningful—and to tap into their abilities to write on a deeper level.

ANALYZE SUCCESSFUL WRITING

The other piece of the puzzle is to analyze how each author of the books you've read has dealt with all the identified elements. You can learn a great deal in a short amount of time by studying how your favorite authors crafted novels, nonfiction books, or poems that you love. One of the best books ever written on screenwriting, *Screenplay: The Foundations of Screenwriting*, by Syd Field, for example, pinpoints when plot twists need to happen, which detracts a bit from watching movies for enjoyment but vastly increases a new screenwriter's ability to understand how a screenplay needs to be structured, right down to the page when a plot twist needs to happen.

Take even one chapter from a book you love and analyze it. To tap into your brain's full resources, pick up your favorite pen and paper (or writing journal) and write down examples of plot, setting, scene, character, dialogue, action, narrative, pacing, and so on. You can also copy pages and use different colored highlighters to identify each element. No matter how you approach the task, you are training your brain to pick up blatant and subtler ways authors use the various storytelling elements to keep a reader enthralled. Keep at it and the input will spark neuronal connections the next time you sit down to write.

There are also books, such as Francine Prose's *Reading Like a Writer: A Guide for People Who Love Books and for Those Who Want to Write Them (P.S.)* (and others like it, such as Thomas Foster's *How to Read Novels Like a Professor: A Jaunty Exploration of the World's Fa-*

vorite Literary Form) that can be invaluable in helping you figure out how authors are so effective. It may feel tedious to do this, but you are programming your brain, and the effort will pay off.

BECOME AN EXPERT ON WRITING

Scientists who study how we learn have theorized that acquiring expertise does, in fact, make us smarter. They have found, for example, that experts don't just know more than the rest of us, they know differently, in ways that allow them to think and act especially intelligently within their domain of expertise. An expert's knowledge can be described in the following way:

- deep, not shallow or superficial
- well organized, around a core of central principles
- automatic, streamlined into mental programs that require little conscious effort
- flexible and transferable to new situations
- self-aware (an expert can think well about his or her own thinking)

Expertise requires time and dedication to develop, but the benefits of broadening and deepening your base of knowledge on the writing elements required for you craft will clearly help your brain work faster and more efficiently.

FIND THE METAPHOR

The fantastically original, brilliant, delightful (and late) Ray Bradbury always urged aspiring writers to "find the metaphor" and said that a large part of his writing success derived from his habit of being "a collector of metaphors." Bradbury didn't go to college and boasted that he "graduated from the library at age twenty-eight" after spending every day there for three to four years. He urged anyone who wanted to write to "pull books down from the shelves, and stuff your head from many different fields (whatever attracts you, whatever you love, whatever captivates your attention)," and specifically offered his ideal preparatory course for writing: "For the next one thousand nights, read one short story (preferably published classics), one poem (lean more towards classic, not "too modern"), and one essay, from various fields: archeology, zoology, biology, anthropology, (neuroscience) and so on." He also advocated reading all the great philosophers. "Stuff your head with as much as you can," Bradbury urged, "and you'll be full of ideas and metaphors and [along with] your own perceptions of life and what you see in yourself and your friends it [all of this input] will bounce around in your head and make new metaphors." He noted, however, that you have to learn to recognize a metaphor before you can create one.

Go Beyond the Literary Metaphor

In general terms, a metaphor means understanding one thing in terms of something else (and not in the strict literary sense of comparing something to something else). Neuroscientists refer to this ability to recognize and think metaphorically as "imaginative rationality," or the ability to see those yet unforeseen relationships between things that may not look related on the surface—something human minds, rather than computers, still do best. Georges de Mestral, the man who created Velcro, was thinking metaphorically when he observed how burrs stuck to his dog's fur and then adapted that thought to create a unique, yet remarkably useful item that never existed before he thought of it.

In the book *A Whole New Mind*, author Daniel Pink noted that "metaphorical imagination is essential to forging empathetic connections and communicating experiences that others do not share"—which is pretty much what writers do. Your task is to start noticing metaphors and working on the creation of original metaphors. When you see, hear, or read a metaphor, write it down, meditate on it. Invest some of the brain capital you've been banking to tweak it, make it even more original. Think hard and expansively. It takes a pretty awesome metaphor to base an entire novel or screenplay on it. Work that muscle like a champ.

Expand the Concept

While you're mining for metaphors, it's also a great idea to spend time working to improve how closely you perceive what's going on around you (or around the world), bolstering your ability to observe and re-member small, telling details, heightening your senses, and pausing to feel emotions more deeply. All of these sensate and brain functions are essential to becoming the kind of writer that maximizes cognitive func-tioning. One way to do this is to keep a "sensory journal" in which you describe, as intricately as possible, one sensory experience a day—the exact way something looked, heard, or tasted, for example. It's not easy to get the description as exact as possible, and making the attempt will help you flex this muscle, according to researchers at Purdue University.

Record Observations

Another idea is to keep a journal in which you record five observations a day (whether it's something silly your cat did or the heartbreaking subtext of what you saw pass between a mother and her teenage daugh-ter). You could also journal about how you resisted every inclination to write, noting exactly how you went about it (also great for understand-ing your process and discovering ways to conquer avoidance). Instead of simply jotting the observations down, use your memory skills to in-clude as many details as you can recall, and then use your imaginative skills to create a metaphor. Write about how something that happened that day tapped into a painful childhood memory, or describe a set-ting that was either strikingly beautiful or repulsive, and use details to show your "reader" what made them so, employing metaphors. In other words, hone your observation, memory, and writing skills by making them a significant part of what you do every day—who you are and how you operate in the world.

YOU'RE SMARTER THAN YOU THINK

For more than one hundred years, scientists researching the brain thought that dendrites—those branchlike projections that connect one neuron to others—were passive receivers of incoming information. But in 2013, researchers at the University of North Carolina, Chapel Hill, found that dendrites do more than passively relay signals; they perform their own layer of active processing. The results, first published in *Nature*, reported that dendrites effectively act as mini neural computers, actively processing neuronal signals. Scientists are now studying this new finding, seeking to discover how your brain's increased capacity for active processing manifests. For now, take heart in knowing that you're likely smarter—or at least more perceptive—than you think you are!

PRACTICE, PRACTICE, PRACTICE ... AND THEN PRACTICE SOME MORE

Writing is similar to other skills requiring coordination. Let's say you wanted to learn to play the piano or make a jump shot from half-court. You'd begin by placing your fingers on the piano keys and learning which key produced which note; or standing at half-court with a basketball and gauging the distance and the amount of thrust that's required to sink the ball through the hoop. Those first efforts would require focused, conscious effort, to determine where you place your hands (and feet), how and how fast you have to maneuver from one key to another (or squat and flex to throw the basketball the desired distance), and you'd make many mistakes. As you committed to physical and mental practice, your caudate nucleus, and nearby regions in your brain, would coordinate what happens in your brain, and, if you kept practicing, these actions would become more automatic, and your brain would be pulling its weight, firing all the synapses you needed to master the skill without your conscious attention being necessary. The same, of course, holds true for writing.

See it in Pictures; Write it in Words

When scientists compared the brain functioning of professional writers to that of novice writers, they discovered differences in the areas involved in speech. They noticed, for example, that during brainstorming sessions, novice writers activated visual centers of their brains (as if "seeing" a scene), while experienced writers activated speech centers (as if "narrating" a scene). The novices were likely seeing a movie in their heads, while the writers' *inner voices* were already using words to narrate the story.

Most striking, however, was that professional writers (unconsciously) activated their brain's caudate nucleus, while novices did not. The caudate nucleus is the region of the brain that assists with coordinating practiced skills into automatic behavior. What it may signify is that there's a real advantage to using words as often as possible, strengthening your inner narrator to the point where he or she spontaneously writes rather than envisions.

Write, Write, and Then Write Some More

Nothing, absolutely nothing, will be more effective than writing as often as possible, and writing in the form you want to master. It's better to write (and complete) five bad novels than to spend years studying, write one, and give up because you haven't mastered the craft. Studying your craft is important, but eventually it's the writing itself that will teach you more than anything else you can possibly do. If you want to learn how to structure a novel, writing and failing will teach you a lot, and, hopefully, one thing you'll learn is that you should never give up. Agents are famous for saying, "If your first novel didn't sell, write another one." In fact, they'll urge writers to keep writing while they try to sell their first book, which not only takes time, but also may or may not sell. That first book doesn't have to represent the sum of your ability. Many well-known writers have shelved books (and sometimes regretted those same books being published after a breakthrough book hits the best-seller lists), and it's not uncommon to write five books before you finally produce one that's exceptional.

REMAIN BI-LITERATE

Humans recently made a huge leap from reading on paper to reading on screens. Scrolling, clicking, jumping, and linking on the Internet, or reading e-mails and text messages, is already making it harder for us to read complex or convoluted sentences and retain what we read. Neuroscientists fear we are creating "digital brains," generating new circuits for skimming through a vast amount of information, latching onto less and less. According to Maryanne Wolf, author of *Proust and the Squid, The Story and Science of the Reading Brain*, this sort of "superficial reading" is creating an "eye byte" culture, one that is constantly looking for and having trouble finding mental markers. Retention is higher when readers opt for print over electronic, prompting some to term this "slow reading." To ward off problems focusing and retaining interest and knowledge while reading, it's highly recommended that you balance your "eye byte" brain by reading classic and more "literary" novels that have all those lovely convoluted sentences. Doing so will keep your brain bi-literate.

STUDY HOW OTHER WRITERS APPROACH WRITING

Because writing is typically a solitary quest, filled with insecurity and self-doubt, it's always helpful to know how successful writers manage to do what they do—whether it's maintaining momentum when everything seems to be going wrong or coming up with fresh ideas after book twelve. Luckily a wealth of resources is available at your local library, in bookstores, online, and on television. Reading, seeing, or hearing what other writers have to say about their individual process is a delightful and informative means of boosting identification, inspiration, and sustenance. "Communing" with fellow writers helps you feel that you really do have a tribe, even if you're never as successful in the marketplace as you'd like to be. Being "with" other writers definitely feels like home—like you're looking in a mirror. Writer's conferences are a great way to find a tribe, but you can also do so in the confines of your own home.

Watch Charlie Rose Interviews

Since 1991 (nationally syndicated in 1993), PBS has been hosting the Charlie Rose show, which airs in-depth interviews with all sorts of luminaries, including writers, screenwriters, playwrights, directors, actors, and many others in the creative arts. Rose's interviews are famous for being well-researched and comprehensive conversations, many lasting an hour with a single artist, which is rare in television. You can access many of the shows for free on the PBS website, and on other websites, including www.charlierose.com and YouTube.com. Because he's intellectually and artistically curious by nature, and a trained journalist, Rose does his homework, which leads him to ask probing questions that reveal a lot about how the various artists think about their work. This can be both revealing and inspiring. I find it surprisingly interesting to listen to actors talk about their craft, how they interpret the complexities of characterization and dramatization that an author or screenwriter has provided and that they often build upon. You'll find many discussions about Shakespeare, and rightly so, but also many other contributors to the arts.

Search his archives for interviews with authors Kurt Vonnegut, Hunter S. Thompson, Jhumpa Lahiri, Aaron Sorkin, Martin Amis, Nadine Gortimer, Margaret Atwood, and a host of others. Remember, your brain will gobble up anything related to creativity. Crossovers into other artistic expressions often offer the kind of surprising insight or inspiration that can fire up your writing brain.

Watch TED Lectures

Ted.com has become a phenomenal resource for all sorts of ideas. Restricted to eighteen minutes per video, people of all sorts offer footage in which they provide tightly focused discussions, most of which are inspirational, technological, and often riveting. Videos have been known to go viral, and many receive millions of views. The good part is that this wealth of ideas and information on all kinds of topics—including the arts—is available for free at www.ted.com.

Just to give you a sample, at the time this book was written, topics included:

- J.K. Rowling on *The Fringe Benefits of Failure*
- Amy Tan on *Where Does Creativity Hide?*
- Isabel Allende on *Tales of Passion*
- Elizabeth Gilbert on *Your Elusive Creative Genius*
- Mac Barnett on *Why a Good Book Is a Secret Door*
- Elif Shafak on *The Politics of Fiction*
- Tracy Chevalier on *Finding the Story Inside the Painting*
- William Gibson on *Riffs on Writing and the Future*
- Chimamanda Ngozi Adichie on *The Danger of a Single Story*
- Lakshmi Pratury on *The Lost Art of Letter-Writing*

In addition to the accessibility of writers and artists of all stripes, you can watch videos on cutting-edge technology, quantum physics, science, cosmology, and all sorts of fascinating topics related to the fast-changing world in which we live. It's an excellent resource for inspiration (nothing like watching successful writers exhibit their ingenuity, originality, specific insights, neurosis, and humor); no writer need ever feel lonely again. I like to watch when I've been alone, writing for days, when my mind is spent … and a little company is welcome.

LISTEN TO OTHER WRITERS

Listening to interviews in which authors discuss their craft is a great way to pick up pointers and to psyche yourself up. Ditto for audio or podcasts in which authors or actors read excerpts or short stories. Here are some to try (these and more are easily found online):

- Brainpickings.org (offers writer videos featuring authors like Ray Bradbury, one of the best speakers about writing ever)
- *Books and Authors* with Cary Barbor
- *Between The Covers*
- *The Lit Show*
- *National Book Awards Author Events*
- *Skylight Books Author Reading Series*

- *The Avid Reader* on WCHE
- *Longform Podcast* (nonfiction)
- *Selected Shorts* (actors read works)
- *The Greenlight Bookstore Radio Hour*
- *New Yorker Fiction Podcast*
- *Slate* Audio Book Club

Besides being delightful entertainment, the interviews and readings can be very informative and can bolster your identification as a writer. Remember, it's always good to connect pleasure to writing. Happy listening!

READ CONVOLUTED FICTION

Before the Internet, the brain read mostly in linear ways—one page led to the next page, and so on. Even if pictures were mixed in, they weren't distracting. Seeing words on an actual page gave us a remarkable ability to remember where key information was in a book, simply by the layout. We'd know a protagonist died on the page with the two long paragraphs after the page with all that dialogue. The Internet, however, has so much information, hypertext, videos alongside words, and interactivity, our brains form shortcuts to deal with it all—scanning, searching for key words, scrolling up and down quickly. Researchers worry that this nonlinear style of reading is not only reducing a reader's overall comprehension (and enjoyment), some studies found that it stunted a person's ability to read complex novels, particularly those with convoluted syntax, such as *Middlemarch*.

Read *Paris Review* Articles

Since 1953, *The Paris Review* has published the work of authors such as Gabriel García Márquez, Alice Munro, Raymond Carver, Jonathan Lethem, Toni Morrison, Carson McCullers, F. Scott Fitzgerald, Ernest Hemingway, William Faulkner, and many, many others. It's also published a series of books containing in-depth interviews with writers, each of which is endlessly fascinating and beautifully written. These books will reassure any aspiring writer that writing is monumentally difficult on occasions (often frequently), but also immensely rewarding and an art over which practitioners struggle. The interviews offer glimpses into the private worlds—and private thoughts—of some of the most talented writers. I keep a stack of them beside my bed, as reading them before going to sleep inspires me to wake up refreshed and ready to write.

They also publish anthologies, with some commentary that can be instructional, in directing your thought to the artful crafting of short stories, essays, and poems. You can receive the interviews each day by following *The Paris Review* on Twitter.

There are, of course, other books, such as *Writers on Writing: Collected Essays from The New York Times*. One that is sure to fuel a fire to write is *To Live and To Write: Selections by Japanese Women Writers* 1913 –1938 (edited by Yukiko Tanaka), which is writing from women who wrote under the most adversarial conditions possible. If they could find the fervor and the brain space to write, you can too!

EMPLOY METACOGNITION

Metacognition (similar to Theory of Mind) is the ability to think (independently) about your thoughts and then *specifically use that ability* to focus on improving your ability to think, or to chart your way to writing a work of art. It involves consciously choosing a strategy to maximize the way your brain functions and using reflection to identify where improvements are needed or to reroute dead ends. To employ metacognition while writing:

- master fundamental—and more nuanced—writing skills;
- organize your work, your work space, and your writing schedule;
- create a "master plan" for completion; create secondary goals for motivation;
- monitor your progress, noting—and celebrating— successes;

- consciously do whatever you can to meet your specified writing goals;
- recognize when your strategy isn't working and make adjustments to rectify;
- when needed, be willing to change course completely.

In other words, you use your brain to drive the momentum you are making toward your goal, using your ability to think to figure out the best route for successful completion. Filter in how your brain works, make choices to maximize your brain's efforts, and reinforce success.

BUILD A BETTER TEMPLATE

One of your brain's primary functions is to predict what will come next; and it bases its decisions on what it knows thus far, what it has experienced, linked, filed away, and reactivated when a stimulus occurred that awoke all the familiar circuits and called upon them to figure out how to predict what needs to be done. To do this, your brain constructs models or templates of the world, and the stronger templates it constructs, the more efficiently it operates.

Action Gamers Become More Adept Learners

A recent study published in *Proceedings of the National Academy of Sciences* found that playing *action* video games improves the specific skills taught in the game—and, more generally, learning capabilities. Researchers had known for a while that playing video games improved many skills, particularly building those brain templates I mentioned in the prior paragraph, but the fact that those who play action video games become better learners was a surprise. The process of navigating the game fosters the development of better templates. When *action* gamers went up against nongamers in the study, they proved to be far better in pattern discrimination tasks, based on their abilities to build better templates for the task at hand. They also have better physical hand-eye coordination and reflexes.

They Develop an Accelerated Learning Curve

In another study, in which participants had little video game experience, half were asked to play action video games for fifty hours over nine weeks, and half were asked to concurrently play more benign video games. Those who played action video games improved their templates, while those who played nonaction video games did not.

"When they began the perceptual learning task, action video gamers were indistinguishable from nonaction gamers; they didn't come to the task with a better template," says Daphne Bavelier, a research professor in brain and cognitive sciences at the University of Rochester. "Instead they developed better templates for the task, much, much faster showing an accelerated learning curve."

Best of all, these improved skills were still intact a year later. Why? Researchers concluded that the fast pace, the necessity to divide attention and to make predictions at different time scales fired up the brain's ability to create templates.

TRAIN YOUR WRITING BRAIN: BUILD AN OPENING TEMPLATE

If the researchers were right in concluding that building templates accelerates learning (we can safely assume they were), one way to strengthen your brain's capacity to create writing templates would be to study your craft as if it were a fast-paced video game. We all know that the opening pages are extremely important, so that's a good place to start:

1. Select five novels that are similar to what you want to write (preferably novels you have not previously read or have not read for a long time). Have some paper and a pen at the ready.
2. Skim read the first five pages of all five novels (about two minutes per novel).
3. Working from short-term memory, rapidly record what you remember about the technical devices used in each novel, in the order each

occurred (setting, characterization, action, conflict, dialogue, voice, and so on). This will be difficult, which is the point of the exercise. You are training your brain to recognize patterns and accelerate its ability to recognize them (and to eventually build upon them).

4. The next day, go back and skim the same passages, and repeat the exercise.

5. Do this same exercise for three more days. Remember, there's no right or wrong. This exercise is about helping your brain recognize, remember, and create templates.

6. Employ *metacognition*: Review your efforts to see if you noticed any patterns in what you missed. (Did you always mess up dialogue? Did you fail to notice scenery detail?) This way you can learn about what you tend to pick up and ignore, and focus on recognizing all aspects of a novel.

7. On the fifth day, start with five new novels and repeat the same exercise. After that round, go back over your notes, with the novels at hand for reference, and fill in the blanks. As you work, study how each author opened his or her novel, identifying the employment and effectiveness of each.

TIP: If you're struggling with one particular aspect of your craft, hone in on that element, be it characterization, pacing, setting, dialogue, narration, and so on. Find examples of that element in works you think are brilliant (or similar to what you want to achieve), and then use the same exercise to bolster your brain's ability to recognize and re-create templates.

EXTRA CREDIT: One way to build a template is to retype the work of your favorite writer—the first ten pages are a good place to start, as the writer's best work should be apparent immediately. If you're struggling with a certain aspect, such as character description, setting description, pacing, etc., retype sections where a writer you admire, or whose work is closest to what you're writing, dealt with the same challenges.

WRITERS ON CRAFT

"It's hard for me to believe that people who read very little—or not at all in some cases—should presume to write and expect people to like what they have written. Can I be blunt on this subject? If you don't have time to read, you don't have the time—or the tools—to write. Simple as that."

—STEPHEN KING

"Peter Yates, the music critic, said that 'the proper work of the critic is praise,' and that 'that which cannot be praised should be surrounded with a tasteful, well-thought-out silence.' I like that."

—DONALD BARTHELME

"When you feel the story is beginning to pick up rhythm—the characters are shaping up, you can see them, you can hear their voices, and they do things that you haven't planned, things you couldn't have imagined— then you know the book is somewhere, and you just have to find it, and bring it, word by word, into this world."

—ISABELLE ALLENDE

CHAPTER 5

JUMPSTART YOUR WRITING BRAIN

Practice the Art of Brainstorming

"Writers don't need tricks or gimmicks or even necessarily need to be the smartest fellow on the block. At the risk of appearing foolish, a writer sometimes needs to be able to just stand and gape at this or that thing—a sunset or an old shoe—in absolute and simple amazement."

—GEOFFREY WOLFF

As we discussed in previous chapters, your brain is capable of many things. Many of these things you likely take for granted because they happen at an unconscious level or because they've become so ingrained in how you function that you've lost awareness of what it took to get to this phase and any effort you have invested. Still, your brain is very active behind the scenes, and in terms of preparing to write, one of its most important capabilities is cognitive processing.

SUMMONING YOUR BRAIN'S INGENUITY

The brain is not only designed to think, it *loves* to think—and there are specific ways you can summon and maximize your brain's ingenuity. Let's begin by clarifying the various abilities and functions the brain performs, and how each will serve your writing.

Perception

Your brain recognizes and interprets sensory stimuli (what you taste, touch, smell, feel, hear, see, intuit, and so on). Just think of how much "raw material" this function contributes! The more your magnificent brain perceives at a minute level, the better you'll be able to write fabulous scenes. Luckily you can both train your brain to be even more perceptive and you can enlarge your hippocampus, where all those lovely memories are processed, just waiting for you to call them up when needed.

Attention

Your brain has the ability to sustain concentration on a particular object, action, or thought. It also has the ability to manage competing demands in your environment. The more you train your brain to focus, and to sustain said focus, the stronger these skills will become. Remember to limit distractions when sharp focus is required—and to tackle one task at a time. Truly dedicate yourself—and all the brainpower you possess—to the task at hand, such as plotting your novel, and your brain will take your quest seriously and "serve up" gems.

Short- and Long-Term Memory

Your brain is capable of juggling short-term/working memory with limited storage (it helps you juggle ideas and information while working—but usually only about seven pieces of information at once), and long-term memory with unlimited storage (that you can call upon when writing scenes and characterizations culled from your own experiences, from stories you've read in the past, or from your imagination). Obviously we have to call on our memory in every level of writing; it's crucial to our ability to craft stories, empathize with characters, and re-create events to illustrate emotional truths. Memories don't become long-term unless you purposefully assign them importance or generate enough sustained neuronal involvement for the hippocampus to know these are memories you wish to store. Writing or speaking about memories helps your brain assign them meaning.

Motor Skills

Your brain coordinates the ability to move your muscles and body, and to handle objects. It's the smooth coordination of motor skills that leads to facile typing. Motor skills are also imperative for walking and exercising—essential to keeping oxygen and blood flowing to your brain. I'm so glad I learned to type while in high school, and if you're a "hunt and peck" typist, it may behoove you to bolster your typing skills. I am known, within my writing circle, for saying that whatever "genius" I have for writing flows from my fingertips, because when thoughts are flowing, my ego leaves the room, and my fingers fly over the keyboard (seemingly with little interference from my brain). It's when I do my best writing.

Language Skills

Your brain's facility for language allows you to translate sounds into words and generate verbal output. With writers, these functions may be—or will become—more highly developed than people who don't write on a regular basis. Reading and playing word games are fun ways to bolster these skills. To bolster your brainpower, don't take your verbal skills for granted. Find ways to challenge your brain—read and analyze works that require massive concentration or engage in wordplay that requires you to think creatively. However, be aware that skills might not transfer—building a better vocabulary won't help you *use* those words appropriately unless you train your grammar centers, too! By the way, it can be beneficial to your writing to review grammar principles occasionally. Books about grammar often hold many useful suggestions, such as limiting adverbs and adjectives, and writing in active rather than passive voice.

WORDS ARE AS GOOD AS CHOCOLATE

A 2014 study published in the *Current Biology* journal found that successfully learning the meanings of new words (or a foreign language) activates the same pleasure-and-reward circuits (ventral striatum) in the adult brain that are stimulated when deriving pleasure from having sex, gambling, or eating chocolate. Researchers think this rewarding feeling may have encouraged the development of human languages, as well as motivate some to learn new languages. "We suggest that this strong functional and anatomical coupling between neocortical language regions and the subcortical reward system provided a crucial advantage in humans that eventually enabled our lineage to successfully acquire linguistic skills," the authors wrote. It may also be why eating chocolate seems the perfect reward for writing.

Visual and Spatial Processing

Your brain has the ability to process incoming visual stimuli and to recognize the spatial relationship between objects. This ability also includes visualizing or imagining images and scenarios, which is crucial to being able to craft stories. This internal "GPS" helps you remember what certain settings looked like and how people moved within the scene. This also has some effect on how you combine words, though most of that will happen on an unconscious plane.

Executive Functioning

Your brain is capable of high-level cognitive processing, commonly called "executive functioning," as it involves the "thinking" functions that allow you to accomplish goal-oriented behavior, such as the ability to generate and recognize ideas, organize your thoughts in terms of all the elements of storytelling (plot, characters, setting, theme, tone, scene creation, etc.), create a game plan for completion, and do what it takes to reach your chosen goal. Without these functions, you'd never be able to write anything cohesive, much less a novel. The specific abilities involved in executive processing include the following:

- **FLEXIBILITY:** the capacity for quickly switching to the appropriate mental mode; from resting to "fight or flight" would be the most dramatic representation.
- **THEORY OF MIND:** the ability to possess insight into other people's inner world, their thoughts, their likes and dislikes, their behavior. It also allows for introspection. It is the part of our brain that allows us to think about our *self*: our mind separate from our brain.

- **ANTICIPATION:** the ability to make predictions based on pattern recognition, what's worked or hasn't worked in the past, in specific or familiar situations. Anticipating pleasure has been shown to be a reward in itself (more on this later).
- **PROBLEM SOLVING:** the ability to define the problem in a way that allows us to generate solutions and (often spontaneously and instantaneously) choose the right solution for the problem. Obviously this task is crucial to the process of writing, when you are constantly solving minor—and major—problems related to crafting the story.
- **DECISION MAKING:** the ability to make decisions based on problem solving, even when dealing with incomplete information and emotions (ours and those of others).
- **WORKING MEMORY:** the capacity to hold and manipulate information in our mind, in real time, which is essential to the ability to write stories. It allows you to hold thoughts about what you've just written, while mining your long-term memory for more input related to what you're writing. This happens both unconsciously and consciously.
- **EMOTIONAL SELF-REGULATION:** the ability to identify and manage one's own emotions for optimum performance. This is a very important function, as it helps you set aside distracting emotions long enough to stay focused on your goal—and writing.
- **SEQUENCING:** the ability to break down complex actions into manageable units and prioritize them in an effective manner. Much of this is done unconsciously, but you can choose to do it consciously simply by mimicking how your brain sequences when making a plan about how you're going to execute a task (such as writing a novel or screenplay, or even crafting a scene). Just break down the steps and proceed to address each task in a sequential manner.
- **INHIBITION:** the ability to withstand distraction and internal urges. Learning to consciously use this skill improves the ability to meet goals. This, of course, has everything to do with your ability to concentrate, and it's a "muscle" you can develop over time.

We should also add the ability to be *original* to this list, as your brain has the ability to make surprising associations, perhaps better known as those "aha moments," when all the thought—research, conjecture, supposition, theorizing, imagining—you've been putting into something seems to suddenly coalesce and a brilliant solution appears, as if by magic. We've all had those moments, which typically come after a long period of struggle and frustration, and often after you've taken a break, to mow your lawn, garden, do the laundry, or wash your car. Halfway through the physical task, while your lovely mind has been blissfully freed from your attempts to steer it in certain directions, a synaptic event occurs (like a lightning strike in your brain, and it really is similar) and the ideal solution emerges. When it happens, it feels like pure writing nirvana, and rather than being elusive, it can be facilitated, which you'll learn and relearn as you progress through this book.

One of the best ways to engage your brain is to call it forth and give it a starring role *before* you buckle down to write—but it's also good to give it break when necessary, so those lightning strikes can happen.

TAP INTO THE PROPER SPECIES

Your complex brain consists of lobes, areas, and layers, some of which are similar to the ocean or the earth, with layers supporting a unique range of life. In your cortex, each layer houses a limited range of specific neuron types, each of which cooperates and competes with others in specific ways. Identifying and enumerating neurons has proved challenging, but scientists are making inroads in understanding the behavior of each neuronal "species." In conceiving, creating, and crafting stories, you are tapping into your prefrontal cortex (thinking), hippocampus (memory), limbic system (emotions), and others. Honor their complexity, and they'll work miracles for you.

CLARIFY YOUR INTENTIONS

One of the best things you can do to get your brain on board is to figure out *what* you want to write and *why* you want to write it. Without clear ideas about these two questions, your brain remains unfocused and unfiltered, which will make it hard to narrow your choices. Instead of knowing what you want it to concentrate on, your brain will sally along perceiving the world around you without knowing what's most important—beyond life or death issues. Basically your brain can be easily distracted and susceptible to focusing on the wrong things.

It's up to you to guide your brain where you want it to go. It's always striving to discern what you want or need, and one way it does this is to "notice" what it's being asked to do on a regular basis. Your brain creates a strong neuronal web for the needs it is asked to fulfill—it focuses on what you direct its attention to, what you direct it to do.

Imagine how hard it would be to go against your desires, to use your writing genius to support something you didn't believe in. You'd encounter substantial resistance and dread every moment spent preparing or struggling to write. Now think about how much easier it will be to write about something that really matters to you, to express something that has been eating away at you all your life, to say something that you know will uplift and inspire others. Having a sense of purpose in alignment with your values gives you a *raison d étre* (a reason for being) and feeds the creative fire. It doesn't have to be noble, but once you delve into the real reasons why you want to write about a certain topic, it clarifies the mission for your brain and facilitates the writing process.

CREATE A SMALL-WORLD NETWORK

When it comes to efficiency, your brain does more with less, partially because it has a dense "local" structure; that is, neurons in the same "neighborhood" are usually connected to each other. Although each neuron has only a few connections, signals nevertheless have the ability to leap from one area to another area in a few hops. Networks with lots of mutual close-range interconnections, combined with efficient, long-range global communication are called "small-world networks"—think Facebook, where knowing one person soon connects you to someone across the sea. In fact, Facebook's global popularity may have skyrocketed because our brains recognized its similar connection pattern. It may also be true that our brains are evolving to keep up with technology, becoming even more efficient at "cost-effective" information processing. What this means for writing and creativity is that the more neuronal growth you create and link to your existing knowledge, the bigger "small-world network" you'll develop.

CHOOSE A TOPIC THAT EXCITES YOU

As we've discussed, your neurons construct elaborate networks in response to frequent cognitive activity, such as writing. The more these neurons are fired up, the more they wire together, formulating a complex, multilayered web of synapses that grow stronger and more complex with use. It's the practice of firing up those neurons that causes them to increase their outreach and to create new and more unique connections. You have writing genius at your disposal, but you have to make a conscious decision to use it to its fullest advantage, and one great way to do that is to choose a topic that really gets your juices flowing, something that has a certain urgency, something you're somewhat obsessed with, something that's important to you.

The passion for what you're writing about will ignite those neurons, initiating the sort of "global excitation" that spurs original thought, surprising and unique connections, and the desire to re-create those feelings. Basically passion energizes your brain, gets it fired up, and makes it sharper than usual. Writing about something you feel strongly about provides the neuronal juice that will make writing a pleasure and will likely result in your best work.

If you have to write about things that aren't deeply and personally important to you, then get excited about the craft and art of writing, and be passionate about your abilities to tell a good story and what your resourceful brain brings to the table. If you can't love the topic, love what you do, and help your brain feel excited about it.

And if all that doesn't do the trick, at least choose something that grips you like a vise.

COMMIT IN WRITING

When you identify the primary motivations related to your current project, journal about it, focusing on details, passions, and fears. By writing it down, you are programming your cerebral cortex and your hippocampus to remember that the story you are creating is important and that you are determined to complete it. You are also alerting your cortex that you'd like help anticipating and resolving problems and your "sleeping" subconscious that you're asking it to offer its import. Before you begin brainstorming, read your entries to fire up all the neurons and synapses needed to do your best work.

BRAINSTORM IDEAS: GIVE YOUR BRAIN FREE REIN

We've all heard about brainstorming, and we've likely all used it, typically when writing essays and reports in school. You likely had a teacher who showed you how to write down the central idea and then create balloons as offshoots to brainstorm ideas for flushing out, illustrating, or refuting the central idea. It may also spark creativity if you incorporate color and use curved or artistic lines from the primary balloon to the offshoots. Using pictures you found in magazines or that you sketch yourself may also spur ideas. This sort of mind mapping exercise (you can find lots of images online) may feel cliché, but, in fact, it remains effective.

But it's also true a brainstorm is what we've already been discussing—it occurs when massive amounts of stimulation (you providing input) produce a tightly woven web of neurons that can be ignited to make writing go well. One way to create a brainstorm and fire up your writing brain is to sit down with pen and paper and start generating as many ideas as you think of related to the story you want to tell.

Gather Your Brainstorming Tools

Now that you've focused your mind and your brain on *what* you're going to write and about—and *why* you are eager to make a massive brain investment in completing the work—it's ripe for the sort of brainstorming that results in plot, characters, theme, structure, setting, and whatever else you need to contemplate to get this story on paper. There are a number of software programs you could use to facilitate this process (and plenty of writers like them), but there's scientific evidence that the old-fashioned way—writing with pen and paper—taps into slow thinking, which is beneficial at this stage.

Spiral sketchbooks with big, white, blank pages—with texture and space—can be very appealing to your senses and can leave your brain feeling like it has plenty of space to roam; that is, it can fill those spaces with brilliant ideas. Some, like me, prefer blue ink pens with a fine-tip point that lets the words flow across those big, white, blank spaces. Many writers have always loved pen and paper and probably still enjoy spending time in stationary stores (lucky you, if there's still one near you) selecting paper and pens.

GO ON AN ARTIST DATE

Julia Cameron, author of thirty books on creativity, developed the idea of going on "an artist date." This doesn't mean you go out with another artist, it means you take the artist in you somewhere special, choosing an activity that stimulates your creativity by bringing your artistic *self* pleasure—examples would be a luxurious day spent exploring a museum or writing at the New York Public Library. Pilgrimages to the homes of famous writers and attending readings are often inspirational. Some writers love running their hands and eyes over handcrafted papers, leather journals, or delighting over writing accoutrements (mini typewriters, plumed pens, paperweights), admiring items that appeal purely to their sense of touch and beauty—and somehow speak to their writing ambitions. If you adore old-fashioned pens and fancy an expensive one, spend a few hours selecting and then gifting yourself the writing tools you deserve—in this way rewarding your creativity. Cameron's books on the creative process are full of ideas. Some of my other favorites include *The Right to Write* and *The Vein of Gold*.

Create the Time and Space for Brainstorming

Once you're ready to fire up your brain, begin wherever you have the most heat, the element that has been driving you to write this particular story, that keeps it in the forefront of your mind, whether it's a compelling situation, a particularly fascinating character, a dramatic and overarching theme, or the climactic and memorable ending. Give yourself at least a two-hour block of uninterrupted time to do nothing more than focus on the expansion of your primary idea. To write a novel, you need an idea that will keep your brain engaged and that can sustain the kind of depth that makes novels and longer works of art necessary, but these ideas often start small and expand as the writer works her magic.

Break it Down and Be Specific

Write down the inciting thought (what attracted your brain to this particular character, situation, or story) and then branch off from there, jotting down any ideas that arise. Don't overthink, just let the thoughts flow, and write down anything that pops in. I suggest starting with the big picture items, such as the basic premise, theme, main characters (and their relationship to each other), and the genre, and giving each one a full page for an expansion of ideas. Big picture elements to break down include the following:

- **BASIC PREMISE:** What is the story about? What happens? What does it prove, or at least illustrate? Why is telling it important? What's unique about your angle?

- **THEME:** Once you have clarified your premise, brainstorm related ideas, extensions, and contradictions. What is the primary message you want to convey in writing this particular story? Which elements (the setting, point of view, the antagonist, the plot and subplot, etc.) will elucidate, amplify, or contradict the theme? What offshoots or subplots are possible?

- **STYLE/GENRE/TONE:** Will it be a comedy or a tragedy? Will it be a young adult novel or a high concept thriller? Will it take place in contemporary times or be historical? Will it be told in first person or third person, subjective, with multiple points-of-view, or only one? No need to narrow it down, but do think about it as your brain may serve up a lovely surprise when you do. This is when you might also decide that your novel or prose poem might work better as a screenplay.

- **PROTAGONIST/MAIN CHARACTER/HERO:** Who will be the primary character, the one who propels the story forward? Create a list of this person's characteristics relevant to what happens in the story. What will serve your protagonist, and what will hamper or sabotage his progression? What is his primary dilemma? What will make the hero unique and unforgettable?

- **ANTAGONIST/SUPPORTING CHARACTER/VILLAIN:** Who will thwart your hero's efforts at every turn? Create a list of the villain's characteristics relevant to the story. What will make this person the perfect foil for your hero? Note: Sometimes the antagonist is the protagonist's own personality or character failings, such as his inner conflict, a drug addiction, or cowardice.

- **THE ENDING:** What happens as a result of what your protagonist does to overcome his challenges? Knowing how your story ends will not only provide lots of ideas and color everything that happens within the story, it will provide the impetus to write.

At this point, keep asking yourself what the story is about and what needs to happen. Concentrate on the broader aspects, but write down any subplots, characters, or scene ideas that occur—and they will. Avoid falling too deeply into one aspect, as doing so may deflect you from creating the broader strokes. When the session feels complete, tuck all the pages away and think about something else. Do, however, thank your brain for being brilliant—and reward it with a glass of wine, a hot bath, or a piece of chocolate perfection.

BRAINSTORM THE WIDTH AND BREADTH OF YOUR NOVEL, MEMOIR, SCREENPLAY, ETC.

For this round of brainstorming, delve a little deeper into your topic/theme/concept. This is when you begin to figure out who else will be in the story, what will happen, and the sequence (this will happen, causing this to happen) and flush out the character's arc (where the character is when the story begins, where he is in the middle, and where he is in the end—and what changes as a result of his actions).

Even if you don't have full confidence in what you've created thus far, release expectations, suppress negative thoughts, and surrender yourself to the process. Thanks to brainstorming, your brain is beginning to make vital neuronal connections, which will spark ideas. Again, this is not the time to reject ideas. Write down whatever occurs to you and welcome surprising thoughts. It's not uncommon to experience the genius your brain possesses. When you feel spent, stop, but be sure to thank (and reward) your lovely brain for delivering up a bounty of ideas for you to ponder further. In the meantime, here's your brainstorming task:

- **REVISIT YOUR "BIG PICTURE" ELEMENTS** (as above) and make any revisions or extensions.
- **PROTAGONIST:** Add to your list of qualities (if needed) and start to think about where the hero will be in the beginning, the middle, and the end. Jot down ideas for what will happen to create her progression or regression. Detail a character arc—challenges that build in strength and often thwart your protagonist, that require proactive behavior to conquer, and that may forever alter your character. Think progression and escalation of action and challenges.
- **ANTAGONIST:** Add more to your original notes. How does this person specifically challenge your hero? What is it about this par-

ticular character that impedes your main character? What will be the antagonist's character arc?

- **SUPPORTING ROLES:** Characters who will add subtext, illustrate themes, create tension, or provide comic relief. Consider their personality traits and anything relevant to the story. Remember, characters have to have a reason to exist.
- **PRIMARY PLOT POINTS:** Write down ideas that would propel the story forward or send it reeling backwards—obstacles/complications/setbacks. Consider how these complications and strategies or solutions to overcome them fit within the theme, but don't censor anything. Remember that conflict, whether inner or outer, is what gives a story its lifeblood.
- **SUBPLOTS:** These are extensions of, or counteractions with, the theme. What's happening beneath the surface that has a trajectory of its own? One of the supporting characters may have a storyline that complements or disputes the theme.
- **SETTING:** Where will it take place, what's significant about the setting (how does it relate to character, theme, plot)? Write down the basic elements: time period, location, weather, occupations, economic status, tone, and so on. Create rudimentary descriptions or list descriptive words.

Once this level of brainstorming is complete, you will have a growing mound of notes to help your writing brain focus on what you hope to achieve. Even while you're sleeping, your brain will be processing all the new information, linking it to what you created earlier and to whatever else is in your storage bin, as a result of your prepping efforts—or what you've encountered in life.

BRING THE HEAT

A single neuron looks like a long, branching vine with thousands of tendrils, or synapses, which connect with other neurons. Tiny electrical currents fluctuate along the neuron's surface. Then, to respond to a stimulus or send a command, the neuron sends a jolt of electric current, or spike, across a synapse and into another neuron. This synaptic process is repeated hundreds of times each second as electrical signals race from one side of your brain to the other, creating ever-changing networks of millions of neurons—and billions of connections—that birth your senses, thoughts, and actions. When preparing to write, fire up your neurons by focusing on bringing your absolute best to the task and consciously calling upon your brain to bring its genius.

USE BRAINSTORMING TO NARROW DOWN SPECIFICS

The third round of brainstorming will focus on specifics. Begin by reviewing all your notes from the previous two sessions and making any changes or expansions that come to mind. Once you're ready, create a page for each major plot point, and be ready to jot down ideas about the essence of what happens and what will change. You may even be ready to create scene pages, describing who is in them and what happens that moves the plot forward. Note that the numbers of pages specified for each section (beginning, middle, and end) are an approximation for novels or memoirs.

- **MAJOR PLOT POINTS:** Create a list of major plot points that might occur (that you can think of without overstressing). Lots of little things need to happen in a book, but this list is about the occurrences that change things or at least propel the story forward (or backward). Remember that everything that happens should be causal and essential. Unless you're writing magical realism, fantasy, or science fiction, coincidence and magical happenings should be avoided. The goal is to put your main character in a situation and then fill his or her path to success with roadblocks that he or she must overcome by taking heroic action (or being an antihero and failing to take action or taking destructive action).
- **BEGINNING/FIRST FIFTY PAGES:** This is where you start to brainstorm scenes and where they belong in the story (ideally, action scenes and quieter scenes will be interspersed to maximize

pacing). In the opening pages, you need an inciting incident (what happens that forces the main character to act and thereby sets the story in motion) and scenes to follow that will establish character, situation, and story, without bogging down the action (i.e., limit backstory to only what's absolutely essential). Keep in mind that scenes must be dramatic enough to sustain interest and that nothing that isn't necessary should be there—no fluff, just plenty of action that reveals character and situational challenges.

- **MIDDLE/NEXT TWO HUNDRED PAGES:** There's no way to make this part easy, so bring your brain to the table and use it to concoct situations that propel the plot, create tension, create complex obstacles, sustain suspense, force your character to act, and reveal growth. Big things need to happen multiple times, and they cannot be contrived but must arise out of a series of situations that escalate as a result of what your characters do—or don't do. Spend as much time as comfortable jotting down as many ideas as possible— and think causal; that is, this happens because that happened and then this happens, which causes this to happen, and so on.

- **ENDING/LAST FIFTY PAGES:** These scenes will lead up to the dramatic climax and a satisfying *denouement*. (Although we seem to prefer happy endings, a satisfying denouement or resolution does not imply "happy." It implies "appropriate for this particular story.") All that happened earlier should lead to a moment when everything is on the line and your protagonist is going to win or lose—dependent upon what he or she does. You need a dramatic, climatic scene that shows the moment it happens (climax), and then you need a few scenes that show what results or comes next (denouement). Keep in mind that all essential plot and subplot elements need to be resolved and that the ending should be as compelling and finely crafted as the beginning.

By now, your story should be taking shape, and if it's not, go back to the first level of brainstorming and keep those ideas flowing. Remember, you're not rejecting or committing to anything. The whole point is to engage your writing brain in the process so that neurons connected to formulating a story will start firing and wiring together. You're creating a strong neuronal network that you'll soon call to duty when the real writing begins.

TRAIN YOUR WRITING BRAIN: BECOME YOUR OWN BRAINSTORMING MEISTER

Advertising and product development agencies have long been known for productive brainstorming sessions. To generate original, inventive, memorable, and marketable ideas in high-pressure situations, they've developed what they call 6-3-5 Brainwriting. They gather in groups of six, and each group has a moderator. One participant is given five minutes to come up with three ideas, which are written down on a worksheet and passed to the next person, who is expected to use the first three ideas as inspiration for three new ideas. After six rounds in thirty minutes, the group has brainstormed 108 ideas.

Okay, you don't have five people to help, but you could try the same concept: Use a timer to give yourself five minutes to write down three ideas—whether it's what to write your next book about, what your character will do next, or what should make up the opening scenes. When that time is up, set the timer for another five minutes and write down three new ideas inspired by your first ideas, and so on until thirty minutes have passed. You may not end up with 108 ideas, but you will see how your brain ingeniously responds—and you may find the germ of a fabulous idea (for your character or plot).

WRITERS ON CRAFT

"Only in men's imagination does every truth find an effective and undeniable existence. Imagination, not invention, is the supreme master of art as of life."

—JOSEPH CONRAD

"The deep self, your true self has to come out. Try word association. Go to the typewriter and type in any old thing that comes into your head. By the bottom of the page, some character will take over and begin to write, and you'll be writing with excitement and passion and all the things in your past that you haven't touched yet."

—RAY BRADBURY

"The mind can proceed only so far upon what it knows and can prove. There comes a point where the mind takes a higher plane of knowledge, but can never prove how it got there. All great discoveries have involved such a leap."

—ALBERT EINSTEIN

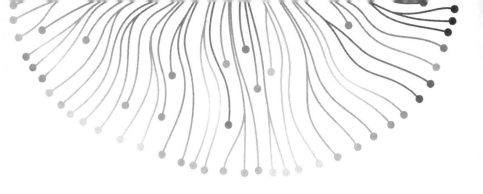

YOUR BRAIN AT THE BEGINNING

"When I write a sentence or a paragraph or a chapter that's good, I know it, and I know other people are going to read it. That knowledge [that] I'm doing this thing that works ... it's just exhilarating. Lots of times I fail at it, but when it's good, it's like going on a date that's going well. There's an electricity to the process that's exciting and incomparable to anything else."

—SEBASTIAN JUNGER

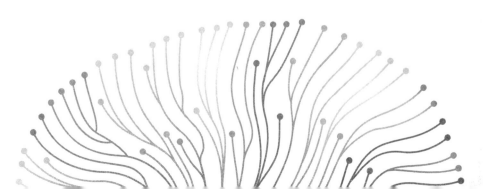

CHAPTER 6

NURTURE YOUR WRITING BRAIN

Lay the Groundwork for Success

"I always get up and make a cup of coffee while it is still dark—it must be dark—and then I drink the coffee and watch the light come ... Writers all devise ways to approach that place where they expect to make the contact, where they become the conduit, or where they engage in this mysterious process. For me, light is the signal in the transition. It's not being *in* the light, it's being there *before it arrives.* It enables me, in some sense."

—**TONI MORRISON**

Now that your marvelous brain has generated brilliant ideas, and you've dutifully recorded them on paper, there are specific writing exercises that will lay the groundwork your brain needs to assist you in the smooth and successful completion of your project. Hopefully your brainstorming sessions have given you a multitude of ideas, some of which you have used to create at least a beginning, broadly focused outline of sorts. I hesitate to use the actual word *outline*, as many feel averse to that process, even though it also works for many writers. Just because you create an outline doesn't mean you have to adhere to it, but many do find that it creates a road map they can refer to when feeling lost halfway through the novel.

PURPOSEFULLY INVITE YOUR BRAIN INTO YOUR WRITING SPACE

Your brain has thousands upon thousands of years in development, yet it still remains primitive in many aspects, one of which is being on constant alert. Our limbic brain's (the lower, more primitive and emotional brain) attention is often on scanning the horizon for incoming danger. It relies upon our primary senses—sight, smell, sound, touch, taste—to notice danger and send alert messages to the higher brain (the thinking neocortex, where executive functioning occurs), which then decides what to do to remedy the situation.

Distract Your Limbic Brain

What this means in terms of writing is that your limbic brain likes to keep all the sensory information pouring in and stay primed for life-saving action, which makes it a challenge to truly focus your brain on something as benign as sitting at a desk, writing—work that requires a narrowing focus. As you move into those first moments of writing, your limbic brain is still scanning the room, as if it expects a villain to emerge from the dusty books stored just behind you. This is a slight exaggeration, of course, but a valid point: If you want to increase your ability to focus, invite your brain into the safety of your writing space and reassure it that you will be safe while working (create an affirmation, such as: *This is my safe place and no danger will occur as long as I'm working*) to help it narrow its focus to what must be done.

WARM UP YOUR BRAIN WITH EXERCISE

Evidence mounts each day that exercise has positive effects on brainpower. The latest findings reveal that the workings of the individual neurons, and the makeup of brain matter itself, are enhanced by physical exercise. Moving your body regularly (twenty to thirty minutes of walking will do) helps your brain resist physical shrinkage and enhances cognitive flexibility. Exercise seems to slow, and possibly even reverse, physical decay of the brain (particularly in the elderly), and it also jump-starts neurogenesis (the birth of new brain cells). If you're feeling grumpy or fuzzy, do something active for twenty to thirty minutes to get your brain fired up—and reap short- and long-term benefits.

Establish a Clear Separation

Some writers like to perform rituals before they begin to write, whether its lighting candles, playing classical music, dancing madly to loud rock 'n' roll music, chanting, meditating, or praying. Some clean their desks, close the door, and turn off their cell phone (a good idea!). No matter which ritual or mind-clearing behavior you embrace, what's important is that you develop a signal to your limbic brain that this is a safe (and sacred) space where you'll be focused on thinking about words and stories. The more you reinforce writing rituals, the sooner your limbic brain will connect that transition from high alertness to confidence in safety, which will free up your cortex to write.

WHAT IS THIS WORK REALLY ABOUT?

We spent some time in the previous chapter deciding what your work is truly about, and we're going there a second time because this is an aspect of storytelling that frequently changes. You think you are writing about a brother betrayed by another brother who never recovers and flees to Nova Scotia to become a poet, or a woman who lost her herself in raising three daughters and has to reinvent herself when her husband dies shortly after the last child moved out, but are you?

You think you are writing about wounded males in a modern society who have difficulty connecting to their brothers, or about a modern woman who surrendered feminism for family and now has to empower herself to create a new life in a confusing new world; but as you work through specifics in this chapter (or while writing), you may find that what you thought was the primary focus is no longer external betrayal, but how one man sabotages himself; or how a woman remarries as quickly as possible so she doesn't have to reinvent herself, and all the repercussions those choices bring.

IDENTIFY A PURPOSE LARGER THAN YOURSELF

A 2014 study of two thousand students, published in the *Journal of Social Psychology*, found that identifying a "pro-social, self-transcendent" purpose, such as gaining skills to benefit society or making a positive impact on the world, helped students study longer and harder. The students who did so were much better at self-regulating their study sessions, resisting interruptions, and sticking with the task longer. Those whose primary goal was to have an interesting or enjoyable career did not produce the same benefits. To keep your motivation strong and your brain engaged, choose a topic that holds deep meaning for you, something that feels urgent in a very personal way—and write about that passion in your journal to bring your brain's attention to your overarching purpose.

Unfortunately (or fortunately), *what and why* becomes less obvious as writing progresses. Just as your characters begin to feel like shape-shifters, going off on their own to do things you did not have in mind, the *what and why* of the work often morphs in response to plot twists you hadn't anticipated—or in response to feelings that arise as you write, as the story reveals itself.

Revisiting the story question of what it's *really* about helps:

- tap into and refine your passion for the subject—and for writing;
- solicit specific ideas for structure, plot, characters, theme, and so on;
- increase and tighten the neuronal network based on your specific motivations;
- help your brain solidify what's important and what's not important;
- motivate you to keep moving forward when you hit roadblocks.

Grappling with these story questions can be highly productive, as doing so both narrows the focus (thereby offering up specific plot points and character arcs) and reinforces your reason for wanting to write this particular work. Knowing—and preferably feeling—your primary motivation for choosing this particular story, these particular characters, in these particular situations is what will inspire you to write whenever time allows and to keep writing when your energy and enthusiasm sags in the middle or drags out the end.

MAXIMIZE THE FAIRY TALE TEMPLATE

In *The Uses of Enchantment: The Meaning and Importance of Fairy Tales,* psychologist and author Bruno Bettelheim says the recurring motifs used in fairy tales—the evil stepmother, the child lost in the woods, the child whose parents cannot protect her from evil—are symbolic of the frightening aspects of being a child in an adult world. Good mothers sometimes flip into angry, punishing mothers, and someone or some situations adults view as normal feel scary to a child. Bettelheim says fairy tales re-create the sort of dramas that lodge in our psyches and offer a way for children to understand that people are rarely all good or all evil, and that they can learn to navigate safely in the world. When crafting your story, don't overlook the underlying meaning or the psychological connections to fairy tales, as those things will add depth to your story and assist your brain in adopting the universal storytelling format.

WRITE DETAILED CHARACTER BIOS, SPECIFY EACH CHARACTER'S ARC

The next step is to nail down your characters: Figure out what your central characters will do and what will happen to them. Many writers find it very useful to write character bios, detailing when and where each main character was born, his family circumstances, what shaped his character, any traumas he experienced, what motivates him, how he sabotages himself, etc. Even if it feels forced, the process can result in greater insights into your character's personality and often provides surprising and welcome ideas for plotting. Remember exercises like these also bolster your neuronal networks, linking personal history, reading and research memories, and original thoughts.

After you've given thought to the characters and the role each will play, it's good to focus on the character arc that your hero or heroine will journey across, an aspect of writing that is essential to good storytelling. The main character should be in a different place from where he or she began, and the changes should result from conscious actions the character has taken—or not taken—throughout the journey, from page one to the end.

Again, many of these elements may change as you write, but just thinking about them—intently focusing your brain on them, mapping them out on paper—will spur ideas. Given the proper input, your neurons will begin sparking and making surprising connections.

GLOBALLY IGNITE YOUR BRAIN

A phenomenon occurs in the brain that scientists call "global excitation," and it happens just as you might imagine: a network of neurons excite each other, which leads to more neurons becoming excited, until a sort of global synchronized activity occurs. It's similar to an audience in which one person claps his hands and then those around him do, and then more and more until it's a unanimous standing ovation. When neurons generate global excitation, which usually occurs from the top—neurons in the cortex—down, they soon begin returning the same level of excitation, which results in an explosion of self-generated activity. The neurons that are strongly connected burst into a high level of self-sustained excitation—if you stay focused, delve deeper, and resist all distractions.

CREATE A DETAILED PLOTLINE AND/OR OUTLINE

Now that you've done a lot of the groundwork, it's time to focus on the plot, or what will happen in your novel (or screenplay, or whatever you happen to be writing) that propels your hero or heroine forward—or backward. Some people love to outline; others believe creating outlines stifles their creativity. If that's the case with you, then please consider that you don't have to draw up an official or traditional outline. Formulating a sequence of what's going to happen, and which actions lead to succeeding actions, gives your brain a template that will help the writing flow. It's good to "feed" your brain ideas about the structure (typically a three-act structure) and the various plot points and plot twists so it begins to create a rhythm for the particular story you're working on.

So if you're one of those writers who loves to outline and your brain readily responds to the blueprint you create, then by all means outline to your heart's content. If you're resistant to the process, at least be open to thinking about the major events and how they will escalate as the story builds. All this can, and likely will, change as you write, but what you're doing is giving your brain something to ponder, to dream about, and to put into action when the actual writing begins. You are helping your brain establish a story pattern, a rhythmical standard that will work small miracles when the real writing begins.

FIND A STORY THREAD

Patti Smith's memoir *Just Kids* chronicles her forays into drawing, poetry, and music—basically how a small town girl became an eclectic artist in the late 1960s through mid-1970s. Living in New York at that time offered a wild mix of experiences and people (who later became famous), but Smith focused on her relationship with Robert Mapplethorpe, the unique and troubled artist she loved. The genius in her memoir—which won a National Book Award—was choosing that focus, that thread, that relationship and using it to knit all the varying experiences together. In this way, she reveals the nuances of their relationship and how it affected her artistic growth.

Search for a thread (an organizing principle, what knits it all together) in your novel or memoir and then create a list of scenes that reinforce the thread. Once you find your thread and bring it sharply into focus, your brain will begin noticing connections and reviving memories. Put it to work and that thread may be the push you need to complete your memoir, novel, or screenplay.

VISUALIZE CHARACTERS, SCENES, SETTINGS IN MOTION

The next step is to take your brain on a visual journey. Although lying back to visualize your characters, scenes, and setting may feel like the

FIRE UP YOUR WRITING BRAIN

sort of daydreaming others (and perhaps you) consider nonproductive, your brain has remarkable abilities when it comes to visualization. Studies have shown that visualizations can effectively trick your brain into thinking what it just experienced in thought only *is* real, particularly if you break down the visualizations into specific, detailed, sequential images (visualizing them as they would happen, in your mind's eye, so to speak).

The value in this exercise is that you are further familiarizing your writing brain with what you hope to achieve in terms of creating unique and memorable characters, embellishing setting to create a desired mood, and imagining a set of sequential actions that will occur in specific scenes. Visualization also aids in memory, so you're likely to remember that great scene longer, too. You are giving your brain images that it can call upon when you sit down to write *what you've already described to it in detail*. Again, how you ultimately write the story may (and likely will) change, but the visualization process helps you bring your ideas into sharper focus, and all this preparation can help you become a more creative, productive, and successful writer.

SPARK YOUR IMAGINATION

Your brain is a creativity machine and needs to be oiled and revitalized throughout your life. Learning how your brain works and what keeps it fired up and fluid is the best thing you can do to bolster your creativity. Try these exercises, or develop some of your own, to fire up and revitalize your creative brain:

- Start writing a story about a character doing something very commonplace, then three pages in, throw in a fantastical twist (the wilder the better). Follow that thread for a few pages and then twist it again (whack it out, by trying something completely illogical or radically different, even something completely ridiculous). Don't forget to include humor—make yourself laugh at your own ingenuity.
- Play *what-if* plotting games and try hard to take them somewhere completely original. Whatever you dream

up, ask your brain to come up with consequences. For example, in the short story "The Curious Case of Benjamin Button," we can only presume that F. Scott Fitzgerald asked himself one day: What if someone aged backwards ... and what happens when that person falls in love? Come up with five *what-if* storylines, each with a few consequences, and remember to imagine outside your comfort zone.

Hopefully you'll find these exercises fun imagination sparkers. If not, dream up your own!

CREATE AN ORGANIZATIONAL SYSTEM THAT FITS YOUR WRITING BRAIN

No one knows your brain like you do. Some people need absolute organization, a clean desk, silence, hours spent alone; some people are unfazed by noise or mess and can snap into writing mode within seconds. This exercise is about noticing what works for you, what circumstances result in your most productive work.

Some writers use writing software to help organize their thoughts, particularly in relation to plots and scenes. Most of the software requires a learning curve, but if that's something that appeals to you, it's worth checking out. These can be very useful if you're writing a historical novel or creating fantasy and science fiction, which often require creation of special worlds, a complex plot, and a cast of characters—far more complicated than writing a novel with a far less complicated plot and ten or so characters. Software programs include WriteItNow, WriteWay Pro, Power Structure, Contour, and Dramatica Pro. Be sure to read online reviews to make sure the one you choose is right for you.

Try Using Note Cards

Some prefer using note cards and a bulletin board or large dry erase board. Some (including me) begin with a large spiral sketchbook in which they write down what will happen in each "act," (first, second, and third or beginning, middle, end) and then break down each section into scenes. Simple wording that is also clear is fine, just enough to remind you later why you included the scene, what is the primary reason for the scene, what occurs, and what results. Once you feel like the story is taking shape, transfer the scenes to note cards (one scene description per note card), which you can then lay out on a floor and move around if you need to, which you likely will. This really helps you with pacing and building tension as the story progresses. You will start to see patterns, such as having too many passive scenes in a row or too many action scenes or just too many scenes (or not enough scenes). At this stage, cards make it easier to shift scenes around, to add and delete, and to see connections and missed connections. Spend a lot of time pondering the cards/notes and while you do, imagine that your writing brain is mapping the storyline and creating a database dedicated to this work, which it is.

Figure Out What Works for You

Some writers like to be organized, which means that this works for them. What you have to figure out is what works for *you*. If you don't know, or feel that whatever you've been doing is not working, experiment, think outside the box, do something new. If you always work at home, take your laptop to a coffee shop for an afternoon; if you never plan ahead, try planning three scenes, visualizing them, writing down the basics, reviewing them before going to bed, and writing them the next morning (before you go to work at an outside job or do anything that requires brainpower). You will soon discover the process that leads to increased creativity or productivity—for you.

Stay Flexible

The goal is to create an organizational method that fits your brain. Once you figure it out, your brain will reward you with productive writing sessions. And nothing ever has to be written in stone. Some books, projects, or different genres have special needs that are speficic to that audience, which is something to consider when you begin the programming exercises.

GROUND YOURSELF AT NIGHT

Your brain creates a hexagonal pattern of grid cells (similar to bees hives) to facilitate the coding of information while you sleep. The *grid cells* help to figure out where your body is in space and time—independent of external clues—and *place cells* organize memories about specific locations you have experienced. Because *place cells* are found in the hippocampus, the brain's memory hub, the brain may use this grid system to create a rich autobiographical "map" that you can mine to navigate life—and to spark memories that have been embedded deep in your hippocampus. Paying attention to where you are in your writing life—and in the story you're writing—before sleeping may help your brain consolidate both narratives and make it easier to start afresh the following day

MAXIMIZE YOUR BRAIN'S ORGANIZATIONAL SKILLS

Your brain never sleeps. While you're consciously zonked out and in REM (Rapid Eye Movement) sleep, your brain is busy identifying and reinforcing connections between events, sensory input, feelings, and memories you experienced that day. Basically it's processing, organizing, categorizing, linking, discarding, and saving information—all based on what you consciously (and unconsciously) experienced that day and how that information fits in with prior experiences and what you have been thinking about or observing that day. The process consolidates your narrative (and also the story narrative of your work in progress) and creates "memory links" that are essential to healthy brain functioning. Memory links improve your waking memory; that is, the ability to spark memories that have been embedded deep in your hippocampus. Sleeping also increases brain connectivity or plasticity, which helps you continue learning and growing as you age.

Summon Your Cortex

During the deeper REM phase of sleeping, your brain is finally "free" to back up its database by:

1. consolidating and processing any and all information you've learned during the day;
2. forming neural connections that strengthen and consolidate memories;
3. replenishing its supply of neurotransmitters, including chemicals such as serotonin and dopamine. These chemicals help all parts of the brain to stay on track—neither too fast nor too slow—allowing the brain as a whole to hum along, doing the best job it can.

In the REM phase of sleep, the pons, located at the base of your brain, sends signals to the thalamus, which relays them to the cerebral cortex, the outer layer of the brain that is responsible for learning, thinking, and organizing information. The cortex is the part of the brain that interprets and organizes environmental information during consciousness. Scientists believe that the cortex tries to interpret the random signals it receives from the pons and the thalamus, essentially creating a "story" out of fragmented brain activity.

Sleep studies have shown that rats who run a maze during their waking hours form a mental "map" that their brains then "relive" while sleeping, perhaps embedding the memory in its hippocampus for long-term storage. They have discovered that the rats will use the "map" when placed in the maze the following day, as a way to figure out where to go next.

Make Your Desires Known

As such, you may well experience major payoffs for organizing your conscious thoughts before crawling into bed. At the end of each day do the following:

- Assess where you are in the writing process. If you have major story questions, journal about them. If you need inspiration, ask for it. If you feel the story's bogged down, ask for new ideas, and so on.

- Sketch out the important elements of the scenes you'll write next, using your software program, journal, note cards, or a dry erase board. Nothing elaborate is needed—just basic information about who's in the scenes, where they take place, what happens, and so on.

Before you go to bed, spend five to fifteen minutes reviewing your notes (and again the following morning) to prep your brain. This doesn't mean that you have to adhere to what you've created, but putting that much thought into what you're going to write—and, in particular, seeing it in print—sparks ideas and makes it easier (and more rewarding) to get to your work space and down to work the next day.

CREATE A CONCRETE, FLEXIBLE GAME PLAN FOR COMPLETION

Another way to get your mind and brain on board is to create a game plan for completion. At this stage, a broad plan will help you tamp down feelings that the task is simply too big or out of your league. Behind the scenes, your brain has been breaking down complicated tasks into small steps since you were born. Huge tasks, such as walking and talking, required the stimulation and coordination of many skills; none were learned overnight and most required lots and lots of practice. You'll likely remember learning to read and can easily imagine all the steps that went into making the act of reading not only possible but simple. In the beginning stages, your brain had to learn all the symbolism, sounds, and meanings, and then how to string together letters to form words, sentences, and so on. The point being that your brain knows how to learn something new, and one way to facilitate that happening more frequently and with greater success is to tackle the task in steps.

JOG FOR FIVE MINUTES

When neuroscientists study brain activity using functional magnetic resonance imaging (fMRI) machines, they are often looking for changes in the levels of oxygen in the blood passing through the brain—because they've found that more active areas use more oxygen, which means oxygen depletion is a sign of brain activity. This is why pausing to exercise or meditating for five minutes can increase blood flow to your brain. If that seems too much, simply pause long enough to slowly breathe in and slowly exhale deep breaths. Imagine the oxygen boosting your brain cells, re-energizing your thought processes, and making you a better writer. Remember: Your brain needs oxygen to function and visualization works!

Break It Down into Tasks

Some writers like to write in spurts, to lock themselves away for a period of days and do nothing but write that novel or memoir or screenplay. However, most writers don't have the luxury of unencumbered blocks of time to spend *solely* focused on their creative endeavors. Still, if you can free up a few days, you can get a lot done, such as creating the backstory for each of your characters (which constitutes research), writing a chapter, or ironing out kinks in the subplot. When you break down everything that goes into writing an entire novel into simpler components, the writing may feel more manageable. You can regularly set and reach goals, and thereby bolster a feeling of success. Remember, wiring success to writing will make it easier to summon your brain for writing sessions. You'll be creating a sense of success that will override a tendency to feel overwhelmed.

Realize Books (and Scripts) Take Time

Even though it's possible to pound out a book (or a play or other work) in two fairly uninterrupted months, most books require a minimum of twelve months and often years to conceive, create, and craft. What you want to avoid, however, is leaving it open-ended, giving yourself a nebulous goal of "however much time it takes" (and thereby never finishing) or setting yourself up to fail. Creating the unrealistic expectation that you can write a novel "in three months," which may be possible, if you're an experienced novelist—and a genius—can actually work against you. It's more helpful to give your brain specific, measurable goals and to reinforce those goals by reviewing them regularly and rewarding yourself for reaching them.

Doing so reminds your brain that you have a *specific* goal that is important to you and you appreciate how beautifully it's working. Remember your brain wants to please you and will work hard to do so. Rewards should be pleasurable enough to awaken your brain's reward center, so it knows to release the *feel-good* chemicals—dopamine, endorphins, serotonin, oxytocin, and others. This release motivates your brain to repeat the same experience, to seek the same pleasure.

Foster a Feeling of Success

You could decide, for example, that you'll have all the prep work (as we've been discussing) done in a month, all the research done in two months (longer, if it's a historical or science fiction novel), and that you'll begin writing in month three and will write one chapter every two weeks. This type of plan will—and should—be individualistic and specific to you, your project, and how much time you have to devote to writing your book (screenplay, play, etc.).

Just remember that speed is not important. What matters is designing a plan that will help you feel successful at every stage and lead you to the finish line. The more successful your brain feels, the better it will perform in helping you meet the goals you have declared most important. Your brain loves feeling successful and rewarded, and will work for you to repeat that feeling over and over again.

CREATE SPECIFIC, ATTAINABLE GOALS FOR GETTING UNDERWAY

If you are, or have been, a journalist for a daily publication, you've experienced the rush of adrenaline that comes when the deadline hour approaches and your editor is literally standing over you, waiting for the final product, pushing you to work fast but still do your best work. Your sense of story and facts had better be in place, and your mind had best be fired up and facile enough to pound out the story. You also know the endomorphic rush that comes after, when you've met the deadline and done an exceptional job. The upside and downside of deadlines becomes your daily life. Deadlines haunt you and serve you; they make you and break you; they grind you down and lift you up.

Make Deadlines Your Friends

That being said, journalists often enter the world of writing novels (or screenplays or what have you) with a strong work ethic, based largely on feeling equally inspired and agreeable to structured deadlines. Some journalists don't find deadlines oppressive. Some actually love having a finite goal, a finish line—unless the editor is expecting too much, too fast. In those cases, frustration and resistance may gum up the works, but the deadline itself may still function as a motivation in a way nothing else can.

For many people, however, deadlines become a fire-breathing dragon. I've known writers who panic as a deadline approaches, even if they've had months to research and write, and the work is far more complete than they think it is. I've known writers to have anxiety attacks and insist that they can't begin to write, let alone meet the deadline.

Flip the Switch to Excitement

The good news for those deadline-phobic, anxiety-prone writers is that all those negative emotions generate energy and focus that can be harnessed. Scientists have confirmed that our brains respond quicker and more attentively to negative emotions—because long ago those negative emotions were likely stirred by an approaching real-life danger in the form of tigers, lions, or bears. In those days, responding quickly to negative stimulants could mean the difference between living and dying, whereas positive emotions were likely signaling that all is well; that is, they were life affirming.

When fear (and adrenaline) surges, it is signaling an opportunity to harness all that brainpower and direct those fired-up neurons where you want them to go—preferably into focusing on completion. Instead of feeling paralyzed, you can *choose* to feel, as President Obama once chanted to his supporters, "fired up and ready to go." I'm not suggesting that it's easy, but it is something you can learn to orchestrate—harnessing and using the energy as fuel to write faster, sharper, more purposefully, and more integrated. Over time, with practice, and knowing that you can consciously choose *how* to use the heightened mental state, you can train your brain to transform paralysis to productivity. I'm not saying you'll grow to love deadlines, but you can learn how to use them to your advantage.

WHEN IT COMES TO GOALS, START SMALL

Again, what's most important is setting realistic goals whose accomplishment will create a feeling of success. You want to reward your brain for meeting your goals, and when you set them too high, you create a feeling of disappointment or failure—and you may even use the inability to meet your goals to berate yourself on a regular basis, which is completely counterproductive.

Remember, *what fires together, wires together.* If you set realistic goals that you continually reach, you are connecting success, and the feel-good brain chemicals (dopamine, endorphins, serotonin, oxytocin, etc.) that replenish your brain when you feel successful, with writing; if you set unrealistic goals, that you always fall short of reaching, you are connecting disappointment and self-defeat with writing. Start with goals you can easily reach, and when you are consistently meeting those goals, you can set new ones a little higher.

REWARD YOUR BRAIN

To create new neuronal pathways that will support meeting your goals, consciously pair up writing with something you consider rewarding. It could be joining friends for a cocktail after a particularly fruitful day of writing or buying your favorite magazine after struggling through a problematic scene or calling a potential paramour after you complete a chapter. Whatever you choose, make it something that brings a genuine feeling of pleasure to you. Also, the reward should take place during, or *immediately after*, the activity. That way, rewarding your brain will link up writing with positive associations and good consequences *for you*, thus reinforcing new, more positive brain connections. Soon you'll be thinking of meeting your writing goals as something you love to do.

THE JOYS AND PERILS OF WORD COUNTS

It's lovely that thousands upon thousands of people all over the world are participating in the National Novel Writing Month of November (popularly known as NaNoWriMo). It's a brilliant concept that has obviously appealed to many aspiring writers, and I know many professional writers who use it to shame themselves into pursuing the creative work that's always getting shunted for day jobs.

It Can Be a Heady Experience

There's something extremely appealing about all that writing energy being exercised worldwide, and many are able to write fifty thousand words in November, which surely feels absolutely amazing. Some who write fifty thousand words do go on to complete and sell their novels (*The Night Circus* by Erin Morgenstern, for example), but a whole lot of people either don't make the goal or, if they do, don't ever go back and edit what they write.

The NaNoWriMo genius is that it encourages creative writers to unleash all restraints (even thinking) and just pound out thousands of words, every day, no matter what else is going on in their lives. The fifty thousand words they create may very well be filled with fabulous raw material, and, hopefully, all who write fifty thousand words will go back to mine those fields, refine, and shape a novel. At the very least, meeting that fifty thousand-word goal is worth a shot, but you may be wiser to participate in one of their "camps," when lower word counts (try five thousand to ten thousand words in one month) can be set—and thus more likely successfully achieved.

Link Writing to Success

Writing groups can, of course, run their own competitions to see how many words each participant can write in a month, and often it spurs action. But what may also occur is that the amount of words doesn't leave them with a completed project, and some will be too hard on themselves for not reaching word counts. Again, they are wiring disappointment— linking a feeling of failure to the *act of writing*. Better to keep word count goals achievable, focus more on the quality of writing, and reward yourself when you reach your goals. Remember, the more you wire a feeling of success to the act of writing, the easier writing will become.

Lay the Groundwork for Ongoing Success

That said, figure out how many words you can realistically write in a week, commit to the amount, and do your best to meet that goal. Keep doing this, and you are laying the groundwork for success because you are repeatedly training your brain to rise to the occasion and to enjoy writing, in real time, while it's happening.

SET REALISTIC GOALS

Worrying about daily word count goals can be counterproductive. If you successfully meet your goals, fine, but if you consistently fall short, lower them to avoid feeling like a failure. Raymond Chandler set the bar at 5,000 words a day; James Joyce strove for two perfect sentences a day. Stephen King aims for 2,000 words (with zero adverbs) a day; Anthony Trollope wanted 250-words every fifteen minutes. Word count goals clearly motivate some, but in the end it's what you can *successfully* motivate yourself to accomplish that matters. That being said, during a first draft, unleash your subconscious and pound out as many words as possible each day. During second (and third, and fourth) drafts, keep in mind that quality is now more important than quantity.

CONSIDER YOUR BRAIN PROGRAMMED

These last three chapters have been all about programming your brain's "software" for the task of writing, whether it's a book, movie, play, or any work that requires extended focus over a long period of time. In the next chapter, we'll focus on reinforcing your own sense of being a writer who successfully writes, which is another step on the road to training your writing brain to become one that conceives, creates, and crafts stories that sell.

TRAIN YOUR WRITING BRAIN: INCREASE YOUR ABILITY TO FOCUS

One negative effect of technology is that our brains have become used to rapid-fire stimulation, a flurry of pictures and words, instantaneous responses via texts and e-mails delivered in milliseconds, the fastest Internet connections one can buy, and screens, screens, *everywhere*, electronic screens. If you're someone who is finding it hard to focus long enough to write, here are a few tips for dialing down stimulation and incrementally increasing your ability to focus.

1. Clear off your desk, or find another space where no clutter will distract you. If you have to dump a stack of books or paper somewhere else, do so. Give yourself as clean a work space as possible.

2. Set aside thirty minutes. Doesn't sound like such a big deal, does it? Still, some may find it hard to completely clear their brain space for the first thirty minutes. If that's you, start with fifteen minutes and do your best, as it will pay off.

3. Isolate yourself and turn off all media. That's right, all media: no television, no Spotify, no iPod, no Internet, no texting or phone calls, no "noise" at all. Turn off your cell phone and e-mail notifications. What you want is absolute silence.

4. To begin, it's best to handwrite on a sheet of paper—this encourages "slow-thinking" and an intimacy with the work that keyboards just can't deliver. Avoid fancy apps, keep the session intimate and low-tech. As you increase the time, it's okay to transition to a computer program—for writing. Clear your mind and ignore distracting thoughts. If you don't know how to brush aside thoughts, refer to the discussion on "Mindfulness" in Chapter 7. Some like to envision thoughts as balloons, floating away.

5. Choose one task: Write a small scene, write a character description, figure out the next plot point, create a list of potent adjectives to replace all the dull or trite ones you used in your last writing session, describe the setting for your next scene. You get the drift: Make it fairly simple and make it directly related to your current writing project. No reading, no online researching (as that quickly leads to distractions). The time is best spent *concentrating*, marshaling all of your mental energy to the task at hand. If necessary, make a spoken request for your brain to "focus, focus, focus," and then notice the moment when it quiets and hones in on the task. This is a muscle you can develop and flex.

6. Stop after thirty minutes and reward yourself for concentrating. The goal is to connect a reward to the session. It could be five minutes of yoga, five minutes of dancing, five minutes talking to your best friend, five minutes to read, five minutes to walk around your neighborhood. Make sure the reward is fun. You can, of course, make it food related, but if you do so, choose a healthy snack or a nourishing lunch to refresh your brain—and then get back to writing!

The next day, increase the time to sixty minutes, with seven minutes of reward; and then move up to ninety minutes with ten minutes of reward. If ninety minutes feels stressful, linger there for a week, writing for ninety minutes each day—and pat yourself on the back after each session for doing what you can. It's all about *linking pleasure to focus*. When you feel relatively comfortable with ninety minutes, go up to two hours. Then increase the time to two and a half hours, and so on until you reach a minimum of three hours. Note that the reward time will pare down related to the time spent concentrating, as the goal is to increase time spent focused and working. As you increase the focused writing session to two hours and three hours, reduce the reward to about five minutes per hour, with the goal of working for three hours at a stretch.

FIRE UP YOUR WRITING BRAIN

WRITERS ON CRAFT

"I jump up in the morning. I can't wait to go see what my characters are going to do today. I get wired up. When my character falls in love, I'm in love. When somebody's heart is broken, or feels jubilation, I feel all of that."

—TERRY MCMILLAN

"I didn't begin with the idea of publishing a memoir, but as I started getting these memories down, they took over. Writers wait for that moment when the material starts to carry them. It happens more rarely than one wants to think, and you're a fool if you don't give in to it when it does—drop everything else and go with it."

—TOBIAS WOLFF

"I like the physical sensation of writing. It gives me a kind of ruddy vigor, like some sort of exercise you want an award for afterward."

—MEG WOLITZER

"I can work anywhere. I wrote in bedrooms and living rooms when I was growing up with my parents and my brother in a small house in Los Angeles. I worked on my typewriter in the living room, with the radio and my mother and dad and brother all talking at the same time. Later on, when I wanted to write *Fahrenheit 451*, I went up to UCLA and found a basement typing room where, if you inserted ten cents into the typewriter, you could buy thirty minutes of typing time."

—RAY BRADBURY

FIRE UP YOUR WRITING BRAIN
Buckle Down and Write

"If you concentrate on writing three or four hours a day and feel tired after a week of this, you're not going to be able to write a long work. What's needed of the writer of fiction—at least one who hopes to write a novel—is the energy to focus every day for half a year, or a year, or two years. Fortunately, these two disciplines—focus and endurance—are different from talent, since they can be acquired and sharpened through training."

—HARUKI MURAKAMI

Now that you've engaged your brainpower—to sort out the details, envision the story, understand your characters and themes—and you have fired up the world's most magnificent writing *machine*, it's time to open the floodgates, buckle down, and get words on the page.

Japanese writer Haruki Murakami, the author quoted above, who has run in thirty or so marathons and written a dozen novels, attributes these impressive accomplishments to his ability to focus. He calls the focus needed for writing "the ability to concentrate all your limited talents on whatever's critical at the moment." Without that, he says, you can't accomplish anything of value. According to Murakami, he spends three to four hours each morning, at his desk, focused totally on what he is writing. "I don't see anything else, I don't think about anything else," he says.

Even in the best of circumstances, focusing for long periods of time is a challenge. Staying alert, keeping your mind razor sharp, generating new ideas, and writing at your peak capacity requires energy and discipline. In this chapter, we'll discuss specific ways you can fire up your brain and keep it focused on writing the best work you are capable of writing.

CREATE THE BEST SETTING TO WRITE

Even if it's a corner of the kitchen table, the place where you write should be treated like a *sacred space*—a place where you focus only on writing, minimize distractions, and honor the craft you are perfecting. Having a space that is readily available will help you transition from "daily life" to your "writing life," and a space in which you can create the ideal working environment for you—whether it's absolute quiet or close to the hum of everyday life or sparsely decorated and clean or lived in and cluttered with books—should feel sacrosanct. It is useful to give thought to your ideal writing environment and to make being in the space enjoyable and rewarding. The more you connect pleasure with writing, the more your brain will be motivated to fire on all pistons, in that space, when you most need it. Loving your sacred writing space also helps conquer writing resistance because you've created a place in which you want to be.

GROUND YOUR BRAIN IN SPACE

Even when you feel a bit spacey, your body and your brain are always intimately connected, but your mind is easily distracted. Thus, when settling in to write, it's helpful to ground your writing brain in time and space. When you enter your writing space, spend a few minutes looking around, noticing what's around you, pausing to gaze at objects that please you, particularly objects you love, your writing tools, your favorite books, and whatever else you've placed around you to help you transition from the outer world of daily life to the inner world of writing. This creates a feeling of safety for your brain and will activate your cognitive writing map, which will foster your ability to transition into focusing on the task at hand—to get busy writing.

CREATE THE BEST ENVIRONMENT

Some writers like noise; others prefer quiet. Some writers write in marathon stretches; others prefer daily, two-hour windows of opportunity. Some writers like to write before the sun rises; some like to write well into the nighttime hours. The point is that whatever works for you is fine. If you're productive and find writing rewarding, then flow with it.

However, if finding time to be truly productive proves difficult, it's important to figure out what isn't working and what *will* work for you. Consider all variables. Your needs may differ for various stages in the process (brainstorming in silence, firing up with loud music, writing with soft music in the background). Don't assume you already know what will work best. Experiment. Notice when things go well and then create more of that environment, situation, and experience. Focus on the positive as much as possible, linking pleasure to writing. The more you enjoy the time you spend writing and the more you feel that your writing sessions are productive, the more you'll want to write every chance you get.

Scientific studies have found that working in a warm environment (ideal temperature around 77 degrees) and working in a well-lit environment (natural daylight is best, even light is also important) is conducive to productive thinking. The gist of it is keep yourself comfortably warm and don't work in a rabbit hole that's dark, repressive, cluttered, and claustrophobic—unless, of course, that's what lights up your brain.

SPEND A DAY AT A COFFEE SHOP

Researchers found that ambient noise, at the level one might experience sitting in a coffee shop, can actually boost creativity. Scientists found that noise around 70 decibels (which they compared to a bustling coffee shop or a television on in the background, compared to 50 decibels, which would be relative quiet) seemed to encourage participants to be more creative on brainstorming or word-association tasks. Once noise rose to 85 decibels (a blender or vacuum cleaner), it proved too distracting. Other studies have found that extreme quiet seems to sharpen your focus, which can hamper your abstract thinking. If you can't go to a coffee shop, you can find ambient coffee shop noise on Coffitivity.com ranging from "morning murmur" to "Paris Paradise." If you're worried that you'd become a stereotypical image of a writer tapping away at a coffee shop, take heart—it benefits your writing brain.

CLEAR BRAIN SPACE FOR WRITING

Substantial research suggests that having a clean work space increases your ability to concentrate. Many writers find it hard to work if their house isn't fairly clean and the laundry mostly done. Yes, doing chores can be a way to procrastinate, but, for many, it's easier to focus on creativity when everyday, real-life things are pretty much in order. It's fine to put things in order before you begin writing, as long as you get around to writing. If this type of fussing becomes procrastination, then you have to stop deluding yourself and either breeze through whatever it is (give yourself thirty minutes to deal with life) or learn to compartmentalize long enough to focus on what comes first—which should always be writing.

Also, it's good to take a break once an hour to stand or, even better, to move around and do something physical. That's the perfect time to vacuum the rug, throw in a load of laundry, pick up the family room, or wash the dishes in your sink. Just remember to keep these breaks short and focused on one task, which will help your brain shift from one task back to the original task of writing.

One way to block the urge to put other things before writing is to create a physical "must-do" list and then prioritize the items on the list by determining what has to be done and what can wait. By the time you've created the list, you will know the tasks you need to do to clear your mind, and which ones can wait, which will help your brain feel in control and confident that everything on the list will be addressed—later.

ENTER WITH INTENTION

Just settling into your writing space should signal that it's time for the real work to begin. The space needs to be at least marginally functional and advantageous to the kind of concentration required to write. Do whatever it takes to create a space and create the kind of ambiance that separates you from your everyday life, whether it's burning scented candles or incense (which many love as a way to "cleanse or refresh energy" and/or create sensual stimulation), softly playing classical music (a gentle way to ease into writing) or rock music (stimulating, at least to get fired up), and the proximity of favorite items, such as a certain pen, a signed, first-edition novel you love, a miniature statue of Shakespeare—whatever you love.

Here's a brief list of what setting a clear intention to write can do for your brain:

- It gives your brain a sense of purpose, perks up receptors and boosts neuronal connections related to writing, which improves clarity, focus, insights, and flow.
- It narrows down the field of awareness and helps your brain dismiss disruptive thoughts, which increases productivity.
- It bolsters purposeful self-observation, helps your unconscious become conscious, and helps you see and address your resistance.
- It helps you notice when you go off task and feel a sense of accomplishment when you stay focused and productive.

Setting an intention doesn't imply anything *woo-woo* mystical, it's merely taking a moment to connect your mind with your brain, thereby uniting them in the sole purpose of focusing only on writing, committing both to whatever mental concentration or power it takes to get into the flow and get words "on paper." It's as easy as speaking aloud one sentence: "I am entering my writing space with the intention of focusing solely on the writing work planned for today—everything else will wait until I [write one thousand words, write two scenes, finish the chapter I was working on yesterday]." Your mind is announcing to your brain that you will now want all of its writing resources to coalesce. It also helps to set a specific time allotment and goal, such as writing two scenes in the three-hour morning writing session.

MEDITATE TO RELAX YOUR WRITING BRAIN

Meditation is a fantastic stress reliever for your brain. When you enter a meditative state:

- The frontal lobe/cortex, the most highly evolved part of the brain (reasoning, planning, emotions, and self-conscious awareness), powers down.
- The parietal lobe, the part of the brain that processes sensory information about the surrounding world (orienting you in time and space), gets a breather.
- The thalamus, gatekeeper for the senses (it's responsible for focusing your attention by funneling some sensory data deeper into the brain and blocking other signals from coming in), cycles down, reduces incoming information to a trickle.
- The reticular formation, the part of the brain called the sentry (it receives incoming stimuli and alerts the brain to get prepared to respond to whatever "new" stimuli excites it), dials down the arousal signal.

Over time, meditation becomes a calming signal for the brain, helping with overall stress reduction, relaxation, and renewal.

USE MEDITATION TO FIRE UP
YOUR NEURONAL NETWORK

Meditation serves as a gateway between the everyday lives we lead and our innermost selves, that which makes us unique and feels most authentic to who we are—in life, and in art. The more access we have to the innermost, sacred parts of our self, the more we are able to express what matters most to us in our work. Meditation can bring clarity, commitment, and calm. Any type of meditation has discernable, positive effects for your brain, but mindfulness meditation has been shown to be particularly effective.

Basically all you need to meditate is a quiet place to sit for ten to twenty minutes. Start with ten and work your way up to twenty minutes; the more you meditate the more you're likely to find those twenty minutes crucial to your sanity—and your writing focus.

Here's how you do it:

- Sit in a comfortable position. If you cross your legs to sit on the floor, perhaps place a pillow under your spine, or sit on a chair with your feet flat on the floor. As you settle in, imagine that a string is gently lifting each vertebra of your spine until your back is straight and your shoulders squared (yet relaxed). The idea is to more fully inhabit your body, to feel your mind, body, brain, and spirit as one.
- Close your eyes and purposefully slow your breathing, noticing your breaths as you gently and slowly draw air deep into your lungs (and down into your belly) and then slowly expel the air. If you prefer, you can also keep your eyes open and use an object as a "soft" focal point.
- When your thoughts wander, bring them back to your breathing. If you like, you can use a ticking sound or soft music in the background to increase relaxation and improve focus—to keep your mind focused only on being fully present in your body.
- If you like, you can softly chant or draw out the sound of "om," noticing how the sound begins to resonate more deeply as your

breathing slows. Some people like to use guided meditation, and you can find a wealth of options online.

- As thoughts arise, gently dismiss them. Some imagine placing their thoughts in imaginary balloons and releasing them. Whatever works, use it to bring your "focus" back to your breath, to the focal point, to the sound of "om," or to the guided meditation. Thoughts will arise, particularly as you remain quietly seated, but the more you practice meditation, the better you'll get at dismissing them.

- Continue meditating until your mind has quieted, your breathing is slow, regular, nourishing, and you feel relaxed. Your mind and brain should feel rejuvenated and free of clamoring thoughts and distractions. When ready, slowly bring your consciousness back to the room. Some like to breathe in deeply and blow it out in a cleansing manner, shake their fingers and hands, open their eyes, or place their hands together in a prayerful way.

While it may feel like you haven't accomplished much, meditating actually provides amazing benefits for your brain. You are training your brain to detach from distracting thoughts and emotions, to let them come and go without latching onto them. This training will help you transition from the demands of your daily life to achieving the mindset to write. The following goes into specific brain benefits, which may help encourage you to embrace daily meditation.

Meditation Bolsters Insights, Ideas, and Connections

Meditation has been widely shown to increase our abilities to be more perceptive and insightful, which is crucial for writing. The more you practice meditation, the stronger those sensory muscles will become. Also, practicing meditation quiets the brain chatter that makes it hard to concentrate and fosters the brain circuits that use a steady *gaze* to look within. Studies have shown that meditation reduces anxiety by calming the amygdala, which is where our brains process fear. During meditation, our brain shifts from the stress-prone right frontal cortex to the calmer left frontal cortex, which facilities greater insights, ideas, and connections.

Meditation Quiets Distracting Thoughts

Meditation is a testament to focus; it's training your mind to quiet itself, ignore distracting thoughts, and focus all attention on the "here and now," what's happening in the present, and how your mind and body are responding to it. Practiced meditators are able to experience the joy of writing in the moment, without attaching expectations or worrying thoughts to the process of writing. They generally experience more moments of flow, that precious time when all sense of time fades and one gets lost in the art of writing. Now that's something well worth pursuing.

Meditation Helps You Bridge the Gap

Meditation bridges the gap between observations—what we see, hear, smell, taste, and touch—and what we can dream, imagine, or create while "in the writing zone" because it does the following:

- creates a receptive state for insights, revelations, and intuition, all of which will add depth to your writing;
- calms an agitated mind and reduces anxiety in general;
- boosts access to your innermost self—what makes you unique in the world—and helps you feel more confident writing from that place;
- helps you move smoothly between three levels of awareness: intellectual/ego, emotional/intuitive, and imaginative/inspirational;
- quiets brain chatter, soothes rattled feelings, and improves the ability to live "in the moment";
- helps you enjoy the writing process as it happens, by focusing thoughts on the present rather than dwelling on the past or worrying about the future;
- improves attention and concentration (The more you meditate, the better you'll become at focusing and concentrating.);

- induces the desirable state of flow, when ideas and words seem to magically appear.

In addition to helping you transition from paying attention to something (or everything) else to paying attention to writing, meditation has amazing long-term benefits for your brain.

MAXIMIZE RESOURCES

Noted researcher and meditation teacher Jon Kabat-Zinn, Ph.D., founded the Mindfulness-Based Stress Reduction (MBSR) meditation program at University of Massachusetts. You can purchase CDs here: www.mindfulnesscds.com; and find out about classes or view webinars here: www. umassmed.edu/cfm/resources/webinars/.

Mindful Awareness Research Center (MARC) at UCLA offers a selection of audio files you can listen to or download at marc.ucla.edu.

Audio CDs and digital downloads on everything from qigong to Taoist to Kabbalah meditations; Tibetan, Buddhist, Vipassana, and Zen practices; and guided meditations from teachers such as Pema Chödrön, Jack Kornfield, Thich Nhat Hanh, Jon Kabat-Zinn, and many others can be found at soundstrue.com.

MEDITATION'S LONG-TERM BENEFITS

Meditation has been shown to provide many health benefits for mind, body, brain, and spirit. Researchers using functional magnetic resonance (fMRI) imaging scans on both experienced and novice meditators found that those who regularly practiced meditation had less anxiety in the "default mode" network of the brain (consisting of the medial prefrontal and posterior cingulated cortex), which has been linked to distraction, anxiety, attention deficit, and hyperactivity. It's also been associated with the buildup of amyloid plagues in the brain that may lead to the development Alzheimer's disease. They found that those who meditated on a regular basis gained the following specific benefits:

- There was a decrease in activity in this default mode network—no matter which type of meditation was being practiced.
- When the default mode activated, brain regions associated with self-monitoring and cognitive control were *concurrently activated* in experienced meditators, helping them suppress "me" thoughts and keep their minds more focused.
- Their brains remained more alert and may develop a "new default mode" in which they maintain more present-centered awareness and less self-centered focus (fewer disruptive thoughts and distractions).

What this implies, of course, is that meditation helps you train your brain to "default" in a way that is more calm, aware, open, and capable of focus. This training could be particularly useful if you're the type of person whose brain defaults to anxiety or scattered thoughts that create an inability to focus on the work at hand. Over time, regularly practicing meditation has been shown to provide the following benefits:

- increase the volume of gray matter in the insula (an emotional center), hippocampus (your memory center), and prefrontal cortex (executive functioning), all of which benefit writing (Increases in grey matter mean increases in the amount of connections each cell is receiving, so you have thus increased your area for creating yet more writing frameworks.);
- boost attention, compassion, and empathy; reduce anxiety, phobias, and insomnia;
- increase the power and reach of fast gamma-range brainwaves, supercharging large numbers of neurons to fire rhythmically;
- reduce cortical thinning due to aging; decrease the amount of stress-related cortisol, which is also aging.

And it doesn't matter what type of meditation you pursue—they're all good for your brain.

TRY SILENT MEDITATION

One radical form of meditation is to spend your day in complete silence. Some people spend a week, or more, at silent retreats where not one word is spoken, even when others are sitting across a table, sharing a meal. Because we're so used to talking and because talking requires your brain to focus on what's required for speech, silence tends to quiet activity in those brain areas and heightens awareness in other areas, such as sights, sounds, sensations, thoughts, intentions, and emotions. If you live and work alone most of the time, you'll have an easier time with silent meditation. If not, at least try to work in complete silence to see if it sharpens your senses.

MAKE WRITING A MEDITATION

The word *meditation* is derived from the Latin verb *meditari*, which means "to think, contemplate, devise, or ponder," which is exactly what one does when writing—or preparing to write. In fact, writing itself can become your mediation, particularly if you sit quietly, slow your breathing, chase away distracting thoughts, and give yourself a prompt, which could be any of the following:

- *When it comes to writing, I feel ...*
- *What matters most to me today is ...*
- *My character's next move will be to ...*

Then, using a prompt, "freewrite" (allow ideas to flow without censure) for at least ten uninterrupted minutes. This will allow surprisingly focused thoughts on your prompt to flow from your mind onto the page. If you find this helpful, buy yourself a notebook and a pen you really like to use as your "meditative writing tools." It is good to handwrite writing meditations, as it helps synchronize body, mind, and brain.

Explore Your Writing Process

You could also set up a series of writing meditations for yourself, such as choosing a topic that will explore your progression, in regards to writing in general, and your current work in progress. Try the following ideas for prompts:

- why I have always loved writing;
- what I love most about novels/screenplays/plays/poems/songs;
- qualities I share with my favorite novelist/screenwriter/playwright/songwriter;
- what I most want to express in this novel/screenplay/play/memoir/poem;
- why I love my protagonist and my readers will, too;
- what my protagonist most needs to learn;
- what my antagonist's most hateful qualities are and why he is also sympathetic;
- why my writing is going well;
- why my writing is falling short of my expectations.

Those ten minutes spent freewriting on meaningful topics could be the place where you clarify thoughts, achieve original thoughts, smooth over frustrations, discover solutions, inspire yourself to new heights, affirm the value of your work, calm and reassure the skeptic inside, and so on. Writing meditations can be whatever you want them to be, but ideally this kind of "soft focusing" on your work as a writer would become a source of renewal and regeneration, which, if reinforced on a regular basis, would bolster self-confidence and make writing more pleasurable and fulfilling.

Make Writing Meditation a Practice

The most important thing you need to know about meditation is that practicing it regularly will provide amazing benefits. Obviously short-term benefits include quieting the mind, focusing on the present, and sharpening focus; long-term benefits would be the ability to more easily transition from a distracted state to a creative space in which ideas flow. Meditating on a regular basis is like building muscle strength: The more you train your brain to meditate on your writing process, the better you will be able to use writing meditation as a way to transition into each writing session—focused like a laser.

EMPLOY MINDFULNESS TO IMPROVE YOUR FOCUS

A recent Harvard study found that our minds wander almost half of our waking hours, and this wandering is usually due to self-referential worrying: *Which bills can I afford to pay this week? When can I finally afford the new computer I need? Will I finish the book on time? Will my editor ask me for a full revision?*

When your mind wanders, your brain actually transitions into your default mode network, which does not occur when the brain is focused on specific tasks. Researchers at Yale University found that mindfulness meditation is effective in limiting activity in the default mode network, and in the medial prefrontal cortex, which governs those inward, self-referential "me" thoughts.

How to Mindfully Meditate

Mindfulness-based meditation is basically choosing to sit quietly for a period of ten to thirty minutes, fostering a nonjudgmental, present-moment awareness; it is accomplished by using objects (or mantras or thoughts) to keep one's attention on the present, on the here and now, while dismissing other, distracting thoughts. When your mind wanders, you intentionally bring it back to what's happening in terms of your breathing, or emotions, or thoughts of the present as you sit in meditation. Instead of thinking about six ways you could put your hero in peril, you sit quietly and focus on the way your breath elevates your chest or how soothing it feels as you breathe out, or even how your thoughts are constantly vying for your attention. Mindfulness-based meditation works by dismissing all incoming thoughts and bringing your mind back to the process of being in the here and now, as opposed to letting your mind and thoughts rehash the past, or worry about the future.

Mindfulness-based meditation, in particular, seems to quiet the mind by training it to acknowledge thoughts (sans judgment) and then relinquish negative, inward thoughts (rather than obsessing about unhappy or stress-inducing thoughts).

How It Helps You Write

Mindfulness-based meditation as a practice has been scientifically proven to:

- Improve function in the anterior cingulate cortex (ACC), which translates into improved self-regulation, or the ability to purposefully direct attention, suppress knee-jerk responses, and seamlessly switch strategies. This will help you resist distractions when writing, learn from past mistakes, and make better decisions.
- Improve function in the hippocampus, which translates into stress reduction, emotional balance, improved outlooks, and memory. This helps you be in more control as you write, have a more balanced perception, and remember and replicate what has worked best in the past.

Neuroscientists have also shown that practicing mindfulness-based meditation affects brain areas related to perception, body awareness, pain tolerance, emotion regulation, introspection, complex thinking, and sense of self. It also improves your brain's ability to screen out distractions and thereby increase productivity and bolster the ability to rapidly remember and incorporate new facts, dramatically improving the ability to mine your memory. Some studies have reflected a growth in gray matter, which bolsters your ability to become a more creative, productive and successful writer.

Mindfulness Becomes Automatic

Other studies found that those who regularly meditated developed the capability to concurrently activate areas important to self-monitoring (to reduce mind wandering that leads to worry about "me" problems) and cognitive control (to direct the brain's attention back to what's happening in the present moment). What's even better is that they seemed to do it without consciously meditating or even thinking about it.

Researchers who studied the brain activity of meditating monks and praying nuns found that they were significantly more adept at activating concentration and attention, while simultaneously deactivating brain areas focused on the self as a distinct entity in an external world. In other words, their thoughts focused less on "me, me, me" and more on the connection between themselves and the world.

The Many Benefits of Mindfulness

Nothing heightens your senses and sharpens your focus more than mindfulness! It helps you remain calm, shed bad habits, improve sleep habits, and feel more in charge of your perceptions, feelings, actions, and so on. Plus mindfulness increases social awareness, attention, appreciation, and affection, which helps you feel more connected with the world. The more connected you feel to the world, the happier and more mentally healthy you will be. Also, mindfulness helps you transition from primarily reactive to more creative. Writing gifts that mindfulness provides are insight, intuition, choice, and creativity.

USE MUSIC TO FIRE UP YOUR WRITING BRAIN

The brain depends on neurons, and whenever we process new stimuli—via our senses—those neurons communicate by firing off electrical impulses known as brainwaves. Processing music and speech is similar because they share three common denominators—pitch, timing, and timbre—and the brain uses the same circuitry to make sense of them all.

Without question, music has an amazing effect on your mood. If you associate it with certain times in your life and emotions that were simultaneously occurring, it stimulates memory in your hippocampus, which can play an important role when it comes to writing about experiences similar to what you've lived.

Because everyone on the planet loves and is often moved by music, the effects music has on the brain has been widely studied, and some of the results illustrate specific ways music can bolster your writing skills.

1. **MUSIC BOLSTERS YOUR VERBAL IQ:** A study of eight- to eleven-year-olds found that those who had extracurricular music classes developed higher verbal IQs and increased visual abilities, in comparison to those with no musical training.

2. **MUSIC FOSTERS AN OPENNESS TO EXPERIENCE:** People who score highly in one of the five personality dimensions called "openness to experience" are likely to feel stronger emotions while listening to music. In one study, people high in openness to experience were more likely to play a musical instrument and more likely to rate music as important to them.

3. **MUSIC AMPS UP HAPPINESS:** Researchers found that participants who listened to upbeat classical compositions by Aaron Copland, while *actively* making an effort to lift their spirits, felt their moods lift more than those who passively listened to the music.

4. **MUSIC HAS HEALTH BENEFITS:** A review of twenty-three studies involving approximately 1,500 patients found that listening to music reduced heart rate, blood pressure, and anxiety in heart disease patients—and what's good for your heart is good for your brain.

5. **MUSIC MAY HELP RESTORE VISION:** Studies have found that when stroke patients whose vision became impaired listen to their favorite music, the "visual neglect" that occurred post-stroke seems to improve.

All in all, few activities you could do would beat out the positive effects of music. If you play a musical instrument, obviously, that's a fabulous workout for your brain; but listening to music can perk up your brain in fantastic ways as well.

USE MUSIC TO REINFORCE MOTIVATION

I have a friend, also a writer, who creates playlists for whatever mood or need she wants to assuage or fire up. If she needs motivation to write, she'll download thirty to fifty songs that fire up her writing energy and inspire her to tell the story she wishes to tell; and if she wants to reward herself for accomplishing goals, she'll download an equal number of songs that she associates with love and happiness.

There's a method to her madness. For instance, if you want to write about a sad time in your life, creating a playlist of songs that were popular during that time, and specifically songs that magnified your sadness when it occurred, stimulates emotional memory in your brain, which will help you make those scenes even more dramatic. Memories will come flooding back, replete with the emotional context, as if it were happening all over again. While you don't want to drown yourself in the same misery, you can mine those emotions.

When you need to feel sad, pick five to ten songs that were popular at the time that focused on sadness, heartbreak, disappointment, grief, and so on; and then pick five to ten epic songs that evoke that same emotion in you. We each have songs that have significant meaning, whether it was songs our mothers loved, songs that were "our song," songs popular when our love was still new, songs that pierced our hearts when that same love came to an abrupt end and we felt lost, confused, hurt, angry, abandoned, and a hundred other emotions. Mine the emotional context of music and use it to add depth to your writing.

MINE THE COMPLEXITY IN MUSIC

Because music is such a personal medium, some musical performances have a multilayered complexity that I call "cross-fire," because the singer's personality and/or the singer's interpretation stir deeper, more complex emotions—firing on more than one piston, if you will.

Which songs become cross-fire songs is completely subjective, but, for me, two examples are Bette Davis singing "I Wish You Love" and Leonard Cohen singing "Hallelujah," of which I own at least three versions. In the case of Bette Davis, her entire persona as a spitfire, a brilliant and unforgettable actress, and someone who appeared to have missed out on a happy love life make her rendition of "I Wish You Love" haunting and sad. It's global in the sense that the mournful wail in the lyrics and her delivery reflect the broken hearts of all those who never found love—trust me, it's *fabulously* sad.

Leonard Cohen's "Hallelujah" is such a reverent, prayerful, and sagacious song that many other artists have recorded it, but it's Cohen's song and the way he sings it—with that time-worn voice resonating deeply in his chest—that makes it like no other. When you particularly love a song, you may or may not consciously know why it moves you so. All you need to know is that, if it evokes a memory, listening to it opens your heart and allows feelings to rush in. There are multiple versions of "Over the Rainbow," but Judy Garland's version seems bittersweet, while Doris Day's version sounds cheerful, so much so one wonders if Doris was capable of being anything but cheerful.

While you don't want to wallow in sadness, music has the ability to stimulate your brain, evoking personal memories, improving moods, deepening thought, soothing feelings, and also serving as a gateway to more philosophical thinking. Listening to—or preferably creating—music helps you feel the despair, the hope, the passion that thousands of human souls feel when buffeted by tragedy, or uplifted by joy, as they progress in their journey through life. Can you see how this can be incredibly helpful to writing?

TRY SYMPHONIC WRITING

Learning to synthesize all the components that go into writing a work—whether it's a short story, an essay, a feature story, a novel, or a script—may feel overwhelming. Let's break it down by including some, but not all, of the steps involved:

- developing an original idea or a unique point of view
- gathering and organizing thoughts to support and refine the idea
- envisioning multiple ways to develop the idea and then narrowing the choices
- researching historical facts, background material, and related topics
- choosing which thoughts or findings or ideas are worth incorporating
- identifying how each element will propel the story forward
- deciding where and how to begin
- getting those first words written

The act of bringing all those elements together comes easier for some, but it is possible to train your brain to perform all of the required skills far more efficiently and creatively. One great way to do that is to break down the various storytelling components into manageable tasks, and then envision all the elements flowing together, as if you were the composer of a symphony, conducting a symphonic performance of your work. Listening to symphonic music may mirror your brain's efforts to bring all the various aspects together, in a cohesive way, building slowly and surely to a symphonic crescendo.

Try Listening to a Symphonic Performance

To further bolster your brain's affinity to symphonic music, try listening to a symphonic performance while brainstorming and while writing, keeping the volume low. Whether you stop consciously listening or not, your brain will continue listening and may begin to synch itself to the swelling music. If it seems too distracting to listen while writing, try listening before writing, as a way to warm up and synch your brain to the task ahead. Experiment and you may just find that symphonic music speaks your brain's language. Some more recent and some very classic symphonies to sample follow (note that you can easily find these online for free listening):

- Stephen Sondheim's *Sweeney Todd*
- Aaron Copland's *Symphony No. 3*
- Rachmaninov's *Symphony No. 2*
- Igor Stravinsky's *The Rite of Spring*

- Carl Orff's *Carmina Burana*
- Hector Berlioz's *Symphonie Fantastique*
- Mahler's *Symphony No. 4*
- Franz Liszt's *Faust*
- Beethoven's *Symphony No. 9*
- Mozart's *Symphony No. 35*
- Tchaikovsky's *Pathetique*

It doesn't have to be classical music; jazz may inspire improvisation or encourage your brain to find connections in the piece you're writing; rock music may fire up your emotions and boost your energy level; lullabies or prayers are soothing and some like to bolster the sacredness of writing by listening to hymns, prayers, gospel music, or other soulful music. Experiment to find what perks you up, touches something in your soul, adds to your pleasure and your productivity.

Use Music to Help You Embody Feelings

Composer Franz Liszt felt the true power of music was that it could do something much more elemental than simply represent or stand metaphorically for ideas or emotions—it could actually *embody them* as experiences. He believed that music possessed a magical power that could transcend other artistic creations by *becoming* the sublime, otherworldly, and transcendent encounters that painting or literature could only symbolize. Scientists have recently found that reading literary fiction can replicate the same experience for the reader, and perhaps, bringing some of the fervor of music into your writing will help you strike those lightning moments when your creativity infuses your work with genius.

TIME TO WRITE

Now that you've done a lot of the prep, including priming your writing pump via meditation and/or music or whatever works for you, it's time to write those opening pages. You'll likely encounter resistance, but push through it in whatever manner works for you because opening pages always change, and the writer who focuses on writing the perfect opening pages may very well become stuck before he's out of the gate. The important thing is to begin and to build momentum, giving your unconscious free rein as much as possible.

There's a time for researching, a time for dreaming, planning, and preparing, a time for writing—and a time for editing. Of those phases, writing and editing are the two best kept separate. Many a writer has been thwarted when her editor (the one in her mind) chimes in at the wrong time, inducing self-doubt when unrestrained creativity is needed. Every writer I know who tries to edit while also writing, writes slower and tends to hamper rather than unleash her genius.

TIME FOR YOUR EDITOR TO DEPART

When it's time to write, first and foremost, kick your editor out of the room until you call for him (or her, however you envision the great scrutinizer who helps you craft your work). Your editor is likely to resist, insisting he plays a critical role in the process—and he does—but not now. When writing, the editor is apt to cripple writing flow by niggling over small details or worrying about something that may be insignificant rather than staying focused on what you're writing at the moment, in the moment. Using your cognitive skills to think hard before you begin writing plays a functional role, but once you're ready to write, thinking hard can interrupt flow. Now it's time to feel confident that you've programmed your supercomputer and you've done your prep work. It is time to unleash your subconscious.

I've known writers who literally don a baseball cap (backwards) when they're editing, giving their editor a costume that denotes importance and a specific role to play. Whatever mental trickery you need to resist editing while writing, do it.

At this point you're ready to begin; your brain is fired up and focused. In the next chapter, I'll discuss ways to keep your momentum going as you edge into "the middle."

TRAIN YOUR WRITING BRAIN: WARM UP YOUR BRAIN WITH KIRTAN KRIYA

The Alzheimer's Research & Prevention Foundation in Tucson, Arizona, has been studying the effects yoga meditation has on the brain and discovered (confirmed, really) that a certain form of yoga meditation, known as Kirtan Kriya, can have immediate, long-term positive benefits for the brain. Practicing this simple twelve-minute yoga meditation has been shown to:

- improve cerebral blood flow (help you think better);
- improve blood flow to the posterior cingulated gyrus (improve memory retrieval);
- increase activity in the frontal lobe (sharpen attention, concentration, and focus);
- replenish vital neurotransmitters and brain chemicals, such as acetylcholine, norepinephrine, and dopamine (which help the brain function more smoothly);
- increase energy levels, improve sleep quality, reduce stress (lower cortisol levels);
- improve both short- and long-term psychological health and spiritual well-being.

Kirtan Kriya is an ancient yoga practice that involves the combination of focused breath work, singing or chanting (and whispering), finger movements (called "mudras"), and visualization. To perform it properly, you use or activate all of your senses, awakening your brain and rejuvenating your energy.

How Does Kirtan Kriya Work?

According to yogi practitioners, Kirtan Kriya meditation stimulates all of your senses and the areas of the brain associated with them. The use of the tongue stimulates the eighty-four acupuncture meridian points on the roof of the mouth, sending a signal to the hypothalamus, pituitary gland, and other areas of the brain. The dense nerve endings in the fingertips, lips, and tongue activate the motor and sensory areas of the brain. Using the fingertips to accompany the sounds activates the occipital lobe of the brain, which improves vision (as in "having a vision") or clarity of purpose—short- and long-term. Like all meditation, this practice can have powerful and positive effects on brain function.

How to Perform Kirtan Kriya

Variations exist, but here's a simple meditation you can do at home:

1. Begin by sitting comfortably with your feet flat on the floor (you can sit in a yoga pose with your legs crossed if you like). Straighten your spine above your hips; breathe naturally, close your eyes.
2. Breathe in and out a few times, until your breath flows easily.
3. Begin by softly chanting "Saa, Taa, Naa, Maa" (together these sounds represent your highest self or true identity). You can recall the familiar children's song, "Mary Had a Little Lamb," using only the first four notes, Mar-y-had-a, to reflect the tempo.
4. Add the finger movements (known as *mudras*). With your arms resting loosely against your torso, place both hands, palm up (you can rest your hands on your lap if you like), and, one-at-a-time, press and release each fingertip, in sequence, to your thumb. On "Saa," touch the tip of your index finger to your thumb; on "Taa," the tip of your middle finger, and so on.
5. As you continue the chants, visualize energy coming down from above (from the universe, or spirit, if you like) into your head, proceeding down through your brain and then dropping and pausing at your "third eye" (considered the site of intuition, located just between your eyes) before beaming the energy out through your third eye (visualize a capital L, if that helps you keep the energy flowing down and through).
6. Imagine the sound you are generating flowing through the same path.
7. Begin by singing the sounds out loud for approximately two minutes (listening and feeling the resonance of the sound as you sing or chant); then sing softly for two minutes; "say" the sound softly to yourself for four minutes; whisper the sounds for two min-

utes; and then sing out loud again for two minutes. You can use a timer, if you like, but soon you'll be able to gauge the length that works best for you.

When you've completed the exercise, inhale deeply, drawing air into your lungs, stretch your arms and hands above your head (gently stretch your spine), and then lower them down each side, in a sweeping motion, as you exhale.

Don't be discouraged if it feels incredibly awkward at first. Over time, your coordination will dramatically improve, and you'll likely find yourself looking forward to these meditation sessions as a way to start, or refresh, your mind, body, and spirit.

Here's an audio you can download: http://yoginsight.com/?p=624.

WRITERS ON CRAFT

"I want to work in revelations, not just spin silly tales for money. I want to fish as deep down as possible into my own subconscious in the belief that once that far down, everyone will understand because they are the same that far down."

—JACK KEROUAC, IN A LETTER TO ED WHITE

"Be regular and orderly in your life, so that you may be violent and original in your work."

—GUSTAVE FLAUBERT

"I never listen to music when I'm working. I haven't that kind of attentiveness, and I wouldn't like it at all. On the other hand, I'm able to work fairly well among ordinary distractions. My house has a living room that is at the core of everything that goes on: it is a passageway to the cellar, to the kitchen, to the closet where the phone lives. There's a lot of traffic. But it's a bright, cheerful room, and I often use it as a room to write in, despite the carnival that is going on all around me."

—E.B. WHITE

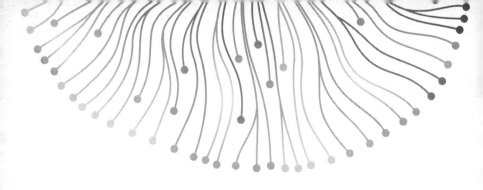

PHASE FOUR

YOUR BRAIN IN THE MIDDLE

"A writer takes earnest measures to secure his solitude and then finds endless ways to squander it. Looking out the window, reading random entries in the dictionary. To break the spell I look at a photograph of Borges, a great picture sent to me by the Irish writer Colm Tóibín. The face of Borges against a dark background—Borges fierce, blind, his nostrils gaping, his skin stretched taut, his mouth amazingly vivid; his mouth looks painted; he's like a shaman painted for visions, and the whole face has a kind of steely rapture. I've read Borges of course, although not nearly all of it, and I don't know anything about the way he worked—but the photograph shows us a writer who did not waste time at the window or anywhere else. So I've tried to make him my guide out of lethargy and drift, into the otherworld of magic, art, and divination."

—DON DELILLO

CHAPTER 8

FUEL YOUR WRITING BRAIN

Get Into a Writing Groove

When writing *Tropic of Cancer* in 1932–1933, novelist Henry Miller compiled a list of writing "Commandments." Here are six items he put on that list:

1. Don't be nervous. Work calmly, joyously, recklessly on whatever is in hand.
2. Work according to Program and not according to mood. Stop at the appointed time!
3. When you can't *create* you can *work*.
4. *Concentrate. Narrow down. Exclude.*
5. Forget books you want to write. Think only of the book you are writing.
6. Write first and always. Painting, music, friends, cinema, all these come afterwards.

So you're up and running with your novel and writing is going well—until it doesn't. Around fifty pages in (if not sooner), most writers lose that first rush of wind. I'm not saying those first fifty pages are easy to write—because they're not—but around page fifty-one, writing a novel or nonfiction book (or play or screenplay) becomes a long-distance marathon. To write novels and other long works you need the ability to push through when inspiration flags, you're doubting every writing decision you've made, the pleasure wanes, and there's nothing to do but just keep writing. Because it can be such a long haul and often leave you feeling like you lost your way, almost all writers experience *a muddle in the middle*—a severe and dangerous case of self-doubt when their vision, their premise, their characters, the plot, their ability to pull it off—*everything*—seems dubious. There's no easy solution for losing steam. You just have to doggedly push through every ounce of resistance and keep writing, using all the prep work you've done to keep pushing toward the end.

Successful, published writers have found a way—*to fuel their brain*—to keep themselves motivated, sustain focus, and persistently push through to the end. Like Henry Miller (as above), you may want to write a list of "Commandments" to keep you motivated when spirits or energy flag—because they will. In this chapter, we'll discuss ways you can keep your brain brimming with energy, inspiration, fortitude, and persistence from page fifty-one to "The End."

SELECTIVELY FOCUS YOUR ATTENTION

Selective attention has the potential to be a powerful cognitive strategy—perhaps even the most essential cognitive strategy—when it comes to achieving writing goals. When you purposefully focus your attention on a writing task, you are calling forth the full intellectual power of your frontal cortex to assist, akin to calling in the troops. Also, people who can direct their attention are better at remembering things and figuring out what new information means and how they can use it; that is, they are better at metacognition and higher-order thinking processes. The challenge: Limit sensory stimulation and emotional distractions, both of which erode focus.

The three brain components involved in selective attention when you are writing are:

1. **THE ALERTING NETWORK** receives sensory stimuli and signals the brain to pay attention to information.
2. **THE ORIENTING NETWORK** processes incoming information and focuses the brain on what needs to be done.
3. **THE EXECUTIVE NETWORK** weighs information and enables the brain to prioritize among competing brain activities. This thinking occurs in the prefrontal cortex and anterior cingulate. It's basically command central, activated when your higher thinking has to decide whether what you've been focused on should be

superseded by a new activity. It also activates when you have to pay attention to something unusual—something that isn't habitual—and decide if it's good, bad, or neutral. It is the system involved in the conscious control of attention, a cognitive function variously termed "effortful control" or "self-regulation.

The ability to regulate one's attention relies heavily on the ability to consciously inhibit what might be a habitual or more immediately rewarding response and to choose another that is more socially appropriate to the situation at hand—or, when writing, to prioritize what you'll choose to focus your brain on and set aside everything else to write one scene, and then the next, and so on.

TRY SINGLETASKING

The problem with multitasking is that you see others doing it and feel like you should be able to do it, too. And it makes you feel good, like you're getting a lot done, but, sadly, the opposite is true. Rather than increasing efficiency, multitasking "splits" your brain. You end up switching from one task to the other, shining a "spotlight" on whichever task is being directly addressed. Whether you know it or not, your brain tries shifting from one to the other task, in milliseconds, which makes it more difficult to give each task its due. Studies have shown that multitaskers are less productive and have greater difficulty filtering relevant information and switching between tasks than those who address things singly. If you're having trouble focusing, revert to absolute silence and block out time where all you do is work on your book—no e-mail, no Internet, no phone calls, nothing but writing your book.

As we discussed in Chapter 7, you can effectively narrow your focus and get down to business faster through the use of meditation, by creating a sacred space, by beginning each writing session with an intention to focus solely on writing and specific goals, and by monitoring your writing process. Now that you're in the middle and the bloom on the rose has faded, go back and try what worked in the beginning.

But most important, keep doing whatever has worked and try new things to make your writing sessions focused and productive. Remember that pleasure is an important component. Reward yourself after writing sessions—take a walk, take a bath, have a glass of your favorite whiskey, phone a friend, etc. Rewarding success breeds success—particularly for your brain.

LIMIT DAILY DECISIONS

Facebook mogul Mark Zuckerberg wears a gray T-shirt to work every day. He buys multiples of the same shirts because he wants to minimize decisions. "There's a bunch of psychological theory that even making small decisions about what you wear, what you eat for breakfast, etc., can make you tired," he explained. "I feel like I'm not doing my job if I spend any of my energy on things that are silly or frivolous about my life, so [I wear the same T-shirt so] I can dedicate all of my energy to [creating and developing] the best products and services to help us reach our goal of connecting everyone in the world." Maybe there'll be a stretch of time while you're writing when you want to try limiting decisions so you can focus on *your* higher purpose.

GET INTO THE HABIT OF WRITING

Because writing a novel (or other work of art) takes time—even in the best of circumstances, it's likely to span a period of months or years—writers have to learn patience and perseverance. When it comes to your writing brain, you want to create a *habit of mind* that facilitates the ability to delay gratification and sustain effort, over a period of time, working toward goals that aren't immediate. This ability begins with critical executive functions taking place in your prefrontal cortexes, in establishing a way of thinking that recognizes the complexities of the writing profession and gears up to generate and sustain sufficient focus, dedication, energy, and confidence to create a work of art, promote it, stay strong in the face of rejection, and believe in what you are doing.

Habit of mind requires the engagement of your executive neural network, specifically as it relates to:

- **JUDGMENT:** Determining that writing a novel will require a long period of time, during which you will have to make judgments about how to best spend your time—when to start, how long to work, what to focus on each day—and about how the work itself is progressing—what's working or not working in terms of story development, characterization, setting, theme, scenes, dialogue, and so on. Using judgment to narrow your choices helps your brain shine a concentrated light on what you've decided needs to get done—and how it needs to get done.

- **ABILITY TO PRIORITIZE:** Anyone who seriously hopes to write a novel has to be willing and able to make writing it a priority. Life places a multitude of small daily demands on us all. Writers have to consistently choose writing. In the same way your neural network has to weigh the importance of choosing one activity over another, your mind will have to repeatedly and consistently place meeting your writing goals above everything else that's clamoring for your attention.

- **ABILITY TO SUSTAIN EFFORT:** Some writers can lock themselves away and complete a first draft in twelve days (some boast far fewer days), but the vast majority of writers don't have the fortitude or the opportunity that requires. Most writers also live complicated lives, with a lot of responsibilities, from marriages to children to everyday jobs. To write a novel, you need to plan for—and commit to—a sustained effort that will take place over months, if not years. Rewards will have to come from smaller goals you set and meet, even if your goal is to write only five pages a week.

What you want is to create a *practice* of writing—similar to a religious practice or a yoga practice—something you choose to do daily, if at all possible. Writing is something you must choose to dedicate your mind, body, brain, and spirit to doing with reverence and devotion. When it comes to your brain, commit to focusing all of your mental facilities to the task, recognizing and rewarding yourself for progress toward the long-term goal of completion. Do your best to honor your commitment to the practice and find ways to link pleasure to fulfillment of daily goals. This way you are embedding and reinforcing the discipline, commitment, focus, and persistence needed to push through the middle to the end of your writing project. When you and your writing practice become *as one*, anything is possible.

ANTICIPATE THE PLEASURE OF WRITING

It doesn't take a neuroscientist to explain that doing what brings us pleasure creates the desire to replicate the experience. Your human brain is hardwired for reward and pleasure, so linking pleasure to writing is far more likely to motivate you than linking displeasure to the experience. Scientists have discovered that *anticipating* pleasure is even more rewarding, as anticipation alone stimulates the release of the neurotransmitter dopamine, which increases pleasure and reduces stress. So, a few hours before you sit down to write, pause to anticipate the pleasure that will come when you're in the zone and words are flowing—or how you'll feel when the session has gone well.

WORK UP THE GRIT TO ACHIEVE MASTERY

MacArthur Foundation "genius" award winner and research psychologist Angela Lee Duckworth believes that self-control and *grit* matter more than talent and IQ when it comes to successfully meeting goals. Self-control obviously has to do with the ability to focus, to prioritize, and to literally show up for work each day. Grit, however, goes beyond self-control into obsessively, doggedly, and persistently devoting yourself to a meaningful goal over a period of time in order to achieve some level of mastery of a task many would find daunting—such as writing a book, a play, a screenplay, and so on.

In describing what equals grit in dance, Martha Graham once said what it takes for a mature dancer to make it look easy is "fatigue so great that the body cries, even in its sleep ... and [suffers] daily small deaths." In other words, mastery requires hard work and grueling practice, practice, practice. Grit is what motivates someone to commit to and stick with an unending round of practice, particularly when failure seems imminent. Keep in mind that feeling confused and frustrated is a sign that you're on the brink of a breakthrough. If you just keep plugging away and keep straining your writing brain to solve the problem, you will likely create your best work possible.

Grit is separate from self-control, the short-term ability to resist temptations that could interrupt your work; grit is the self-determination that takes you the distance. Studies have consistently shown that being smart, talented, and curious doesn't guarantee that you'll reach your full potential. What's needed is the grit that indicates you'll work harder and resist setbacks, pushing ever forward until you've done your best work.

WALK A MILE A DAY

One of the largest studies ever conducted monitored health and lifestyle habits of 121,000 nurses. Data collected on 18,766 of the nurses (who were then ages 70 to 81) revealed that the group who maintained a median level of walking for six hours a week were 20 percent less likely to show cognitive impairment than those who exercised the least. Another long-term study of elderly volunteers, published in the journal *Neurology*, found that those who walked the most cut their risk of developing memory problems *in half*. The optimal exercise for cognitive health benefits, the researchers concluded, was to walk six to nine miles each week.

CREATE THE MINDSET TO WRITE

Education researcher and author of *Mindset: The New Psychology of Success*, Carol Dweck, attributes success to something she calls a "growth mindset." A growth mindset equates to believing your brain capabilities are malleable, as opposed to being fixed at birth (which, of course, neuroscience has proven to be true). Dweck teaches young children to think of their brains as something that grows and changes, and she provides pictures of neurons making connections so the kids can literally "see" a brain in action. She also shows them videos of older children talking about how their capabilities grew and has the older children write to the younger children about specific ways their brainpower has grown.

FIRE UP YOUR CURIOSITY

Researchers have found that once a subject's curiosity had been piqued by the "right" question, they were better at learning and remembering completely unrelated information. Curiosity creates a sort of brain vortex that sucks in whatever you feel most motivated to learn, along with ideas that may be floating around your environment. The spark of curiosity lights up the hippocampus (where the creation of memories occurs), and the reward and pleasure brain circuits, which release dopamine. So if you want an alert brain, start your day by immersing yourself in something you find fascinating and mysterious. Pique your curiosity enjoy the natural high, and learn something new.

Commit to the Mindset

Dweck's goal is to teach children to accept personal responsibility for the level of self-determination that will drive them to work hard and do whatever it takes to overcome all obstacles to success. She encourages her own children to choose one hard thing they want to do—that requires a level of mastery—and then asks them to commit to deliberate, focused practice in pursuit of their goals, expecting nothing less than vigor and determination. She forewarns them that feeling frustrated and discouraged—experiencing all those small daily deaths Martha Graham described—while working toward a goal that is truly hard to achieve is normal. Rather than quitting when things get hard, she urges them to engage in more deliberate practice.

Recommit to Your Mindset

Writing a book (novel or nonfiction), writing a play, a screenplay, or a TV script is the kind of goal that requires a well-thought-out and long-term commitment. Months will be spent researching, outlining, preparing, writing, and rewriting. A writer should "go in" knowing that it's going to get hard—very, very hard—requiring far more energy, brainpower, dedication, and flexibility than ever imagined. Everyone experiences some false starts, many rewrites, and times when frustration spikes and quitting seems like the only sane and viable option. Writing is not for sissies, so when it bogs down, think back to how far you've come, reward yourself for how much you've accomplished, and then consciously recommit to doing whatever it takes to get back on course—even if it's working twice as hard.

CHALLENGE YOURSELF

The posterior cingulate cortex (PCC) lies along a midline between the ears, near structures related to rewards, and is considered a kind of a nexus for multiple systems connected to both learning and reward systems, called the "default mode network" (activated when the mind slacks off or wanders). When this area begins to deteriorate, early signs of cognitive decline occur. In a study reported in the journal *Neuron*, monkeys used their eyes to repeatedly spot the target (among distractors) that resulted in a reward. Researchers expected the PCC to activate *before* a choice was made or the reward was received, but found it activated *after* the feedback—particularly when the monkeys got it wrong—in other words, neurons in the PCC responded strongly when the monkeys needed to learn something new. Researchers concluded that rather than the PCC being the cause of poor performance, it summoned more resources for a challenging cognitive task. It is important to note that this experiment worked only when the reward was adequate to motivate the effort. Moral: *Do things related to writing that challenge you to learn something new and then reward yourself well.*

ENVISION YOURSELF A WRITING SUPERHERO

Which comes first: Being powerful or thinking you're powerful? According to some scientists, thinking you're powerful comes first. Studies have shown that feeling powerful changes the way people think in specific ways:

- They are better at focusing on relevant information.
- They are better at integrating disparate pieces of knowledge.
- They are better at identifying hidden patterns.

Basically, when people think they're powerful, their brains reflect superior "executive functioning," which also means they are good at concentrating, warding off negative thoughts, and adapting to change. This type of mental flexibility is what makes power players feel like they *are* powerful. They're not weighed down by self-doubt and negative self-talk.

Adam Galinsky, a professor at Columbia Business School, reported in the journal *Psychological Science* that "a sense of power has dramatic effects on thought and behavior." He found that being in— or experiencing—a high-powered role transforms one psychologically. Here's how:

- The social roles people in power "play" change their perceptions of themselves. Studies show that people assigned to a managerial role (whether they are truly managers or not) immediately act more decisively, take risks, show more persistence and follow through, and think more abstractly and optimistically. These are all cognitive functions that play a vital role in creative writing.
- Those who experience feeling powerful can re-create the feelings in different situations. Studies have shown that merely remem-

bering a time when you felt powerful in a situation can regenerate those feelings and help you feel powerful in all situations—even during intimidating situations, like script meetings or when negotiating with your editor.

- They can feel powerful by taking a powerful stance. That's right, stand up, plant your feet onto the floor, and whip those hands onto you're hips, *à la* Superman. Studies found that standing or sitting in an expansive or powerful way, helps people to concentrate, to be bolder in their choices, and to have increased abilities to identify patterns, that is, to be mentally sharper.

Time to don that "secret" superhero costume squished into a box in your closet. Time to take on the mantle of being a *Super Star Writer*. If you have an imagination—and you so do—approach this exercise with an open-minded enthusiasm. You may be surprised how, well, strong, clear, and confident you feel when you sit down to write.

WHEN WRITING, PRACTICE ACTIVE SITTING

I'm not the first to phrase this, but I love its motivating simplicity: *Sitting is the new smoking*, linked to increased risk of diabetes, cardiovascular disease, and early death. Slouching while sitting causes physiological changes, weakening tissues and leading to degeneration, but even if you maintain good posture, simply sitting for long periods of time—over time—leads to muscle and tissue degeneration, similar to what happens when one of your bones is set in a cast.

The bad news is that simply hopping up regularly won't do the trick alone. What's needed is something called "active sitting." Here are four ways you can actively sit while actively writing (do each three to four times—or more—during your normal working day):

1. **ROLL YOUR FEET.** Get a small massage ball (or anything similar), take your shoes off, and roll your feet slowly over the ball (one at a time or together, if space permits), repeatedly massaging the arch, loosening the ankle and calf muscles, and, more important for your brain, increasing circulation.

2. **PAUSE TO DO A FEW WALL SQUATS.** Plant your shoulder blades and hips against a wall, plant your feet 6 to 8 inches from the wall, and, with your legs about the same width apart as your hips, slowly lower your body down and then push it back up. Do this at least three times.

3. **DO A FEW LUNGES.** Step one leg forward, and lower your other leg, again about a 90-degree angle, and hold briefly; repeat three times for each leg. This helps stretch your hip flexors and quads, which become tense when you sit too much on a regular basis.

4. **STRAIGHTEN UP AND ROTATE YOUR SHOULDERS.** Working, particularly on a laptop, can lead to rounding shoulders and jutting necks out and forward. Take a few minutes to sit straight over your tailbone, drop your arms to your sides, take a deep breath in, turn your palms outward, and rotate your shoulders back. While holding this pose, widen your hips by rotating your feet out. Hold for ten seconds and repeat ten times.

What's good for your heart and your body is good for your brain—and exercise may be the most crucial necessity in maintaining brain health, and, unfortunately, as writers, we have to sit more than we like, far more than is good for us. Practice active sitting when working, and remember to reward your hardworking brain with at least a half hour of vigorous exercise a day—whether it's walking, washing your car, or scrubbing your bathroom: *Move it or lose it!*

FOSTER THE FLOW THAT COMES WHEN WRITING GOES WELL

Hopefully all writers experience "the flow" (also known as "the zone"), typically a brief period of time when every aspect of writing progresses easily, the ideas, the words, all the elements required, and even the typing simply floats along, sometimes at a brisk pace, other times at a little slower, but no less productive, pace. It's a blissful state, one in which time and space appear seamless; sometimes hours pass and thousands of words pour onto the page. When "the flow" dries up, the writer may suddenly feel fatigued and often disappointed. Where did it go? When will it come back? Before we discuss how to create this ideal writing state, let's describe how you recognize it. When you're in "the flow":

- You feel energized, alive with creativity; the closest you'll come to feeling like you were always destined to become a writing genius.
- Suddenly every impasse you've been struggling to breach breaks open.
- Ideas, scenes, and words seem to magically appear (or flow through your fingertips and onto the page, as if your writingbrain has banned your distracting ego from the room).
- Writing feels effortless, yet intensely exciting.
- Your productivity skyrockets, so fast you struggle to keep up.
- Time seems to slow, and, after a while, you lose all awareness of time passing.
- Everything you write seems brilliant (though you do not pause to reread anything).
- You feel like the muse you've long courted has alighted onto your shoulder.
- Every good idea leads effortlessly to the next good idea.
- You're barely thinking at all; your writing instincts are at their highest.

Oh, the ecstasy of it all! One could describe this kind of flow as orgasmic or rhapsodic ... and for some it lasts relatively as long. For many, pursuing flow becomes their primary goal, with some even feeling that they're not *really* a writer if they can't "get into the flow" or that they can write only when they are in the flow (hence a lot of excuses for why they aren't making progress on their project).

But *flow* is not some esoteric, impossible-to-catch specter that comes and goes without reason. In fact, well-known psychologist Mihaly Csikszentmihalyi wrote, in his seminal works on creativity and flow, that it basically comes down to three things: enhancing focus, increasing concentration, and minimizing distraction. He also writes that flow tends to come when we're feeling particularly challenged by our work. Hardly orgasmic, but then again, what's good for your brain is good for your flow.

FOCUS YOUR NEURONS

When global ignition occurs, the brain is not globally excited—a very precise set of neurons is excited, which defines how an individual experiences consciousness. The neurons can be incredibly precise. Researchers have found that many people have a set of neurons that only respond to Bill Clinton's face, and merely suggesting that these people imagine Bill Clinton's face is enough to activate those *particular* neurons. The majority of anterior temporal neurons exhibit that same selectivity for actual and imagined images—and memory recall can also activate them. That being said, conscious information is distributed within a myriad of neuronal cells (millions upon millions of neuronal cells). So what to do? When working on your book, do some stimulation prepping to focus your neurons and literally rile them up. Once global ignition occurs—whether it's focused on characterization, plots, setting, and so on—firing up the particular neurons connected to the task can fuel your imagination.

AVOID THE OPPOSITE OF FLOW

The opposite of flow—*blocked*—is also familiar to every writer I've ever met or listened to or read about; even the most prolific writers occasionally bog down. Before we discuss why using "writer's block" as an excuse is totally bogus, let's describe how it feels when you're blocked:

- Every inch forward drags you backwards; it's like swimming upstream in a river of molasses—or worse.
- You have to force yourself to your writing desk and bully yourself into writing.
- Writing becomes literally painful: headaches, bellyaches, backaches, and even toothaches become a recurring problem.
- You don't want to talk to anyone about your work in progress; in fact, you don't want to talk about writing period.

- You are beginning to question your entire premise and your artistic vision.
- You shun hanging out with your fellow writers, who know you're making pathetic excuses.
- You feel exhausted, discouraged, pessimistic, and caustic.
- You spew petty criticisms about people who seem able to work when you can't.
- You begin to wonder why you ever thought you were a real writer, or a writer with more than one book, play, movie, poem, or song in you.
- You lapse into depression and overindulge in alcohol, drugs, or food.

Small wonder that we all hate feeling blocked. For a writer, it's about as bad as one can feel—and it happens to the best of us, which you may find reassuring. It has been suggested that writer's block may be a form of "brain block," too. Under stress, a human brain will shift control from the cortex to the emotional limbic system—which gets caught up in habitual behaviors and is looking for a quick release from stress—which further inhibits writing, since whatever behavior it indulges in usually does not provide the sought-after "quick fix." In her 2004 book, *The Midnight Disease: The Drive to Write, Writer's Block, and the Creative Brain*, Alice W. Flaherty has argued that literary creativity blockage may be a direct function of activity "blockage" in the cerebral cortex.

Rarely, however, is feeling blocked a sign that you aren't meant to be a writer, particularly if you've written a lot up to this point in time, some of it quite good, perhaps published, or perhaps not. The trick is not to buy into the mythology of "writer's block." Here's a simple fact to remember: Writer's block is not a legitimate excuse for not writing or working on your project. You can be challenged, temporarily stalled, confused, uncertain, underprepared, out of fresh ideas, or even lazy, but you—and your ability to write—are not "blocked." You may just need to get your cerebral cortex firing again, and I've given—and will continue to give—you lots of tips on how to do that.

KEEP FAMILY PHOTOS NEARBY

A study at Massachusetts General Hospital found that mothers looking at pictures of their children (or their dogs) showed increased activity in the amygdala, medial orbitofrontal cortex, and dorsal putamen, areas that process emotions and rewards. These same areas were not activated when mothers viewed photos of children or dogs they didn't know. Conversely, the midbrain—specifically the substantia nigra and ventral tegmental area—lit up when mothers looked at their children (but not when they looked at their dogs)—bathing the brain with feel-good chemicals like dopamine, oxytocin, and vasopressin. If you're feeling stuck, try leafing through your children's baby books or family photo albums.

BRING BACK THE FLOW

Flow happens when what you are doing naturally suits your personality. If you are trying to force yourself to write fiction, for example, and you're finding that you simply don't have an affinity for it, flow is likely to remain elusive. If you're the most talented and prolific novelist on the East Coast, and you love what you do, flow may visit often. That being said, flow also comes when you've done a lot of preparation, and both programmed and fired up your brain. There's no question that your brain plays a starring role in achieving flow, and if primed and rewarded, your brain gets better and better at re-creating flow—or you could just keep waiting around for some magical muse to show up at your doorstep.

The magic, aspiring and/or stalled writers, is in your brain. In the next chapter, we're going to go into detail about how you can train your brain to achieve flow—and surrender all mythology around "writer's block."

FOCUS ON SOMETHING ELSE FOR A WHILE

Even if you have zero affinity for drawing, perhaps you love and appreciate artists who draw beautifully and the breathtaking work that is available via a quick Google search for images. Maybe you own an art book that you bought at a museum exhibit long ago. If so, there's a good chance looking at the photographs in the book will remind you how stimulating you found that exhibit at the time or how much you enjoyed talking about it with the person who accompanied you to the museum and joined for lunch afterwards. Maybe you'll also remember how thrilling it felt to see a masterwork up close—the brushstrokes, the brilliance of the color, the originality, the outspoken themes, and the richness of expression that mesmerized your senses. Maybe you'll recall a distinctly pleasant feeling you experienced while viewing it, like you'd met a kindred spirit.

TAKE A VISUAL BREAK

If you don't own any art books, go outside and stroll around your yard or neighborhood. Notice colors, shapes, trees, flowers, leaves, bees, and other creatures—all of nature's handiwork. In addition to seeing, take time to touch, smell, listen, and "drink" it all in. You'll find giving your brain a respite that doesn't involve language or "thinking" will make returning to a writing session feel invigorating. And, no, watching movies does not qualify as a visual break, as your brain will focus on the words and all the subtext it observes. Better to keep it purely visual and wordless.

WHY YOUR BRAIN RESPONDS TO ART

If you've ever been moved by a beautiful piece of art, you're actually following a natural biological inclination.

We now know that man has been making art for thousands upon thousands of years, using it to tell stories about their lives, but also, it seems, to reap the benefits of appreciating the art itself. Thomas Merton once said, "Art enables us to find ourselves and lose ourselves at the same time." And he was really on to something. According to a new field called neuroaesthetics, the human brain is drawn to and uniquely responds to viewing art. Several studies have discovered multiple ways the brain responds to art—and to *making* art.

- A University of Toronto meta-analysis, published in the journal *Brain and Cognition*, found that viewing paintings not only "switched on" the visual cortex, but also those parts of the brain linked to inner thoughts and emotions, movement regulation, and learning.
- As reported in the journal *NeuroImage*, Emory University School of Medicine researchers found that the ventral striatum and the hypothalamus, parts of the brain involved in making decisions, taking risks, and experiencing pleasure, are activated more from viewing paintings than photographs that represent similar themes.

Scientists believe that the brain is more interested—and intrigued—in *how* an image is depicted than it is in the image itself, hence the activation in cognitive functions. They also found that viewing visual art activates the brain's reward circuit, which has evolved to provide reinforcement when what you're doing creates benefits, or pleases, the brain.

Interestingly, studies have also shown that we're mostly drawn to curved lines rather than hard lines and angles; perhaps because viewing curved lines seems to calm our brains while viewing a sharply angled line is associated with rising tension.

And—to absolutely no one's surprise—creating visual art is even better for your brain than simply viewing art. A recent German study, which divided twenty-eight newly retired people into two groups, found that those who produced original art displayed significant gains in psychological resilience and "functional connectivity" in the brain than the half that only analyzed paintings. The study's researchers suggested that improvements derived from a combination of motor and cognitive processing, as well as the necessity to stay fully and creatively engaged while working on their art projects.

Also, art therapy has been proven effective in helping people with Alzheimer's disease and dementia, because making art stimulates the senses, triggers memories, and invites social connections through conversation.

Like writing, creating art engages your brain and your mind in multiple ways. The static nature of paintings, for example, like novels, invites your brain to explore its appreciation and curiosity in your own way and time, and from different angles. You can ponder not only how the artist created a unique work, but also explore the meanings and emotions viewing it generates.

BECOME AN ART ENTHUSIAST

When your creativity needs a boost, visit an art gallery and take time to pause and consider brushstrokes, color selections, form, function, aesthetics, and emotion. Give your brain time to ponder not only how, but why the artist created this particular work of art and how it makes you *feel*. Take a journal along with you to write down observations and thoughts. Observe others around you (and listen in on conversations) to see how their responses differ from your own. Later, take fifteen minutes or so to reflect on the experience, as a whole, and on how certain works of art trigger memories and other associations. This will help your brain create synapses based on personal experience and possibly lead to fresh ideas. Better yet, create a work of art yourself—just for fun!

FIND OTHER WAYS TO STIMULATE CREATIVITY

When your mind is mush or ideas are not flowing, and you suddenly despise your characters or start second-guessing yourself and doubting the importance of completing the work, the simple fact is that your brain needs a rest or inspiration. The simple act of making a cup of tea (or pouring a glass of wine), retrieving that beautifully printed art book, and spending an hour on the couch (feet up!) will not only soothe and refresh your writing brain, but will also awaken your senses. Indulge for a while, savoring each aspect of the respite, and you'll likely return to writing with a more lively sense of setting, design, or beauty—and your writing may be infused with more depth, better descriptions, and the slowness that comes with pausing to appreciate nuance, shape, color variations, and so on. In admiring the way lines flow and the subtlety of how colors blend, you've relieved your brain of the necessity to think—and it will definitely reward you.

If art or visual appreciation doesn't do it for you, then do something that stimulates your senses:

- Go to an auto or boat show to admire the latest sleek designs.
- Go to a movie or a play to soak up someone else's brilliance.
- Visit your favorite bookstore just to run your hands over the books.
- Spend a few hours playing music or listening to music that thrills your soul.
- Pull on waders or rent a rowboat and go fishing on a quiet, cold lake.
- Take a walk deep into the woods where the hushed silence and sound of crackling twigs underfoot will soothe your frazzled nerves.
- Walk along a seashore or river, searching for shells or rocks that feel good in your hands.
- Knit a scarf or bead a necklace or sand down a dresser you want to refinish or cook a gourmet meal full of delicious smells.

In other words, do something (other than write) that pleases you because it soothes your brain and stimulates your visual, auditory, taste, or tactile sensations.

The next day (or hours later, if you feel like it), go back to writing as usual, and you'll likely find that your brain is fired up and ready to focus. You may even discover some surprising connections occurred while you thought you were off having fun, not thinking at all.

TRAIN YOUR WRITING BRAIN: EXERCISE YOUR CREATIVITY

Artist Lisa Congdon has created what she calls a "Creative Unblock Project" to explore the interplay between structure and imaginative play. She has students choose one thing they love to draw or paint—and feel comfortable drawing or painting (as in, it's their thing)—and for thirty days, they are to draw or paint the object thirty different ways, a new idea each day, using different mediums, colors, styles, or whatever they can come up with to break out of their conventional style. Most important, perhaps, they are to get a little crazy and, as Ron Zak, my talented photography professor used to advise: *whack it out.*

The idea is to break out of your comfort zone or whatever creative rut you may (consciously or unconsciously) be in, to stimulate your creativity, to create new neuronal pathways that spark new ideas. So, why not apply the same idea to writing? Why not take conventional writing and find unique ways to break free of your usual style, to *whack it out*?

For ten days, write a scene (or a short, short story of 150 to 250 words) ten different ways: change the point of view, change the setting, change the main character, flip the character roles, change the characters into aliens, rely solely on dialogue, use no dialogue, write the story as a movie scene, as a poem, as science fiction, as a western, and so on—whatever your brain comes up with to *whack it out.*

Remember that having fun is fabulous for your brain, so the weirder the better.

EXTRA CREDIT:

- Write character descriptions twice: first use a focused 150 words and then use only 30 words, doing your best to compress as much of the essential information in those 30 words.
- Write a scene in three pages and then compress the same scene into one paragraph, again capturing the most essential elements of the scene by selectively choosing details, actions, dialogue, etc., to convey the same event.

MAJOR BONUS POINTS:

- Spend fifteen days coming up with alternative ways of telling the story you are currently writing. In this case, create lists of the fifteen ideas in your writing journal and spend some time each day envisioning how each would change the story.
- Sketch pictures of the pivotal moment in fifteen scenes in graphic novel style. Crudeness of sketching doesn't matter; the point is to stimulate another area of your brain, to stimulate a fresh approach to storytelling, and to see your work in progress in new and refreshing ways.

The whole point of "whacking it out" is to invite fresh ideas in. Have fun!

WRITERS ON CRAFT

"When I was in the middle of writing *Eat Pray Love* ... I fell into one of those pits of despair that we will fall into when we're working on something that's not coming and we think 'this is going to be a disaster, this is going to be the worst book I've ever written—not just that but the worst book ever written ... '"

—ELIZABETH GILBERT

"There's a marvelous sense of mastery that comes with writing a sentence that sounds exactly as you want it to. It's like trying to write a song, making tiny tweaks, reading it out loud, shifting things to make it sound a certain way. It's very physical. I get antsy. I jiggle my feet a lot, get up a lot, tap my fingers on the keyboard, check my e-mail. Sometimes it feels like digging out of a hole, but sometimes it feels like flying. When it's working and the rhythm's there, it does feel like magic to me."

—SUSAN ORLEAN

"If a writer stops observing he is finished. But he does not have to observe consciously nor think how it will be useful. Perhaps that would be true at the beginning. But later everything he sees goes into the great reserve of things he knows or has seen. If it is any use to know it, I always try to write on the principle of the iceberg. There is seven-eighths of it underwater for every part that shows. Anything you know you can eliminate and it only strengthens your iceberg. It is the part that doesn't show. If a writer omits something because he does not know it then there is a hole in the story."

—ERNEST HEMINGWAY

CHAPTER 9

REFRESH YOUR WRITING BRAIN

Overcome Writer's Block

"When you are stuck in a book; when you are well into writing it, and know what comes next, and yet cannot go on; when every morning for a week or a month you enter its room and turn your back on it; then the trouble is either of two things. Either the structure has forked, so the narrative, or the logic, has developed a hairline fracture that will shortly split it up the middle—or you are approaching a fatal mistake. What you had planned will not do. If you pursue your present course, the book will explode or collapse, and you do not know about it yet, quite."

—ANNIE DILLARD

We're going to go there, right now, even though it might lead to automatic resistance: *Writer's block is a myth.* It is not something that always existed; in fact, the concept originated in the early nineteenth century when the English poet Samuel Taylor Coleridge first described his "indefinite indescribable terror" at not being able to produce work he thought worthy of his talent. Romantic English poets of the time believed their poems magically arrived from an external source, so when their pens dried up and the words did not flow, they assumed the spirits, the gods, and/or their individual muses were not visiting them with favor. French writers soon latched onto the idea of a suffering connected to writing and expanded it to create the myth that all writers possessed a tortured soul, unable to write without anguish. Later, the anxiety (the artistic inhibition) that often accompanies writing was blamed on, or turned into, neurosis, depression, alcoholism, and drug addiction. On good days, writers suffered for their art, and never so much as when they allowed psychological issues to thwart their ability to write.

But this is a book about neuroscience and writing, so false mental constructs will be appropriately dismissed. Here's the simple truth: The very nature of the art of writing incorporates uncertainty, experimentation, and a willingness to create art from the depths of who we are. Writing is a mentally challenging occupation which requires more hard-core, cognitive expenditure than many other lines of work. Here's another truism: Lots and lots of adults don't like to think; once they have an occupation that provides a living and keeps them relatively happy, they prefer to live in a mentally remote world where they have a job they can do, sans hard-core thinking.

SHINE A LIGHT ON THE SUBJECT

If you're having trouble deciding what goes into your novel (or any work) and what doesn't add anything essential, try thinking of your mind as a spotlight. It can only focus on what's lit up within the beam. What's on the periphery is easily missed and probably should be missed. This is also a good technique for focusing your attention in general. The next time you sit down to write, turn on your spotlight and shine its white hot light on creating unforgettable scenes.

But writers have to think and *think hard*—and we have to think beyond mastering craft into creating works full of meaning, purpose, and nobility—and then editing and selling them. So, to even assume that this should go smoothly—particularly in the slogging middle—is to be misguided. Writing is not for sissies, and if you intend to write novels, screenplays, or plays, it will not be easy, and you will often come up against a wall of resistance. Just don't call it "writer's block," call it what it is: *not being prepared to move to the next level*.

That being said, a discouraging loss of steam strikes even the best and most prolific writers. Even though it's natural, and fairly predictable, one must never linger, which is why this chapter will offer a spate of ideas to break the spell and get your writing brain back on track. But we begin, of course, with reasons why all writers get stalled.

FIGHT COGNITIVE INERTIA

Cognitive inertia occurs when you pursue the same line of thinking, failing to open up all the possibilities and allowing ideas to flow. Your brain, with all its genius, keeps going down the same neuronal path, leading to frustration. What's required is time for actual *thinking*, actively engaging your emotions, memories, thoughts, and imagination to focus on the generation of new ideas. Begin by writing down the problem, specifically naming the roadblock, and then give your brain free range to come up with a multitude of solutions—the wilder and more off-course the better. Even if you don't walk away with an immediate solution, all the neurons you fired up will keep searching for new synapses until a brilliant idea emerges. Your job: Write down whatever pops up. It may or may not be the solution, but it's a sign for your brain that you take the work seriously. Your writing brain will continue to work on finding a solution as long as it receives feedback that this line of thinking is important.

YOU'VE LOST YOUR WAY

All writers reach a point when they lose their way, their work veering off into unforeseen directions or experiencing a surprise (like when a character you didn't anticipate shows up). Rather than permitting this to sabotage your momentum, take a day or two to rethink your story (or project). Identify the holdup, and loosely dance around it a few days. If it's a character issue, go to the library, pull some of your favorite books off the shelves, and see how writers you admire dealt with similar problems. If it's a setting issue, visit the place in question, or a similar site, and spend some time absorbing elements that you can weave into the story.

REVISIT PLACES LINKED TO POTENT MEMORIES

In order to remember a speech, ancient Greeks used to think of a familiar path they frequented and mentally attach segments of speeches to each location along the path. Memory experts also use a system like this to remember names, faces, and dates (a common one is to think of associating a person's face with a place in your house, for instance). It turns out this may reflect how our brain's *place cells* assist with memory. Using the "grid system" that encodes memory with space, it seems the best way to truly remember experiences may be to travel to where they occurred. While this may seem particularly useful for all writers—save some fiction writers—it could also be important to any writer who wishes to mine personal experiences to re-create similar happenings in fiction. The best way to truthfully represent emotional truths may be to revisit places where you experienced *what* you're describing.

Do the Opposite of What You Typically Do

With fiction, some writers do a lot of prep work (creating character bios, plotting out the storyline, researching for authentic elements to integrate, visiting possible settings, and so on); some writers create broad outlines consisting mostly of major plot points and/or scenes; some writers create detailed outlines that include every scene they want to write; and some writers start with the germ of an idea (a beginning scene, the ending, a character, a situation, a real-life event), sit down, and let the words flow onto the page.

If you're stalled because you lost your way, try the opposite of what you usually do—if you're a plotter, give your imagination free rein for a day; if you're a freewriter or a pantser, spend a day creating a list of the next ten scenes that need to happen. This gives your brain a challenge, and for this reason you can take heart, because your billions of neurons love a challenge and are in search of synapses they can form. You can practically feel the dendrites fluttering their spiny little arms.

DRAW IT OUT COMBINATORY PLAY

Memories are one of the best resources you have in your brain. Everything you've ever encountered and processed through your prefrontal cortex (at the front of your brain, where we "work with" new memories) is accessible via your hippocampus, and it's the connections those memories make that offers up a wealth of ideas. When all goes well, those connections happen spontaneously, but occasionally it's necessary to "prime the pump." One way to do that is to use another creative medium, such as sketching or drawing a scene, a road map of your plot, or a family tree for your main character. It works by waking up your prefrontal cortex and spurring new neuronal connections that may just serve up the fresh idea you need.

Look at the Big Picture

If you're having trouble identifying the problem, your perspective may be too constricted. Try pulling back, both mentally and emotionally. Go as far back as it takes for you to be able to view the work as a whole and, hopefully, view it more objectively. Think about how the story is working on a larger scale, give yourself credit for getting this far, and then hone in on what you think may be the hitch. Maybe you think your character has turned into a caricature or the plotline is too weak. If that's the case, look through the previous fifty pages for ways you can tweak it to achieve what you want. Often the brilliance is right there, just waiting for you to claim it. And once you've fixed the perceived problem, your flow will likely return—along with a fired up writing brain.

CALL IN THE NEURONAL TROOPS

The prefrontal cortex, located just behind the forehead, plays an essential role in information processing and making decisions, but when studying what role neighboring

FIRE UP YOUR WRITING BRAIN

regions play, scientists discovered that neurons in the orbitofrontal cortex monitor and represent the current state of the monkey assigned a difficult task (that's you writing). If the level of conflict is high, it sends a signal to other parts of the prefrontal cortex to "think harder." So when you need to figure out a snag in your work, alert your brain that it's time for your orbitofrontal cortex to summon the cavalry. How do you do this? Remove distractions and focus your mind on the problem until you feel somewhat agitated—and then concentrate even harder. If you stick with it, the troops will arrive and a higher level of executive functioning will kick in. The orbitofrontal cortex is also important in making value judgments—and the more it's activated, the more likely it is that your writing brain believes you are making a valued decision. Moral: *Activate it often!*

Give Your Brain a Puzzle

Sometimes, even if you're someone who hates anything that smacks of an outline, thinking about scenes, plot points, character arcs, subplots, the climax, final scenes, and so on will spark new ideas. Remember, your brain responds to stimuli and seeks to create patterns. If you delineate what the problems are and put some thought into how to solve them, your brain will start searching for links, combing memory, forming new synapses, and serving up fresh ideas. Just give it the input it needs, a little time, and maybe a night's rest, and it will come to your rescue.

YOUR PASSION HAS WANED

It happens. Because writing a novel requires immersion—thinking about it, crafting it, dreaming about it, obsessing about it—your brain may be on overload or just bored. It doesn't mean that your writing is boring; it means that you've worked and reworked the material so much that it now feels, sounds, or reads boring—to your mind. A pair of fresh eyes would likely have a more objective opinion, though it's not time to ask for outside eyes. Asking now may invite uninformed opinions (no one will have invested as much as you have to date) that make you question everything, and editing while writing can stifle creativity. Wait until the first draft is complete and it's time to edit, before allowing yourself, or others, to question your creative decisions or, worse yet, to nitpick. Usually it's best to just keep writing forward. Whatever you imagine to be a problem will likely iron itself out in the rewrite—and yes, you will have to rewrite, likely more than once.

STEP AWAY FROM THE DESK

Studies reported in *Journal of Personality and Social Psychology* (in 2004 and 2007), on the effect of spatial distance on creative cognition and insight problem solving, found that when the creative task is portrayed as originating from afar rather than a close location, participants provided more creative responses and performed better on a problem-solving task that required creative insight. What this means for your writing is that you may be feeling "too close" to the problem. Try putting some physical and psychological distance between the roadblock and your brain, giving your brain the opportunity to process its thoughts while you are "off somewhere else."

Don't Make It a Pattern

Lots of writers discard projects at this stage, often lamenting that they just lost the juice they needed to keep going. They chalk it up to choosing the wrong project, the wrong genre, the wrong topic, the wrong characters, or whatever. That may be the case, but if feeling bored about a third of the way in becomes a pattern, it's likely more about you than about the story, characters, or subject matter. Either that, or you need to spend more time thinking and prepping before you commit to a project. Remember, your writing brain looks for and responds to patterns, so be careful that you don't make succumbing to boredom or surrendering projects without a fight into a habit. Do your best to work through the reasons you got stalled and to finish what you started. This will lay down a neuronal pathway that your writing brain will merrily travel along in future work.

Go Where There's Heat

When it comes to writing a nonfiction book, such as this one, the publisher requires a detailed outline, as well as a formal proposal, before they contract to publish a nonfiction book. Convinced their "good idea" and any kind of writing résumé should be sufficient, new writers moan about having to create a formal nonfiction book proposal (including memoirs), especially that detailed outline. Creating the outline (and proposal) can feel like a lot to do upfront, as it requires research, contemplation, planning, concentrating, and commitment— with no guarantee that it will be purchased; but, in truth, the formal proposal and outline provide a road map, which usually helps the writing proceed much more smoothly.

When the writer bogs down halfway, he can use the outline to help him get back on his feet by writing at a different place in the book. He can simply read down the list of topics not yet discussed and choose one that holds more appeal, or that doesn't require as much concentration. An outline can also help the writer go where there's "heat" (something that excites the brain) and avoid the need to push through rough patches. This really helps your writing brain stay engaged and helps you avoid getting so stuck that you lose momentum.

DO WHAT A GENIUS DOES

If you're stuck and out of ideas about what to do, try doing what a genius would do:

- Albert Einstein famously attributed some of his greatest breakthroughs to his violin-playing breaks, which he believed connected different parts of his brain in new ways—and his hypothesis has since been scientifically proven.

- Vladimir Nabokov secretly and regularly indulged in collecting and studying butterflies, which he believed helped him develop his deep passion for detail and precision. He became particularly deft in those areas.
- Madeleine L'Engle believed that getting stuck occurred when the conscious mind overtook the unconscious mind, stemming the flow of ideas. She found playing the piano helped her "break the barrier between the conscious and subconscious mind"—a method that is also scientifically sound.

As you can see, whatever passion or talent you possess outside of writing may be the perfect ticket out of the hell that comes with feeling stalled.

Reexamine Your Motives

If you've lost steam and fear it's because you've chosen the wrong subject, take a day or two to do, read, or think about something else. Before you go back to the manuscript, ask yourself these three probing questions to reveal the real reason you chose this topic, these characters, this storyline, this theme, and so on:

- What drove me to write about this in the first place?
- Why did I feel that this was worth a year of my time?
- What is it that I wanted the world to know?

If your reasons remain solid, true, and important enough to you, you'll likely spark a few "grass fires" into your neuronal forest, which will send you rushing to your desk to get words on paper.

Reexamine the Work Itself

Perhaps you're more frustrated than bored or uninspired, and are giving up too easily? Perhaps you've come against an element that feels too challenging? Perhaps you've been letting someone else's opinion into the room? Review the work itself. Often there is an element that needs to be reworked and you just haven't wanted to dig into it—easier to start over with something new, or at least that's what you tell yourself. Some people find it easier to get fired up about a new idea than to plunge ahead through the laborious middle (and this pesky setback called being stalled); but if you consistently abandon projects, you're not likely to complete one soon. Remember that it's important to set yourself up for success—to set your writing brain up for success. You don't want to link "failure" with writing.

STRAIN YOUR BRAIN

It's making the effort that reinforces the way our brains think. Researchers have found that we learn best when the learning requires excessive mental effort—what we struggle to learn, we retain longer. In fact, it's the incubation period, between posing the questions and allowing your neuronal network to seek the necessary connections, that leads to increased curiosity, productive thinking, and creativity. When your brain is searching through its various networks to find connections, the thinking itself deepens and broadens, often leading to surprising connections and epiphanies. Moral: *When your writing brain bogs down, think harder.*

YOU NEED A MUSE

If you fancy thinking that an angel—or muse—stands just behind you, guiding, protecting, and perhaps inspiring you, well, it's a lovely thought. In fact, neurologically, these types of feelings or sensations often occur when someone is under extreme duress, is sleep deprived, or has been isolated for too long. It also occurs with mental disorders, such as schizophrenia.

Under these circumstances, the brain may lose oxygen and shut down the "rational mind" which can lead to hallucinations—thought to be our mind's way of re-remembering what it feels like to be around others. And the psychological construct that creates our sense of self (as separate from our brain, which it's not; it resides primarily in our left temporal lobe), is activated and it "feels" like another being is standing, sitting, breathing beside you. Your psychological sense of self, often referred to as "the mind schema," coordinates the many independent neural networks that simultaneously process stimuli and coordinate actions in daily living so that you feel like you possess a single mind (and not a bunch of neurons firing in disparate groups). So, when you feel a presence outside of yourself (you could even feel like someone is touching you), it's basically that internal sensory input temporarily confuses your brain, and your mind goes to work constructing an explanation.

BECOME YOUR OWN MUSE

A sleep-deprived Charles A. Lindbergh wrote about sensing presences during his transatlantic flight to Paris: "The fuselage behind me becomes filled with ghostly presences— vaguely outlined forms, transparent, moving, riding weightless with me in the plane ... conversing and advising on my flight, discussing problems of my navigation, reassuring me, giving me messages of importance unattainable in ordinary life." These kind of hallucinations can occur when sleep-deprived, which is not recommended, but when you're in a pinch, why not envision a helper, an angel, or a muse standing just behind you? Anything that bolsters your confidence and lessens resistance or fear is a good thing, so have fun, give her a name, have tea with her, do whatever it takes—as long as you're clear who is actually writing.

Neuroscientist Michael S. Gazzaniga calls the mind schema that creates these sensations "the left-hemisphere interpreter"—the brain's storyteller, because it pulls together countless inputs into a meaningful narrative story. Your brain fills in the details from past memory, and you may feel more comfortable, or simply enjoy, imagining the sensation as that of a separate being and thinking of it as an angel, a muse, a ghost, your dead grandmother, or some sort of spirit guide. The good news: There's no harm in imagining an angel or muse if doing so helps you become the best writer you can be. Just remember that you are creating the illusion and projecting what you desire onto the construct. Whatever wisdom and brilliance you ascribe to the presence already resides in your writing brain.

Own it and call it forth, from within.

YOU'VE SPENT TOO MUCH TIME ALONE

Writers are, by necessity, solitary beings. Some writers pair up or write as one cog in a team, but most writers write, think, and create alone. Successful writers (successful in terms of completing their work) either love or have made peace with solitude, because we know that's where the genius arises. Solitude becomes the best way to minimize distractions, to quiet emotions, and to focus the mind. When we are alone, our innermost self feels brave enough to crawl out of the shade into the light. If we're ever going to hear our innermost self "talking" to us, it will occur in solitude—and we need that voice to make our work original, remarkable, and ingenious.

Still, unless you're co-writing or part of a writing team, you have likely been sitting in a room alone, scorching your brain cells, pounding out words for hours, and often days, on end. This is, of course, particularly true when a deadline is approaching and you're holing yourself up in a room, forcing yourself to churn out words at a breakneck pace, working deep into the night.

If writing grinds to a halt, it's highly likely that what you need most is a break, a chance to let in sunshine and someone else's voice for a spell. Being around other people is always refreshing, but never more so than when you've been working like a maniac behind closed doors.

STAY ACTIVE AND SOCIAL

It's very important to remain "cognitively engaged" as you age, but the highly advertised "brain games" (computer-based, cognitive-training software) are not proving effective in keeping brains supple enough to meet the claims of preventing or reversing Alzheimer's disease or dementia. In fact, most studies using data from websites such as Lumosity have shown that playing such games only increases your ability to perform *on the particular task you're playing*—the cognitive increases don't "spread" to other demands or cognitive/behavioral skills, because the games are too focused. What does help maintain brain health is remaining engaged—thinking, learning, and exposing yourself to new ideas and experiences that force your brain to make new connections. Going places, doing things, and remaining actively social (carrying on complex conversations) may be more effective than any sort of "brain game." Although, if you really like playing computer and video games, or doing crossword puzzles and Sudoku, they can be stimulating— just don't believe the hype that promises they'll improve your overall intelligence and memory.

YOUR EXPECTATIONS ARE TOO HIGH

A mistake many novice writers make is in setting their sights too high, expecting perfection when they have yet to write a complete novel or screenplay. The best advice anyone can give inexperienced writers is to write a first draft as quickly as possible, as good books are not written, but rewritten and rewritten and rewritten. Once you have a first draft, you have a solid base on which to build, and all the "problems" you anticipated will work themselves out as you massage and craft your raw material.

What stops many writers midway is attempting to make the first draft the best they can write. Some believe it's the way real writers write, which is generally *not* true; and some believe that perfecting each chapter will relieve them of the need to rewrite, which is also *not* true. Imposing this unreasonable need for perfection is bound to cause anxiety—and a great deal of frustration.

TRICK YOUR INNER CRITIC

We all have a critical voice within that questions what we're doing. Jungian analyst, and *mythopoetic* author Marion Woodman once likened this to a demon on your shoulder, whispering that "you're wasting your time, that nothing will come of this, that you may think you're special, but you're not," and so on, echoing whatever your inner, self-berating voice says. She suggested the best way to fight off this demonic heckling was to cheerfully announce that you're just playing, that this isn't serious work. Then, she says, the pesky demon will scamper away.

YOU'RE CREATING YOUR OWN ANXIETY

Frustration and anxiety are what can lead to a debilitating state of mind. In effect, you are setting your writing brain up for an emotional meltdown. The more pressure you put on yourself, the higher your anxiety level rises and the more writing becomes a signal of danger, which transmits a message straight to your limbic system, triggering fight-or-flight reactions. When that happens, the limbic system stops forwarding messages to the cortex, which is where conscious thought, imagination, and creativity are generated. Instead, your amygdala releases stress hormones, like cortisol and adrenaline, and soon, your heart rate is skyrocketing, your ability to feel emotionally safe enough to write is eroded, and your ability to concentrate vanishes. Who wants that? Who wants to re-create that? Small wonder that you are feeling a resistance to writing.

What you need to do is release those inappropriately high expectations and just pound out that first draft, as fast and furiously as you can. Once you have the bones of a story down, it will be far easier to craft your novel, with a lot less anxiety to gum up the works.

Instead of setting your sights too high, give yourself permission to write anything, on topic or off topic, meaningful or trite, useful or folly. The point is that by attaching so much importance to the work you're about to do, you make it harder to get into the flow. Also, if your inner critic sticks her nose in (which often happens), tell her that her role is very important to you (and it is!) and that you will summon her when you have something worthy of her attention. That should divert her attention and free you to dive back into the writing pool.

LIGHT UP YOUR RESTING NETWORK

There are two types of meditation: concentrative (which includes external directions for focusing thoughts on breathing or a sound, as a way to suppress thoughts) and nondirective meditation (which encourages the person to focus on breath or sounds, but does not provide direction and thus allows the mind to wander). In a study, those practicing nondirective meditation had more activity in the part of the brain dedicated to processing self-related thoughts and feelings (introspection) than those practicing concentrative meditation. This "resting network" has its highest activity when we rest, because it takes over when external requests do not require our attention. So when you want to be introspective, spend a few minutes focused on your breath, while allowing your mind to wander.

YOU ARE BURNED OUT

It is quite possible that you've simply tapped yourself out. We all have our limits, be they physical, mental, emotional, and all of the aforementioned. If you've been pounding out your novel—in addition to working full time—your body and brain may be sending you a potent message to slow down. In a frantically paced life, you may be pushing too hard, raising your expectations too high, and putting too much pressure on yourself. Eventually your body, brain, or emotions are going to rebel and insist on downtime, which may come in the guise of what you may call writer's block.

But keep this in mind: *You aren't blocked; you're exhausted.* Give yourself a few days to really rest. Lie on a sofa and watch movies, take long walks in the hour just before dusk, go out to dinner with friends, or take a mini-vacation somewhere restful. Do so with intention to give yourself—and your brain—a rest. No thinking about your novel for a week! In fact, no heavy thinking for a week. Lie back, have a margarita, and chill. Once you're rested, you'll likely find the desire to write has come roaring back.

Stop Thinking

Have you ever wondered why ideas seem to come easier when you've stopped concentrating and gone off to rest, shower, or mow the lawn? When you're working on a task that requires higher level cognitive functioning, like writing, which requires intense concentration, your brain focuses like a laser on the task at hand, blocking out distractions and relying on existing neuronal connections. But when you break concentration and do something that doesn't require focused cognitive functioning, your brain is more susceptible to distractions and thus "lets in" a broader range of information, which can lead to imagining more alternatives and making more diverse interpretations—fostering a "think outside the box" mentality and creating the milieu for an aha moment. Scientists have even found that when your brain is a little fuzzy from exertion, it's a lot less efficient at remembering connections and thereby may be more open to new connections, new ideas, and new ways of thinking.

Take a Nap

Daytime naps have long been a part of many cultures, just not so much in America. In fact, daytime naps have been shown to improve perception and keep you more alert, boost your memory and your creativity, reduce stress, increase optimism, and improve stamina.

Naps can also be beneficial in assisting your brain's processing of information. When a memory is first recorded in the hippocampus, it's still tentative and can be easily forgotten, especially if your brain has been busy processing (or being asked to remember) additional stimuli. As with sleeping at night, during naps, your brain is sorting and processing stimuli that occurred before the nap, making decisions on what should be linked and what should be moved to long-term memory or discarded. Studies have shown that participants asked to remember information prior to a break will remember the information far better if they napped for thirty to forty minutes before being asked to recall what they learned. By taking a nap, you may wake up feeling refreshed and often you'll have a fresh idea because:

- Ideas, thoughts, and associations that don't pertain to the task at hand were released.
- Important learning has been distributed to, and integrated within, the cortex.
- Existing, relevant synapses were strengthened.
- New neuronal connections occurred while you napped.

Daytime naps may also improve your motor skills, enhance your sex life, and aid in weight loss. Scientists say a five-minute nap is too short (it doesn't give your brain time to transition into a restful state) and a thirty-minute nap may be too long (the brain may begin transitioning into deep slumber, leaving you drowsy afterwards, instead of refreshed). They say ten to fifteen minutes is just enough to refresh and renew your brain. So, determine what works best for you, and then set aside time for a midday nap to reap cognitive (and other) blessings.

YOU'RE TOO DISTRACTED

Few of us have the luxury of being free from distractions. Most of us have jobs, spouses, kids, and responsibilities that occupy a huge amount of our brain space. If your productivity has stalled, or your frustration level has peaked at a new high, it may be that too many other things are on your mind. For many, bill paying and prior commitments begin to nag. There's just "too much" on your desk— and in your brain. When those distractions mount, it's often easier and more productive to just stop writing and go take care of your life, to do whatever it is that is causing you to feel pressured.

Identify Your Distractions

If it's a persistent problem, then you'll want to figure out what you need to do to dedicate yourself to writing. Maybe it's hiring a babysitter four hours a day for a few days each week; or maybe it's inviting all your friends to lunch rather than parceling out time for each of them; or maybe it's rearranging your schedule so you can squeeze in an hour's writing time each morning or evening. Maybe going away alone for a weekend to write would help?

MAKE A "TO DO" LIST FOR YOUR LIFE

Often, feeling blocked is really all about feeling stressed—not just in relation to writing, but to your life as a whole. Studies show a direct correlation between feelings of psychological empowerment and stress resiliency. Empowering yourself with a feeling of control over what's happening in your life can help reduce chronic stress and give you the confidence to figure out what's bugging you so you can get back to writing. Make a prioritized "to do" list for everything that's on your mind, thereby reassuring your brain that you'll get to all of those things in due time. If you still can't focus, strike a few things off the top of the list and try again.

Manage Your Distractions

Few of us have the ability to minimize outside stressors, so moving forward relies on your ability to find a creative way to free your mind long enough to work productively. And, to start, stop berating yourself for having too much on your mind, too many responsibilities, or too many tasks left undone. Better to take action and address each distraction as best you can. Include time to do what you have to do—pay the water bill, figure out your taxes, plan a party for a loved one, scrub the floors, rake the leaves. In fact, clearing the decks (and often just doing something physically tiring) will leave your writing brain feeling refreshed and ready to write.

Give Yourself a Break

Take note that, unless you're just one of those rare birds who always write no matter what, you will experience times in your life when it's impossible to keep to a writing schedule. People get sick, people have to take a second job, children need extra attention, parents need extra attention, and so on. If you're in one of those emergency situations (raising small children counts), by all means, don't berate yourself. Sometimes it's simply necessary to put the actual writing on hold. It is good, however, to keep your hands in the water. For instance, in lieu of writing your novel:

- Read novels or works similar to what you hope to write.
- Read books about the setting or historical context of your novel.
- Keep a designated journal where you jot down ideas for the novel (and other works).
- Write small vignettes, poems, or sketches related to the novel.
- Whenever you find time to meditate, envision yourself writing the novel.

Instead of feeling like a failed writer, be patient and kind toward your writing self until the situation changes. The less you fret and put a negative spin on it, the more small pockets of time might open up. And, since you have been wise in keeping your writing brain primed, you may find it easier to write than you imagined.

YOUR BRAIN HAS SHUT DOWN

To access the pathways to the prefrontal cortex and ignite your higher thinking processes, your brain requires a low stress, positive emotional climate. The amygdala, a switching station deep in the brain's emotional limbic system, determines whether information will be transmitted to the higher prefrontal cortex where long-term, retrievable memories are developed, or to the lower brain where you react but do not learn. When stress levels are high, the amygdala adopts a one-track approach, directing all stimuli responses to the lower brain.

Boredom and Frustration Create Stress

Frequent and sustained boredom and frustration also create stress that encourages the amygdala's hypermetabolic state and blocks input being channeled to the higher prefrontal cortex's executive functions. Because input isn't reaching the prefrontal cortex's emotional control center, the lower brain responds with fight-or-flight responses, rather than nuanced, "thought-through" responses. If you want to focus at this stage, you have to stimulate the brain, draw it out of its reactive mode so messages will again be directed to your prefrontal cortex. Doing something pleasurable is a great way to do it.

Spark Your Brain by Doing Something Fun

Focus on a task that piques your curiosity or delights you, and give pleasure its due by noticing the feelings and staying in the moment long enough to consciously register pleasure. An equal mixture of delight and relevance should break you out of the boredom spell and get your prefrontal cortex in control and firing on all pistons.

PAMPER YOUR WRITING BRAIN

If you want your brain to be brilliant, you need to create the ideal conditions for your mental processes to be refreshed and expanded. A smart writer knows that pampering the brain increases the odds that it will be ready and eager to assist when the next writing session arrives. Even if your brain is working just fine, writing genius isn't something that happens to you: It's something you can teach your brain to deliver. Here are some ways you can make sure you're giving your writing brain what it needs to make your ongoing work stellar and to ensure that you keep growing as a writer:

- **REST:** Sleep matters!
- **MEDITATE.**
- **KEEP YOUR BRAIN NOURISHED:** Eat foods known to benefit brain health: Fish (wild salmon and sardines in particular), tree nuts (walnuts and almonds, in particular), berries (blueberries, in

particular), extra virgin olive oil, beans (lentils and black beans, in particular), mushrooms, cruciferous greens (spinach, broccoli, and kale, in particular), dark chocolate, avocados, seeds (chia, flax, and sesame seeds, in particular), wheat germ, quinoa, beets, coffee, green tea, garlic, turmeric, and cinnamon.

- **DRINK LOTS OF WATER TO KEEP YOUR BRAIN HYDRATED.**
- **REWARD IT:** Find something you really want. I've chosen white gold, wedding band hoop earrings as a reward, because I saw Diane Sawyer wearing similar ones on television, and I coveted them. I have priced them and posted a picture of them on my desktop so I see them every time I sit at my computer. I've wanted them for a long time, but they are such a luxury for me that I haven't been able to justify buying them, so instead I use them as a carrot—when I finish the first draft of my novel, I will buy them for myself, and, more importantly, for my writing brain.
- **REINFORCE SUCCESS:** Pause to mindfully acknowledge your brain's contribution to your work; when something is working, keep doing it and reward your dedication and persistence.
- **EXPAND CAPACITY:** Stretch your output.
- **STRENGTHEN CONNECTIONS:** Read about the topic you're writing on. The Internet is fantastic for this; go online at the end of your workday (or just prior to beginning work) and Google your topic. Even if you click on items that don't seem relevant, your brain may think otherwise and link the info in surprising ways. Have fun with this, welcome absurdity or obscurity. You never know what might pop into your consciousness as you progress through your work: a fully formed metaphor, for example, or the sudden appearance of a thread you hadn't planned. Your writing brain is a wonder, feed it well.
- **CREATE NEW SYNAPSES:** Think outside the box, look for original ideas or associations, and play.
- **DAYDREAM:** This is your brain and your creativity playing; don't tell anyone (i.e., your brain) that you are, in fact, feeding it images that can be mined when you write. You are recharging your crea-

tivity, sparking new synapses and associations, and planting seeds for future brainstorming sessions.

- **KEEP A WRITING JOURNAL:** This gives your brain official space to grapple with the process of writing. Use it to record gripes, frustrations, disappointments, challenges, hopes, and anything and everything that involves process, including inspiration. Not only will a journal give your multitude of thoughts and emotions an outlet, your brain will reward you for taking your work seriously and using all resources available to grow as an artist.

If you're pampering your writing brain, it will very soon reward your efforts with increased brainpower and energy.

Push on Through to the End

Now, *whew*, pushing through the middle is hard, and you've done it. All that remains is to write the end—and then edit. But let's not get ahead of ourselves. For now, celebrate; tomorrow, back to writing!

TRAIN YOUR WRITING BRAIN: GIVE YOURSELF AMPLE CREDIT

Take fifteen minutes to write down everything others have said that's good about your writing, being as specific as possible. Think hard if you have to, but come up with something. Then write down your own thoughts, recognizing how far you've come. If all you can credit yourself for is reading a few books on writing and writing one thousand words in the last month, focus on the positive aspects. Instead of berating yourself for what you may perceive as shortcomings, give yourself credit for whatever you've done, even if the only thing you've done is get enough sleep. Write the affirmations in positive language:

- I sleep eight hours a night to keep my writing brain refreshed and ready to write.
- When I walked for two miles today, I felt blood and oxygen flowing into my writing brain, which will soon be percolating with ideas.
- I honor my subconscious by keeping a journal by my bed to jot down ideas when I wake.

- I journal about my writing process every day, seeking a way to get back on track.
- I'm proud of what I've done so far; all I need is a final push toward completion.
- I'm confident the story will come together and that I'll be able to fix anything that needs fixing on the next draft.
- I'm feeling excited, renewed, and confident, trusting that my brain is on the job, even when it doesn't appear to be.

The singular goal is to bolster feelings about you and your writing process. After you complete the list, read it over a few times and recognize how good it feels to validate your efforts. Do this once a week, and you may see a big boost in confidence—and word count.

WRITERS ON CRAFT

"[If] in the middle of writing something you go blank ... You're being warned, aren't you? Your subconscious is saying 'I don't like you anymore. You're writing about things I don't give a damn for. You're being political, or you're being socially aware. You're writing things that will benefit the world. To hell with that! I don't write things to benefit the world ... I set out to have a hell of a lot of fun' ... If you've got a writer's block, you can cure it this evening by stopping whatever you're writing and doing something else. You picked the wrong subject."

—RAY BRADBURY

"By [the] middle of the novel—I mean whatever page you are on when you stop being part of your household and your family and your partner and children and food shopping and dog feeding and reading the post—I mean when there is nothing in the world except your book, and even as your wife tells you she's sleeping with your brother her face is a gigantic semicolon, her arms are parentheses and you are wondering whether *rummage* is a better verb than *rifle*. The middle of a novel is a state of mind."

—ZADIE SMITH

"I learned to produce whether I wanted to or not. It would be easy to say oh, I have writer's block, oh, I have to wait for my muse. I don't. Chain that muse to your desk and get the job done."

—BARBARA KINGSOLVER

CHAPTER 10

SUSTAIN YOUR WRITING BRAIN
Get a Second Wind

"Over the years, I've found one rule. It is the only one I give on those occasions when I talk about writing. A simple rule. If you tell yourself you are going to be at your desk tomorrow, you are by that declaration asking your unconscious to prepare the material. You are, in effect, contracting to pick up such valuables at a given time. Count on me, you are saying to a few forces below: I will be there to write."

—NORMAN MAILER

You're nearing the finish line and feel like you need a final push forward to reach completion. You've slogged your way through the long, seemingly interminable middle, and your energy has flagged. Writers often experience self-doubt in this stage (worrying that it won't come together well), and some have issues with finishing things. Your writing brain, too, may feel weary at this stage.

Writing a novel, a nonfiction book, a screenplay, or a TV script is no easy feat. You and your brain are in for the long haul of writing, and naturally you—*and your writing brain*—get weary. To push on and stay fresh, let's discuss specific things you can do.

IF YOU READ IT, IT IS SO

When your brain reads about an event or experience, the same neurological regions are stimulated as if it happened to you. According to Keith Oatley, an emeritus professor of cognitive psychology and a novelist, this vivid simulation of reality "runs on minds of readers just as computer simulations run on computers." This is one reason why written fiction, with its sensory details, imaginative metaphors, and particular, observant descriptions of people and their actions, offers far more reality—and depth—than watching movies. Unlike visual fiction, novels go beyond simulating reality to giving readers an experience unavailable off the page: the opportunity to enter fully into other people's thoughts and feelings.

BOLSTER MOTIVATION

This is great time to revisit all the reasons you wanted to write this book in the first place—the underlying, important motivations that set you on this path and fueled the fire, right up to this point. In fact, the writing will have revealed emerging themes or underpinnings you hadn't even thought of when you first began preparing to write— and you will have figured out what's been working or not working in terms of your writing progress (how you write, what could make it go smoother, and so on).

A new probing of motivation and process will also help you pause to evaluate your writing process as it relates to this specific work. So, without going back to review your original list, begin by creating a new list of answers:

- Why does completing this particular story/project matter to me?
- What drives me to make it the best work I can perform?
- What is going really well in the writing process and why?
- What's proven a struggle, and how can I overcome it?
- What can I change to be more productive?
- How can I keep motivating myself to write?
- What needs more attention as I move forward?

Sounds simple, but please don't rush through this process; spend some time thinking—and feeling—on a deeper level. Maybe you'll want to meditate before you begin, or at least mindfully clear your brain of competing thoughts and distractions. This exercise will be more effective if you speak to the innermost part of yourself, the voice that guides you through life—in other words, take time to commune with your heart and soul on the depth and complexity of your work in progress. Hopefully you are motivated to do the very best work you're capable of doing, and, if you are, completing this exercise will train your writing brain to take the process of writing even more seriously.

Now, retrieve your original motivation list and compare the two, noting diversions (surprising directions the work has taken) or the clarifying and strengthening of themes. This contemplation will not only clarify your motivation, it will generate new ideas. Hopefully you'll feel that rush of energy that comes with a sense of purpose and a clearly defined goal.

BRAINSTORM ON WHERE TO GO

It's a brainstorming session with a massive amount of new material (that you and your marvelous brain have created) to record and mull over. Fresh ideas regarding what you've written so far and what needs to be in the closing chapters will seem to pop into your head, and, in a way, that's exactly what they do—it's your brain linking all those thoughts together and sparking new neuronal connections. Your brain has been as focused on this work as your mind (more so, if you add in what happens in your unconscious mind), and if you simply award your writing brain the time and attention it needs to process all this new input, it will light up and weigh in.

SET YOUR WRITING BRAIN ON FIRE

Receiving "random" fluctuations in information (from outside stimulation) increases the possibility neurons will burst into a state of global ignition, which helps imprint the experience. It is interesting to note that the unpredictable fluctuations in neuronal firing sometimes fit exactly with the incoming stimulus (making the processing of the information smoother), and sometimes fight against it (making it more difficult to process)—conflict happens, even in your neurons. Conscious perception seems to occur when your preexisting biases and new incoming stimuli (especially new information your neural activity "fights," because it's different!) combine into a full-blown global ignition. When you're writing, global ignition is highly desirable, and you can create this by stimulating your brain as much as possible (using the many techniques included throughout this book).

REVIEW YOUR PLOT

A great way to get revved up again is to review whatever planning or plotting device or method you used to get started. You don't have to labor over this; just glance through your notes to see if you lost a thread or missed something important. The idea is to stimulate your memory, marshal your thoughts, and use the refresher as a way to generate new ideas and build momentum as you proceed downwind from *the muddle in the middle.*

If You Used Note Cards

If you used note cards, take them out and go through each one, evaluating which scenes made the cut and which did not—and why. If you've been using the cards all along, and they've worked well in terms of priming your brain for writing sessions and providing a map for the storyline, character arcs, and scenes, then bravo! If you haven't been referring to them, reading them will likely come up with fresh ideas—be sure to jot them down on new cards. Even if you don't refer back to the cards, the thinking and decision-making process will program yourwriting brain for the work ahead.

If You Used a List of Plot Points

If you used a list of plot points at the inception, go back and review them, noting where you contracted or expanded events. You'll likely discover how inventive your brain has been in creating ideas as you worked—and you may be delighted to discover that it's popping in with ideas during this process. Give your magnificent brain an appreciative nod and jot down any ideas that spring forth from this review.

If You Used a Detailed Outline

If you used a detailed outline (or some sort of plotting software), you've probably reviewed it often and know exactly where you are. However, as you move into the final stretches, reviewing what's ahead is like priming the pump, and you'll likely reap a burst of energy in response.

LOOK AT THE BROAD STROKES

You can use the same review process to focus your brain on how all the elements that need to coalesce in the closing chapters are coming together. Note: This is not time to go back and start editing. What you are doing is looking at the overall work in broad strokes to determine if you're on course—and to fire up your brain for more writing. The goal is to use this exercise as a way to move *forward*, not to look backward. You don't want to suffer the fate of Orpheus, who lost his beloved, Eurydice, when he lost faith and turned his gaze backwards.

The point is to spend some time *thinking* through all the elements that you are *prepping* to write:

- **THE STORYLINE:** How has the plot progressed up to this point? What's missing, what needs to be maximized going forward?
- **THE PROTAGONIST:** Is your hero proactive, multidimensional, and engaging? Is his character arc nearing its peak? How is he growing, stepping up, overcoming the obstacles that threaten to destroy him? What does he need to do (or conquer) to bring the story to a climatic and just ending?
- **THE ANTAGONIST:** Whether it's an external person (remember that your antagonist needs to be a worthy opponent, as complex as your protagonist) or inner conflict (the protagonist's failings), is the conflict rising in intensity, repeatedly challenging your heroine in new ways? What needs to happen for your heroine to triumph?

- **OBSTACLES:** Is your protagonist constantly tested and required to conquer multiple, escalating obstacles? Is he proactive in doing so? What will be the final test, and are the stages leading up to the dramatic, make-it-or-break-it contest increasing in intensity?
- **SCENES:** What has yet to be dramatized? How can you maximize action, pacing, and rising tension to best dramatize the remaining scenes?
- **THEME:** What needs to happen in the closing chapters to strengthen and prove (or disprove) your themes?

I am not encouraging you to delve in too deeply. You are still in writing mode, not editing mode. What I encourage you to do is to prime your mental pump by gaining a fairly comprehensive view of where you are in the broader terms of fulfilling the story and getting clear on what you need to add to bring it to fruition. Once again, you are programming your writing brain for the immediate work ahead: crafting the realized, climactic, and unforgettable ending your story and/or protagonist deserves.

If you spend a few highly focused hours reviewing the elements I've suggested, your brain will absorb the fresh input and begin the process of linking your present thoughts to everything you've done up to this point in time. Synapses will start firing in new and surprising ways; and you'll excite your brain—and your mind—for the task ahead.

REMIND YOUR BRAIN THAT A REWARD IS COMING

We now know that rewarding yourself with something pleasurable leads to a dopamine release, but studies have found that *anticipating the reward* elicits more dopamine than receipt of the actual award. What does this mean? Before you sit down to write, promise your brain a specific reward, within a specified timeframe. You might want to post a reminder that pops up on your screen that says, "three hours until chocolate, two hours until chocolate, thirty minutes until chocolate ..." (or a walk, a movie, whatever creates a dopamine drip in your brain). This way, you'll be perking up your brain throughout your writing session.

INSPIRE YOUR WRITING BRAIN

This is also a good time to fire up your brain by reinforcing what matters most to you. Go back to your writing journal, find quotes you love, copy them onto cards, and then post those cards in places you will regularly see, such as your bathroom mirror or your refrigerator. And when you do see the quotes, nod in appreciation and affirmation. Congratulate yourself for becoming the writer you've always longed to be and for joining the ranks of writers you most admire.

Identify with Authors You Admire

If you're struggling to write the ending, find quotes from writers who also struggled to write their story's ending. You're in the same situation every successful novelist has experienced, so find snippets of authors discussing the undercurrents and how they traversed those dangerous waters. Absorb this as if they were giving you a personal therapy moment. Take in their wisdom, humor, dedications, persistence, and determination and claim it as your own.

CALL UPON COGNITIVE EMPATHY

There are two kinds of empathy: affective and cognitive. Affective empathy is just like it sounds: an emotional identification with someone else's pain; cognitive empathy has more to do with being able to imagine someone else's pain— to walk a mile in their shoes, if you will. Both kinds of empathy are part of a normal, healthy, and moral personality. Understanding others' perspectives is central to emotional intelligence, but affective empathy can be very selective; you're most likely to feel it solely for loved ones or those suffering in your line of sight. It can also lead to what is called "empathic distress," or identifying too closely and mirroring the other person's emotions—which can lead to a blurring of boundaries and stalker-like behavior. Cognitive empathy, on the other hand, is more removed but plays a central role in writing in that it allows us to imagine what someone else may be feeling in a situation.

Allow Their Works to Inspire You

This is also the ideal time to reread endings you've always loved from authors that you admire and authors whose work is similar to what you're working to achieve. Spend some time studying how they wrote sensational endings and what elements contributed to making them sensational. Then think about how your ending can be as effective and memorable as the ones they created.

This exercise is not meant to encourage you to copy what someone else has done; it's merely to offer your brain examples and to plant some seeds that will blossom when you sit down to write your ending. So notice how your favorite authors successfully wove all the novel elements together to craft an ending that brings a satisfying, surprising, or heartbreaking close. You can also read endings that didn't work, as sometimes it's easier to notice what went wrong than it is to ferret out how a talented author wrote a nuanced, succinctly crafted ending.

READ SOMETHING ABSURD

Several Canadian studies found that people like feeling that whatever they are reading has "meaning"—and that your brain will search for meaning if it's not obvious. Your brain loves patterns. In a study, participants who read an absurd Kafka parable (without obvious patterns), they performed better on a pattern recognition test (the search for meaning in a task) than those who had not read Kafka. Further, those who read an absurd Monty Python parody only engaged in compensatory affirmation (the search for meaning in response to chaos) if they had not been forewarned that their brains were about to experience something absurd. Another study confirmed that those who view absurdist art (i.e., unstructured, abstract) experienced a heightened need for meaning. All this means is that your brain will work harder to find meaning and patterns after going through an experience where obvious patterns do not exist. So, if you're feeling disconnected emotionally from your work, try reading or viewing something absolutely absurd, unstructured, and abstract that will leave your brain on the hunt for patterns and meaning. You can also try viewing abstract artwork.

GET MORAL SUPPORT

If you stall as you round the corner to completion, it may be helpful to find allies who are familiar with the highs and lows of the writing process and can urge you toward the finish line. I'm not advocating that you share your work with peers—yet. I'm a total believer in incubation periods and keeping the specifics under wraps until your idea and your work in progress is virtually complete. Creative projects—books, screenplays, TV scripts, nonfiction books, memoirs, plays, songs, and poems—are like seedlings:

- They need time to germinate, take root, and grow.
- They need the proper amounts of attention, soil and water, and fertilizer.
- If you don't bury them deep enough, they can be easily uprooted.
- Without the aforementioned fertilizer and nutrients, they won't blossom into fully developed, magnificent plants.
- Like a hothouse flower, they are unique, delicate, and rare, something that needs protection until its strength surpasses its vulnerabilities.

Also, it's too easy to tell the story rather than write the story, and often, if you go around telling it to friends and family or fellow writers, the energy and heat the story brings may dissipate. Also, it's best to keep your own voice prominent as you write that first draft. Otherwise you may fall sway to other people's opinions and their thoughts, and even their words could start to seep in.

Until your work is truly on solid ground, what you can do is find like-minded people who will offer moral support and encouragement. If you're feeling like the finish line is near and the story so fully developed that you won't fall sway to outside opinions, then you may find it helpful to discuss the story in general or discuss particular topics within the story.

CONSULT SOMEONE YOU RESPECT

The human mind is very adept at looping in our bodies, our tools, and even other people to use as instruments of our own thinking. Often in couples, one person keeps track of items related to the upkeep of cars, while the other assumes responsibility for keeping track of important events. This type of cooperative thinking is called *transactive memory*, and it's just one of the ways that relationships with others can make us smarter than we would be on our own. If you feel stymied, talk over the reasons with the one person in the world who helps you make your way through life. He or she may have a surprising perspective and excellent ideas that will inspire you both.

Find Allies in Writing Groups

All that said, there comes a time when input from the outside world is welcome, when it could play a crucial role. Not so much for the content of your work, but for you, as a writer. Many find belonging to a writer's group helpful, as being around others who understand what you're willing to put yourself through to write alleviates the isolation that can come from the many necessary hours spent alone at your computer. It can be very useful to develop mutually beneficial relationships with other writers whose work you respect. Asking for feedback on the work in progress does come into play eventually, and perhaps you will find that you need an outsider's opinion as you draw to the conclusion.

Up until then, why not join a writers' group for emotional support? You won't find anyone who understands what you go through more than fellow writers do, particularly those working in your genre. Then, if you sag at the end, they can be the ones who spur you on, reassure you that you're on the right track and all you need to do is finish, get it all on paper, and ready to edit.

Also, a 2013 University of Virginia study validated that the human brain is wired to connect with other humans so strongly that it can feel what the "other" feels, as if it were experiencing the same event. If a friend's book just hit the best-seller list, your brain can feel the excitement that she is experiencing, as if you, too, were elated about being on the best-seller list. People you are close to "figuratively" become a part of you. The more bonded you become to the other, the more neural representations you form—through empathizing with them, understanding their point of view, and seeing the world as they see it. So hanging around with writers who write and produce marketable and successful work can effectively rub off on you.

IMAGINE THE FUTURE

A team of researchers at UC Berkeley's Gallant Lab discovered a way to map neural activity in a person's visual cortex (which is easier to decode than other areas) using an fMRI. They then used that visual data to reconstruct the "scene," that is, whatever that person had viewed, in a crude video re-creation (facial features and other fine details were lacking). This means that neuroscientists may someday have the ability to map and recreate what we have seen in our minds—or to implant "scenes" that never happened into our memory. Think about how far science has come, how imaginative and perhaps on target the movie *Eternal Sunshine of the Spotless Mind* actually may become, and celebrate your ability to re-create events in your mind.

FIRE UP YOUR WRITING BRAIN

Pause Ten Seconds to Let Positive Feedback Settle

Ever notice how quickly people brush aside a compliment—or worse yet, counteract it with denial, failing to consider that their protests call your perception into question? Many of us were taught to be humble, but too much humility can deny your brain the opportunity to process and retain positive experiences, as well as internal and external validations. You may even brush your own good thoughts aside.

According to Rick Hanson, neuropsychologist and author of the book *Hardwiring Happiness*, it's important to let yourself linger in the moment of a positive experience—and not just because it feels good (though that should be reason enough). Hanson notes that pausing to recognize how good it feels gives your brain time to hardwire that feeling. What's desirable is to linger in the limelight for a good ten seconds, preferably more, so your brain has to time to transfer what's happening in the moment from short-term memory to long-term memory, where the feelings can be reexperienced the next time you feel good about yourself. Ideally you'd think about that moment all day and dream about it at night—making the tracks to long-term memory more durable and permanent.

BE MORE OPTIMISTIC

A University of Illinois study of 5,100 people found that optimistic people are twice as likely to have healthy hearts and less likely to be obese, smokers, or lethargic. Makes sense as chronic stress causes the body to enter into a state of perceived danger. Nerve signals and hormonal fluctuations lead to an excess release of adrenaline, which raises heart rate and blood pressure, and cortisol, which slows down digestion and the immune system function to focus on fight or flight. Over time, these levels of stress cause sleeping problems, digestive issues, anxiety, weight gain, memory issues, and heart disease. Identifying stress triggers and rewiring how you respond to emotional challenges can generate more positive thoughts. If you're feeling stressed, do something to dial it back—a healthy heart is essential to a healthy writing brain.

Remember What Fires Together Wires Together

Relishing the way it feels to have someone recognize that your work is fabulously creative and brilliantly written is the type of strong emotion that will cause neuronal synapses that fire together to wire together. In other words, you'll bolster your brain's ability to connect each new compliment (and realistic assessment) with what has come before, creating a stronger and more confident writer. The more you learn to savor and take in the positive feedback or reinforcement you receive, the more your brain will recognize those moments when someone has validated your work, and it will link them all together, helping you feel better about yourself—and your writing.

GET BACK TO WORK

Now that you've primed your brain, refreshed your creativity, and formulated clear pictures about the closing chapters, it's time to set new, realistic goals for completion. Because it's challenging to bring a book to a close (just think how much you dread it when a story you love inhabiting comes to a close), you need to set goals that will encourage you to steadily push forward but that also allot you breathing space. Remember, a stressed brain is a far less productive brain. If your limbic system feels pressured, it overrides your prefrontal cortex (executive functioning) and all cognitive abilities are negatively affected. What you want are goals that encourage you without pressuring you—and then you need to hold yourself to those goals, because writing "The End" is not going to be as easy as you imagine. Still, you must do it, so you can proceed to editing.

DO SOMETHING PLAYFUL

When you do something that you find particularly joyful (and, ideally, physically active), it stimulates your basal ganglia (coordination of movement and feeling) and your deep limbic system (emotional intensity and passion). Their combined stimulation alerts your prefrontal cortex (thinking cortex) that you're having fun! Soon after, dopamine is released, along with oxytocin, vasopressin, and endorphins, all of which reduce stress and bathe your brain in pleasurable chemicals—giving it the type of cognitive vacation it deserves. While playing, enjoy yourself, trusting that your writing brain will respond with greater concentration when you need to get back to work.

RECHARGE YOUR BATTERIES, AS NEEDED

Getting to the final stages of writing a novel (or other work of art) is somewhat akin to getting battle fatigue—you've been at it a long time, struggling with a familiar (though no less demanding) challenge, and your endurance is waning. This is a good time to do things that recharge your brain. Sometimes that means taking an actual vacation or a few days to do something completely unrelated to the work.

It's also a good time to step up your meditation sessions and reward your brain for the hard work it's been doing. Good nutrition and plenty of restful sleep, on a fairly regular schedule, is also good. Working late into the night and disrupting your regular schedule is rarely a good idea, as your brain actually prefers routine. The fastest way to burn out is to push your brain beyond the bounds of reason. Your brain may continue performing for you, but it won't be long before you're not getting optimum brainpower. Best to pamper your brain— give it your best, and it will give you its best, as always.

TRAIN YOUR WRITING BRAIN: CREATE A VISUAL ROAD MAP

Even if you didn't create a visual "road map" when you began, creating one now could add significant momentum for your push to the end. Sketch out what will be happening in the chapters yet to come. If you can draw, literally sketching scenes is a great way to stimulate your brain in a new way (offering it words and pictures to contemplate); but if you don't draw, sketch it in terms of a list (or use note cards) of the remaining scenes: This will happen, which will make this happen, which will make this happen ... and so on, to the end.

PLAY A MOVIE IN YOUR MIND

Also, if you don't draw, you could spend an hour or so envisioning what will happen, as if you were watching a movie of your characters in motion. Imagine who's in the scene, where and when it takes place, what's happening around the characters, what are they doing and saying, etc. This kind of visualization creates a visual road map for your brain. Don't overdo it, unless you're all set to go right from the visualization to writing, in which case, full speed ahead. This is more about playing a movie in your head that gives you a broad view of what's yet to be written.

CHART IT ON A WHITE ERASE BOARD

One way to keep your writing on track is to use a white erase board to plot each scene. One scene at a time, write down the basics: who is in the scene, what happens, what results. This "visual list" helps focus your writing brain on what needs to be written.

REWARD YOUR WRITING BRAIN

Remember that it's important to reward yourself for progress forward—including completion of this exercise. When you write a scene, erase its listing from the board, and do a small celebratory dance. By that I mean actually dance; then do something that helps you feel *good about yourself*, whether it's a fifteen-minute walk through your neighborhood (to say hello to your neighbors) or a pause to savor a glass of your favorite wine. What you are doing is reinforcing your efforts and rewarding your writing brain, which will then reward you by rising to its genius capabilities.

WRITERS ON CRAFT

"What I try to do is write. I may write for two weeks 'the cat sat on the mat, that is that, not a rat.' And it might be just the most boring and awful stuff. But I try. When I'm writing, I write. And then it's as if the muse is convinced that I'm serious and says, 'Okay. Okay. I'll come.'"

—MAYA ANGELOU

"I've never aborted or abandoned anything, perhaps because everything I've written has been well prepared in my mind. I write the complete first draft before returning to the beginning, though of course I'm working from a fairly detailed synopsis, so I'm sure of my overall structure . . . the use of the synopsis reflects, for me, a strong belief in the importance of the *story*, of the objective nature of the invented world I describe, of the complete separation of that world from my own mind."

—J.G. BALLARD

"The writer who cares more about words than about story—characters, action, setting, atmosphere—is unlikely to create a vivid and continuous dream; he gets in his own way too much; in his poetic drunkenness, he can't tell the cart—and its cargo—from the horse."

—JOHN GARDNER

"The refusal to rest content, the willingness to risk excess on behalf of one's obsessions, is what distinguishes artists from entertainers, and what makes some artists adventurers on behalf of us all."

—JOHN UPDIKE

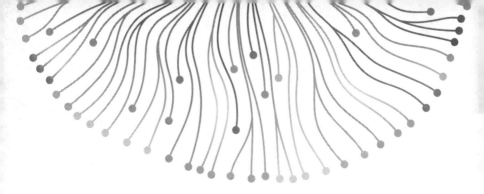

PHASE FIVE

YOUR BRAIN AT THE END

"As I move through the book it becomes more demanding. At the beginning, I have a five-day workweek, and each day is roughly ten to five, with a break for lunch and a nap. At the very end, it's a seven-day week, and it could be a twelve-hour day. Toward the end of a book, the state of composition feels like a complex, chemically altered state that will go away if I don't continue to give it what it needs. What it needs is simply [for me] to write all the time. Downtime other than simply sleeping becomes problematic. I'm always glad to see the back of that."

—WILLIAM GIBSON

CHAPTER 11

REWARD YOUR WRITING BRAIN

Cross the Finish Line

"It's often the case that the most strained moments in books are the very beginning and the very end—the getting in and the getting out. The ending especially: It's awkward, as if the writer doesn't know when the book is over and nervously says it all again. Sometimes the most useful thing you [as an editor] can tell a writer is, 'Here's where the book ends—in these next two and a half pages you're just clearing your throat.'"

—ROBERT GOTTLIEB, EDITOR

The end is in sight and you—*and your brain*—are panicking. Convinced you'll never successfully wrap this up, or that it won't be the satisfying ending you envisioned, or that you will finish and will never have another original thought, you let insecurities smother your flame, bringing work to a halt. Luckily there are ways to soothe your addled brain and bring everything to a cohesive and satisfying close.

VISUALIZE YOURSELF AS SOMEONE WHO FINISHES

As we've discussed throughout, visualization is a powerful tool—if you visualize something hard enough and long enough, your brain will believe it is true, experience it as if it were true. You create your brain's reality, and you determine how your brain views your *self*. If you want to be someone who finishes the book she started, then spend a week's worth of meditation sessions on visualizing yourself as someone who has finished her novel—or finishes a series of novels.

You may, or may not, be old enough to remember *Romancing the Stone*, a charming movie in which Kathleen Turner, a romance novel writer, ends up on a perilous adventure with Michael Douglas. It opens with Kathleen at a typewriter, writing the last few sentences of her latest novel. She narrates the last sentence, and then types "The End." She then lights candles, opens tuna fish for her cat, and a bottle of champagne for herself. It's memorable to writers because anyone who dreams of becoming an author dreams of writing those final scenes going just that smoothly—and privately ending in such a pleasant way.

In fact, a fabulous visualization is to imagine yourself in exactly that situation: *writing the last few sentences*. What would your environment look like? Would you feel a rush of excitement or an overwhelming feeling of relief? Would you weep with joy? What kind of happy dance would you do? Would you have champagne on ice? Who would you call?

When you meditate, create pictures of your scene in your mind's eye and reinforce them with additional meditation sessions. Have fun with it, but do try to feel what the experience would be like for you. The more you can create an experience for your writing brain, the more it will help you fulfill the dream.

Those last two words you'll type are like catnip; once you get a taste of them, the more you will crave them. So use the visualizations as a way to envision you reaching that point and anointing those words—"The End"—with the power to push you forward—rapidly or slowly, but forward nevertheless. The speed with which you arrive is not nearly as important as writing the best closing chapters possible; but you do want to overcome any tendency to linger and instead to push yourself to bring the story full circle. Even if you aren't confident about the ending, it's better to write *something* to avoid stalling. Everyone rewrites, no matter how good he or she thinks they are, or how good he or she is. It's not uncommon to rewrite three to five times—perhaps not the whole novel, but large portions of it will require substantial revision. That's how you make it the best work you can possibly achieve. And each time you rewrite, your writing skills gather strength and clarity.

THINK WITH YOUR BODY

Scientists are studying what they call "embodied cognition." The basic idea is that human intelligence supersedes abstract processing power because it is a result of the interaction between our minds, our bodies, and the environment we live in. Which means that our minds are inherently embodied, thought is mostly unconscious, and abstract concepts are largely metaphorical (i.e., reason is not based on abstract laws because cognition is grounded in bodily experience). Under this theory, metaphors are more than mere language and literary devices, they are conceptual in nature and represented physically in the brain. If you want to goad your brain to race toward the end, try racing around the block, or rapidly jogging in place for ten minutes. The idea is that the physicality of motion will help your writing brain embody your desire to finish, and it will also boost brainpower to the levels needed to do so.

Things You Could Envision and Practice

Remember, if you envision it hard enough and long enough, your brain will assume it's real. Try imagining:

- you at your writing desk feeling satisfied and jubilant about the last scene
- you typing "The End," and then raising your fists in a Rocky-like celebratory manner
- you holding the entire printed manuscript in your hands, clutching it to your chest
- you showing your spouse and children the completed manuscript
- you signing a publisher's contract
- your book on a best-seller list

Some people will make collages, and a favorite is clipping out a copy of best-seller lists and pasting their book at the top of the list. Use your genius to come up with inventive ways to stimulate your writing brain to push on through to the end.

LOCK YOURSELF AWAY

In the fall of 1830, with a novel due in less than six months, Victor Hugo bought an entire bottle of ink and locked himself away, keeping only one, large gray shawl that dragged on the floor to wear (to prevent him from succumbing to urges to leave his room). He finished the book—and used up the entire bottle of ink—weeks before deadline. Reportedly he toyed with titling it *What Came Out of a Bottle of Ink*, but settled instead on *The Hunchback of Notre Dame*. I'm not recommending that you lock yourself away with no wardrobe, but sometimes completing a book requires drastic measures and only you can determine what it will take to push on through to the other side.

PRINT OUT YOUR MANUSCRIPT

Unless you are a writer who has written a book of 80,000 to 100,000 words, you may have no real idea of what a massive effort is involved in completing a novel. Now that we've come this far in the process, and you are about 10,000 words (or less) to completion, I hope you'll have a real appreciation for what you've accomplished—before you even reach "The End."

See It, Touch It, Feel It

One way to psych yourself up for the final push is to print out what you've got so far. Just seeing those paper pages piled up validates for your brain that you've almost written a book. I'm a fan of the cardboard boxes that we used to use to mail manuscripts to agents and publishers, and thus prefer to lodge my printed pages in one; but a stack held together with a large clamp or a rubber band is also fine.

- Admire the beauty of your dedication and effort. Run your hands over the pages; pick them up and hold them; put your hand on them and offer a prayer of thanks (or whatever celebratory gratitude you prefer).
- Feel the joy and pride of accomplishment, because you have, indeed, done something that is hard, that is often discouraging, and that many try and a far fewer succeed.
- Enjoy the moment and use that feeling to fire yourself up to write the closing chapters. If it feels good to be seven-eighths of the way through, imagine how great it's going to feel when a complete first draft is on your desk.

Whatever You Do, Don't Edit

Leaf through the pages, but ignore the temptation to read through them with an editor's eye. You're still not at the editing stage, and it's too easy to redirect your attention to fine-tuning when what you really need to do is to keep writing. If you want to refer back to something, seeing it in print may spur ideas for the closing chapters, but resist all urges to edit—better that you continue writing in a mad heat to the end ... and then edit the entire book. Trust me on this: Do not edit at this stage.

RECOGNIZE AND REWARD YOURSELF

Yes, you have made tremendous progress, and you do deserve a reward, or at least recognition. What you want to do is bring to consciousness your recognition of the hard work you've done to reach this point. Sometimes writers psychologically batter themselves for what they see as a failure to write as well as they think they should or to write faster, tighter, smarter, more successfully (in whatever terms they use to gauge success). We know how to berate ourselves, belittle our efforts, and thrash ourselves for being shortsighted in some regard, but we don't know how to recognize or appreciate our hard work.

A Happy Brain is a Productive Writing Brain

Bringing this appreciation to consciousness reinforces and rewards your brain's efforts. The more you create a pleasurable experience focused on rewarding yourself for the hard work, the more you'll bathe your brain in feel-good neurotransmitters. Remember, a happy brain is a productive brain—one that is motivated to re-create those same feelings and the rewards that come with them.

So, Give Your Writing Brain a Party!

And, no, you don't have to wait until you're 100 percent done. You should also party then, but partying before you write those final chapters can fire up your brain. Besides, getting this far was hard work, and you've both maximized and nurtured your brain along the way, so please pause for acknowledgment and do something fun. It doesn't have to be big, but do something that brings you pleasure, whether it's inviting friends over for dinner, going to a great new restaurant (or your favorite restaurant), or buying yourself a gift.

Mindfully Savor Your Success

Be mindfully aware of how good it feels to have reached this stage, and imagine how that joy will quadruple upon completion of that first draft. Feel the joy in your body and try to sustain that glow as you work your way through the final, closing chapters.

WRITE AN UPDATED BIO

If you haven't written a writer's biography, pause to craft one. Focus on the writing and life experience (relevant to the novel in progress) that's brought you to this point, and add to it the completion of this novel, screenplay, play, or TV script. Be sure to add lots of detail about the various writing talents you possess (and are honing). Write as if it's complete and you are "out there" being successful in the wider world. This is another visualization that reinforces your new status in your brain. Remember, if you dream it, envision it, meditate on it, write it, speak it, and *experience* it, your writing brain will believe that it's true—and then it will help you make it true.

PLAN THE BIG CELEBRATION

Now that you've celebrated being in the final stages of completion, it's time to plan ahead for an even more special way to celebrate completion, the time when you legitimately type "The End." Give some thought to what would feel really celebratory, special, and an appropriate reward. Think about the details you desire—where, when, how, with whom—and take time to fantasize and to research. Remember that it should be something that will feel very rewarding for you and for your lovely brain.

Once you have something definite in mind, do some visualization meditations and envision it happening, step-by-step, detail-by-detail. Remember that your brain will not only experience this as reality and produce all these feel-good chemicals, but it will use this fodder as motivation. When you dangle the carrot of a fun celebration in front of your brain, it wants to make that happen and actually "anticipates" the joyous celebration.

Remember also that the celebration should occur upon completion and not be held off until you've edited the first draft. What you will be doing is rewarding yourself (and your brain) for concluding the process of writing a novel (or screenplay, etc.), for taking a project from conception through completion—for crafting a fully formed and unique work of art. You have every right to feel proud of your accomplishment and to savor the recognition—from yourself and others. It's a major challenge to write a book, and you will have done it.

WRITE IT WRONG IF YOU MUST, JUST WRITE IT

Many writers, as they approach the ending, experience the same sort of paralysis that can accompany writing the opening chapters. Just as the beginning carried a huge responsibility—in creating a storyline, characters, setting, theme, and all the elements that will captivate your readers—the ending, too, presents a daunting task. Your readers expect you to leave them feeling satisfied (inspired, encouraged, justified, and so on), so crafting the ending is not easy and may feel more challenging than getting yourself through the middle. For one thing, it can feel finite. You may even have a small demon on your shoulder that doesn't want you to bring the story to a close and will whisper the reasons why. Or, you may feel as overwhelmed as you did in the beginning.

WHEN YOUR FIRST DRAFT IS COMPLETE, CELEBRATE!

Whew, you've finally written the entire first draft—huge congratulations! Now it is time to print out the manuscript (I did not yet say that it is time to edit). All manuscripts benefit from a "resting period," and I'm referring equally to the author needing a mental rest and the manuscript needing time to germinate. The time spent between completion and editing is best spent celebrating your accomplishment. Remember that you promised your brain you'd reward it in specific ways; and you spent time planning and envisioning the celebration, so if you want to fire up your brain when it comes time to edit, it's important to follow through on your promise.

Too many authors skip this part and shortchange themselves and their brains. They can be too focused, even obsessed, with pushing right on through to editing and submitting to agents and publishers. This equates to burnout and isn't likely to produce your best work. Pause to experience and savor how it feels to have written a complete manuscript, as this is what will ultimately motivate your brain to embrace the tasks ahead, with vigor, with balance, and with inspiration.

REFRESH YOUR WRITING BRAIN

Now that you've wrapped the first draft, it's time to "move that body!" Studies have shown that aerobic exercise (something that gets your heart rate up for an extended period of time) helps build new neurons and connections in the brain that will counteract the effects of stress. People who rarely exercised showed greater stress-related atrophy of the hippocampus (memory retention) compared to those who exercised more. Regular exercise also promotes quality sleep, reduces depression, and boosts self-confidence through the production of endorphins. So now that you've depleted your brain's resources, kick up the exercise a few notches and get it ready for the round of edits to come.

SAVE THE EDITING FOR ANOTHER DAY

Because you've likely been living with the story for months (or years), it's incredibly hard to be objective when assessing its strengths and weaknesses. You're just too emotionally invested, which can lead to blind spots, rigidity, and both overvaluing and undervaluing the final product. Give yourself a period of several weeks or a month to create the kind of distance you need to evaluate with an editor's eye, one that is more objective and sharper at noticing the kind of detailed review every novelist (or screenwriter, scriptwriter, playwright) needs to polish and shine the final manuscript.

Reading the work with a "cold eye" creates the kind of objectivity that will serve you well, as you evaluate how the story works as a whole, how your protagonist and antagonist (and all characters) evolve or devolve as a result of their proactive behavior, and if you have achieved the level of craft required to make this particular story as compelling as possible. If you start evaluating (or editing) too soon, you are far less likely to see what needs to be done; and it's also possible to be too critical of your work.

You need time to feel great about your productivity and possibility, and to shift from a writer to an editor, which requires a different skill set. Imagine how your gears would grind if you downshifted from fourth gear to first gear, or vice versa. Your engine would likely stall, or at least protest in a gruff manner. Give your writing brain time to switch gears, and it will perform magnificently.

So, pat that completed manuscript, press your palms against it, and feel really, really good about having a first draft. Remember also that books are not written; they are rewritten and rewritten and rewritten. When you feel properly objective, it's time to edit.

TRAIN YOUR WRITING BRAIN: PRACTICE WHAT YOU'VE LEARNED

Many writers stall as they approach the end, and that's perfectly understandable; how your book ends is important and nearly as hard to write as the beginning. That being said, please notice (and appreciate) how the actual act of writing has become easier for you and congratulate yourself on all the skills you've honed along the way. Whether you realize it or not, you've grown as a writer, and you have all the brainpower and genius needed to craft the ending.

That being said, if you feel stymied, or find yourself making excuses, it's time to work on motivation again—just as you did early on.

- Clarify your intention in regards to this particular work of art.
- Clear brain space for writing, uncluttering your workspace and your brain.
- Use some sort of ritual to transition from a distracted state to a focused state.
- Set goals for your daily writing, without making them so out of reach that they create stress.
- Meditate on what's holding you back (is it your mindset or the challenge?).
- Determine what you need to move forward, or choose (try) something/anything to get rolling again.
- Use music to alternately soothe and fire up your moods—and your neurons.
- Chase your premature editor/nagging tormentor/demon out of your writing space.
- Make writing a priority and practice writing as a meditation.
- Get words on paper, sans judgment about their worth.

If you've forgotten how these motivational methods can help, Chapter 7 spells out their benefits. To rev up your brain for the challenging task of writing a fantastic ending, go back and take yourself through the process again, replicating what worked and maybe trying things you didn't try on the first go-round. Don't forget about the hand/brain/mind coordination exercise of Kirtan Kriya, which can also focus your brain before editing sessions.

WRITERS ON CRAFT

"Struggling through the work is extremely important—more important to me than publishing it."

—TONI MORRISON

"The great mass of human beings is not acutely selfish. After the age of about thirty, they almost abandon the sense of being individuals at all—and live chiefly for others, or are simply smothered under drudgery. But there is also the minority of gifted, willful people who are determined to live their own lives to the end, and writers belong in this class. Serious writers, I should say, are on the whole more vain and self-centered than journalists, though less interested in money."

—GEORGE ORWELL

"I find that when I'm vulnerable, when I take risks emotionally, when I decide to take an open stance instead of a closed stance, when I offer my hands instead of close them into fists, good things come."

—CHERYL STRAYED

FIRE UP YOUR WRITING BRAIN

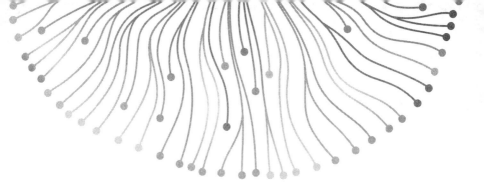

YOUR EDITING BRAIN

"In my experience of writing, you generally start out with some overall idea that you can see fairly clearly, as if you were standing on a dock and looking at a ship on the ocean. At first you can see the entire ship, but then as you begin work you're in the boiler room and you can't see the ship anymore. All you can see are the pipes and the grease and the fittings of the boiler room and, you have to *assume*, the ship's exterior. What you really want in an editor is someone who's still on the dock, who can say, 'Hi, I'm looking at your ship, and it's missing a bow, the front mast is crooked, and it looks to me as if your propellers are going to have to be fixed.'"

—MICHAEL CRICHTON

CHAPTER 12

CALL IN YOUR EXECUTIVE BRAIN

Don Your Editor's Cap

"You need a certain head on your shoulders to edit a novel, and it's not the head of a writer in the thick of it, nor the head of a professional editor who's read it in twelve different versions. It's the head of a smart stranger who picks it off a bookshelf and begins to read. You need to get the head of that smart stranger somehow. You need to forget you ever wrote that book."

—ZADIE SMITH

All writers benefit from the ministrations of an editor. While the writer is the artist, the editor is the mechanic, or the craftsman of the final product. The editor works in tandem with the writer, bringing unique talents and a fresh and more comprehensive perspective.

Few, if any, writers whose work sells to a publisher are not edited. The level of editing required fluctuates, dependent upon the artistry and craft of the writer, but even the most accomplished, most talented, most prolific authors work with an editor who scrutinizes his work. For every great book written, one can rightly assume that a great editor helped the author craft the final version. In fact, when authors begin to think they don't need any editing and rebuff suggestions, their work typically suffers.

Thus two things you can do to vastly improve your chances of being published are to conscientiously edit and rewrite, rewrite, and rewrite. It's one thing to complete a first draft and think you're such a genius that it's ready to go as is, and quite another to complete a first draft and proceed to invest equal time and effort in editing and rewriting until it's as good as you can make it. Lazy writers rarely become professional writers; and editors of all ilk dread working with a writer who thinks all she has to do is spew out words and have the editor, dazzled by her genius, do all the grunt work.

Even if you're lucky enough to be able to hire a professional editor (from whom you can learn how to become a better writer and self-editor), self-editing skills play a significant role in the true crafting of the work. Professional editors (of which I am one) need you to give them your best effort. If the first draft falls far short of the end goal, they won't be able to help you craft something spectacular. Unless you're already a writing genius, a mediocre first draft that is not then revisited is not likely to be published or to gather flattering reviews if published.

TIME FOR THE EDITOR'S CAP

Your editing brain is not the same as your writing brain, which is why you kindly ask the editor to step outside while your more imaginative and spontaneous brain is writing the first draft. You call in the editing brain when you've had a few days, weeks, or months to gain a modicum of emotional and intellectual distance from the first draft. Your more focused, more methodical, detail-oriented brain is better suited to editing than your more creative, spontaneous, emotional brain. One delivers the goods; the other crafts and perfects the goods. The brain you need for editing is your executive brain; so let's discuss how you, as the first editor, can successfully edit and rewrite.

SPEED UP DECISION-MAKING

According to a Princeton University study, making decisions is painful. Paradoxical feelings arise—even when either choice is a winner—and "excite" two brain circuits. Researchers determined that feelings connected with excitement originated from the lower portion of the brain and the prefrontal cortex; those associated with anxiety originated in upper regions (the anterior cingulate cortex seemed to calculate how conflicted the person felt about the choice). These parallel feelings occur because one part of the brain is trying to figure out how difficult the choice is, while the other is evaluating what you're about to receive. The anxiety didn't lessen, even when participants were told that they had nothing to lose; and being given more time to decide didn't elevate anxiety—the pain arose from having to decide at all. This may help explain why bad news often accompanies good news. The higher the level of anxiety in a person's life, the more likely they were to change their minds. Rather than linger in a state of anxiety, make your editing decisions and move on.

VIEW THE WORK MORE OBJECTIVELY

The executive brain is the one you can train to view your work objectively, sans emotion, and prejudgment. Although it seems odd, it's most helpful when you can read and reassess the work with complete objectivity—almost as if someone else wrote it and you are seeing it for the first time. Naturally, that's not an easy thing to do, but doing whatever you can to come close to the level of objectivity is desirable.

READ MORE FICTION

Mirror neurons allow us to experience the emotions of another person, like feeling sad when we see someone—whether it's in real life or in a movie—emoting sadness. Researchers who study the effects of storytelling on the brain have found that people who read a lot of fiction tend to have higher levels of empathy and better social skills than those who don't, probably because they've developed stronger mirror neuron responses.

Wait a While Before Reading Your Book

The best way to achieve this is to wait a while before settling in to edit. Spend time generating new ideas, plotting new books (or screenplays or plays), or writing something else. Why not spend a few weeks composing essays on the writing process you've just experienced for your website? (Yes, you will want a writing website.) Or you could spend a few weeks researching a new topic or doing additional research on the book you're about to edit. The thing is: resist temptation to dive back into crafting the story too soon.

Print a Copy to Read

As we discussed in the previous chapter, printing a copy of your book offers your brain a visual of what those three hundred or so pages look like piled up. It's also a tactile experience, particularly if you love the feel of paper and writing on paper. In addition, studies have found that reading books on the screen is different from viewing them on paper. Reading on paper makes it *stick* longer than reading on the screen. It's even better if you take notes while you read, as you're interpreting it for yourself, and that makes it stick best of all.

READ IT ALOUD

Author Margaret Atwood recommends reading your work aloud as an editing technique, and she says it best: "Black marks on a page are like a musical score. And because those letters on a page are just a score, they don't come to life until they are being played. A score for violin is not actualized until somebody takes up a violin and plays the music. That's when it turns back from paper and ink into music. Pages are like a magic freezing mechanism whereby you take a voice and you put it into a score on a page—it's a score for voice, it always is—and it becomes actualized again when somebody reads it and turns it back into a voice." Reading your work aloud helps you spot the places where your voice and the story's voice are not fully represented on the page. You will hear all kinds of errors your eyes would otherwise glide right over.

Skim Read the First Time Through

To view the work objectively, try to set aside emotions, particularly fear. Release any strictures or precepts (set ideas) that someone else may have told you, and keep the responsibility on this first read-through light. Instead of honing in on details—nitpicking word choice, for example—read the story as you imagine a reader might, with a fresh eye. At least try pretending that you've never seen, or heard, the story; and read through it as fast as you can (skimming or fast reading instead of slow reading). Don't even take notes on the first read-through. What you are seeking is a nonjudgmental feel (an intuitive feel, rather than an emotional feel) for the story and how well you've captured what you wanted to capture.

VIEW THE WORK WITH A CRITICAL EYE

Critical thinking involves analyzing, synthesizing, and evaluating information as a guide to behavior and beliefs—thinking about the way you think. It serves as a way to regulate the way we think by exercising purposeful judgment. We accomplish critical thinking by reasonably considering evidence, contexts, conceptualizations, methods, and criteria. This thinking also involves interpreting, verifying, and reasoning. When editing, consciously choose critical thinking as a way to dig beneath the surface and further strengthen why you wrote it the way you did.

CONDUCT A MACRO-EDIT: FOCUS ON THE WORK AS A WHOLE

After the first general impression read-through, read the work again, but this time, widen your focus to include assessing how each component works within the whole. Basically you're conducting a *macro-edit*, focusing only on the larger components of structure, style, tone, theme, pacing, character arc, and so on.

Use a Checklist

Using the checklist below, see how you're faring on each element. This time read with a pen or pencil in your hand so you can jot down notes. However, we're still talking broad notes, focused on structure, so don't lapse into changing sentences. For example, begin by looking for a three-act structure, noticing how the story ebbs and flows within each act.

- ☐ Does the first act open with a bang in the first ten pages, luring the reader into your lair?
- ☐ Is your main character/protagonist and his situation someone and something a reader will want to follow for three hundred or more pages?
- ☐ Is the protagonist being forced (or about to be forced) to take action to overcome life-changing challenges?
- ☐ Does he have a worthy antagonist or opponent (unique and fascinating in her own way)?
- ☐ Is there enough opposition, emanating within the protagonist or from the antagonist, to create and sustain conflict?
- ☐ Does the first chapter of the first act draw the reader into the story by establishing compelling characters, a gripping storyline, a meaningful setting, theme, tone, and so on?
- ☐ Is the story grounded in a time, place, and situation that are all central to the story?
- ☐ Does the second act (the middle) reflect the growing complexity of the plot?
- ☐ Is character motivation, or what's at risk, sufficient to continue propelling the plot forward?
- ☐ Is your protagonist being constantly challenged?
- ☐ Is the action, tension, and conflict escalating due to what your protagonist and antagonist do or don't do?
- ☐ Is the action causative and causal? This happens, and then this happens as a result of that?
- ☐ Are the stakes becoming higher; is your protagonist in peril?
- ☐ Does enough action, or rising tension, occur in the middle to sustain reader interest?

☐ Is your protagonist rising to the occasion, growing as a result of his actions?

☐ Is your antagonist equally drawn, sufficiently counteractive?

☐ Does the third act quickly build toward a climax?

☐ Is the climax the pinnacle of conflict? Does it change everything for your protagonist?

☐ Does your protagonist prevail, due to his own efforts?

☐ Has your character undergone a life-changing experience or epiphany?

☐ Does the story have a satisfying ending (not necessarily happy or sad, but satisfying)?

Remember, you are building and reinforcing your executive brain's editing skills by gathering information on a macro-level. Soon you'll be honing in and making actual edits, but at this stage, it's more important to conduct a global assessment. Viewing and reviewing your work, as a whole, broadens your perspective and will provide significant insights that your brain will reveal when rewriting.

TRANSPORT YOUR READER

When you create characters, settings, situations, and scenes that really resonate or intrigue readers, you achieve what is called "transportation." Neurologically, the reader is transported from his "real world" into your "fictive world," in which he feels like he is the one hanging on the edge of a cliff about to tumble to his death. When writing a story (whether it's a novel, a poem, a song, a play, or a movie), imagine that you have the capability to dismantle and disintegrate all the particles that make up your reader's reality, and reintegrate or materialize the reader into the world you've created. Write scenes to accommodate the fresh eyes of your transported reader.

Look for Consistency in Style

As you macro-edit, also notice style. Whether you purposefully adopted a particular style or tried to mimic a certain style, you will want to make sure stylistic devices are consistent throughout the book. Begin with these questions:

- Did I achieve a singular, strong voice? Is it consistent throughout the work?
- Is the entire book written in past tense, or did I flip to present tense here and there?
- Is my point of view consistent throughout the book? Did I primarily use first-person narration and occasionally flip to third-person limited point of view or to omniscient point of view (or whatever the case may be)?
- If I switched point of view, did I do so effectively? (General rule of thumb: one point of view per scene; no more than three per chapter.)
- Is the tone of the book consistent? If it changed, was it evident when and, more importantly, why?
- Is the theme fully represented? Is there an evolution, or revolution, of thought?

What you are doing is assessing a deeper layer of the work and determining whether it's effective. Again, this is not the down 'n' dirty stage of editing; this is still a macro-edit. By breaking down the editing process, you are helping your brain take in as much information as possible, which will boost its executive functioning when you begin editing and rewriting. Remember, your executive brain likes input—as much relevant information as possible that relates to the task at hand—and spending time to conduct this broad review can be more helpful than you may realize. Often our creative brain surprises us with genius, and it's important to notice where genius occurs, as well as the places where it falls short.

DEVELOP YOUR INNER MOUSE

A University of Minnesota study found that people who practiced yoga and meditation—at least two times a week, for an hour, for at least a year—were able to move computer cursors using only their minds, faster and better than those who didn't practice yoga and meditation. Over the course of four weeks, in which they wore caps that picked up brain activity, participants tried to move a computer cursor across the screen by imagining (*but not executing*) left- or right-hand movements. *No mouse allowed!* The yoga/meditation people were *twice as likely* to complete the brain-computer interface task by the end of thirty trials, *three times faster* than those in the other group. Researchers noted that the ability to achieve an undistracted mind and to sustain attention likely played a significant role. Time to roll out that yoga mat and spend twenty minutes meditating each day.

PROCEED FROM A MACRO- TO A MICRO-EDIT

Once you've printed, read aloud, and assessed the work from the perspective of a broad overview, it's time to transition from a macro-edit to a micro-edit. This is when you want to focus your brain on paying attention to all the elements that create a work of genius: scenes, pacing, conflict levels, characterization, setting, narrative, dialogue, and so on.

Give Your Brain Directives for the Rewrite

Remember that you're engaging your executive brain (the prefrontal cortex) and want to avoid having your emotional limbic brain barge in. To do this, focus solely on mechanics, reading with a slow, cold eye. Here is some "shorthand" you can jot down in the manuscript to alert your brain to the changes you need to make when it's time to rewrite:

Where there's too much narrative	*Scene needed*
Too much telling	*Show*
Where there's a weak scene	*More conflict, more action, more inner thoughts, more setting, mood (and so on, as needed)*
Mundane dialogue	*Beef up or Delete*

All surface conversation	Add inner thoughts (that reflect inner conflict or motivation or resolution)
Goes on too long	Tighten
Dramatic events not mined	Expand or Dramatize
Doesn't add to story or reveal character	Delete!

In other words, read like an editor, one who is noting what works and doesn't work, what needs additional dramatization or what isn't contributing something vital. You should begin to see the weaknesses, as well as the strengths, in the work and to develop a much clearer idea of what you need to do to make it better. If you insert notes on the pages, you are helping your writing brain knuckle down to make thoughtful revisions when you rewrite.

FOCUS ON EMOTIONS

While you don't want to be manipulative in your storytelling, keep in mind that it's the *emotional experience* the reader covets. When you write scenes, use all the methods you can to help your reader feel the emotion you want him to have—sadness, anger, confusion, mistrust, love, lust, envy, greed, and so on. If you want the reader to hate your character, show him being despicable to someone who doesn't deserve his wrath or to someone he supposedly loves. Show how the fear, anger, fury, and desperation the abused character surely feels in response manifests—via action, not thoughts, wishes, or rumination. The more you draw the reader into the emotional experience, the more the reader will engage, and the more likely he'll want to read your next book—or catch your next film.

REFINE AND REWRITE SCENES

Once you've made your global edits and inserted notes as a road map to rewrite, it's time to focus in on scenes. Strong scenes are crucial to the novel's (screenplay's, play's, etc.) success. To double-check and make sure each scene establishes a particular *situation* (plot point or scene), ask yourself the following questions:

1. *Who* are the characters involved in the situation?
2. *When* and *where* does this event happen?
3. *What* does each want and how does it support or clash with what the other person wants?
4. *What* is the (inner or outer) conflict that takes place during the situation?
5. *What* is the source of tension between the protagonist and antagonist?
6. *What happens* as a result of this conflict?
7. *Why* does this event need to happen?

While the first six will help you set the parameters for scenes, create new scenes, expand existing scenes, and create stronger characters, the last one—*Why?*—is most important. *Why* is important because each scene has to justify its existence. When you review scenes, ask yourself these questions:

- Is there a reason for this scene to exist?
- Does it reveal crucial information about the characters or the plot?
- Does something *meaningful* happen?
- Does it propel the plot forward?
- Does the action challenge your central characters?
- Does it include conflict and rising tension?
- Does it have consequences that determine what comes next?

Scenes can be very short, but they should be structured: with a beginning (an inciting incident), a middle (conflict and rising tension), and an ending (a consequence that leads to what comes next). Keeping scenes around three to five pages is a good idea, unless there's so much potent activity and dialogue that a longer scene is justified. Concentrate on keeping them focused on what's most important, and that will help you pare them down when needed.

Also, in general, it's rarely a good idea to leisurely lead your reader into a scene; it's much more effective to jump right into scenes. Start with the "inciting incident." The best way to jump into a scene is to use potent dialogue or action. Scenes don't have to end with resolution, but they do need to either resolve the immediate situation or stop at a place that creates a logical transition to the next scene (or have a transition at the beginning of the next scene to indicate a new time and place). Remember that it's good to surprise your reader occasionally.

Why Rising Tension Matters

Scientists have also found that rising tension in the storyline is essential to brain participation. Just as with any form of brain engagement, the brain needs ongoing stimulation to continually focus its attention on what's happening. If the brain is bored, it's far more likely to disengage. Also, the points when the heroine is at peril are the points where primal brain responses cause us to *care* about the character, to essentially *feel* her pain. If you make your reader feel the pain your character is experiencing, she will also feel relief and pleasure when all turns out well. It's this fulfilling experience, which may happen unconsciously, that fuels the market for new stories, surprising stories, triumphant stories, and so on.

While you want tension in your story, feeling tension creates cortisol, the brain chemical associated with stress. Fortunately cortisol alerts your brain to pay close attention, as if the events are actually happening and *you* need to take real action. Cortisol baths can be unsettling, of course, but once the character is out of peril (due to the heroic actions he takes to overcome the obstacle), the feeling of relief releases oxytocin to counteract the cortisol, and all balances out again—and the reader experiences a sense of relief and camaraderie with the character.

If the story has a happy ending, it lights up our limbic system, which produces the very pleasurable chemical dopamine that restores our sense of justice, beauty, and harmony. Happy endings make us, well, happy—and optimistic, which is good for your brain.

CREATE INSPIRATIONAL CHARACTERS

Stories encourage growth in terms of opinions, attitudes, beliefs, and the way we typically act and react to situations and people. Characters and events often mirror our reality (or not!), stimulate our imagination (What if this happened to me? Would I respond the same way? What's the hero going to do to save himself, and those he loves?), and stir our empathy (or our disdain!). Character-driven stories help us make sense of situations that may make no sense at all (it's become harder and harder to grasp what's happening in our modern world), and they often "complete us" in terms of identifying values that stir our souls. Think Sally Field in *Norma Rae*, Denzel Washington and Tom Hanks in *Philadelphia*, Tom Cruise in *A Few Good Men*, and so on. Use your writing genius to create characters whose actions stimulate your readers' brains.

Why Character Identification Matters

Scientists have found that *character-driven* stories tend to create more oxytocin in the brain. They theorize that the pleasing "chemical bath" both reflects and generates a sense of identification—she's just like me!—and thereby engages empathetic feelings. Oxytocin also creates a sense of bonding—both in real life, between parents and children, and romantic partners—as well as with fictional characters. If there is oxytocin, there is a sense of emotional connection. We begin to care deeply about what happens to the characters, and if the story is gripping enough, we'll read long into the cold, dark night, worried about their fate and hoping for their triumph—or their demise, in the case of dastardly villains.

On the flip side, some studies have found that oxytocin also serves us in identifying and remembering enemies, by triggering an important signaling molecule, known as extracellular signal-regulated kinases (ERK). Once activated, ERK lights up your brain for six hours and appears to stimulate the brain's fear pathways, many of which pass through the lateral septum, a region of the brain that processes emotional and stress responses. In these cases, oxytocin seems to intensify fear and to imprint memory of the event (or person) that caused the pain.

So what does this mean for your writing? It means that when you need to amp up the scenes involving love, you could increase your oxytocin levels by watching romantic movies; and when you need to fire up action scenes, in which the hero's life is in danger, you could boost your "vigilant" oxytocin by watching movies in which villains wreak havoc.

AVOID OVERWRITING

Overwriting refers to being exceptionally wordy, incorporating excessive detail, too much repetition, an overwrought or exaggerated narrative (or dialogue), and stilted or overworked sentence structure. Some overwriting occurs when an author is trying to sound "intellectual" or academic, but most overwriting results from a lack of editing skills. The more you learn of the basics, the better you will become at editing—if you invest time and energy and look at your work with a critical eye for improvement. Overwriting is often, quite simply, lazy writing or lackadaisical editing.

REFINE AND REWRITE DIALOGUE

Dialogue is a crucial element of any novel, screenplay, or play. Dialogue should always be interesting, revealing, potent, focused, and, occasionally, at least somewhat unique to your character. It's one of the most potent tools you'll use to reveal crucial information. You can almost always strike out any pleasantries (greetings, farewells) or everyday, ordinary conversations about nothing of importance (like what someone is ordering for dinner).

You've probably heard that dialogue needs to be "realistic," but that's not precisely true because most of what people say in real life isn't sharply focused or dramatic (except on rare occasions). It's the author's task to *craft* dialogue, focusing on what's important within the conversation, choosing an interesting, revealing, or confrontational way for the characters to say it, and deleting whatever feels ordinary or boring. In other words, it should be realistic—but exceptional—specific to story or character development.

A lot of the underpinnings regarding conflict and the particularities regarding character are revealed in dialogue. As a reminder, dialogue should do at least one of four things (and preferably more than one of these things at the same time):

1. Reveal character
2. Convey important information
3. Create, sustain, escalate or resolve tension between characters
4. Move the plot forward

Make sure your dialogue is not too pedantic. Work on making it more potent, more revealing, and more individualistic. While steadfast rules don't exist in creative writing, here are a few tips that will help you refine dialogue:

- Avoid introductions: Cut right to the essential information.
- Avoid standard greetings: No hellos and goodbyes, unless something exceptional occurs.
- Avoid ordinary exchanges (chitchat about weather or anything that isn't important to the plot or character): Dialogue needs to be potent and focused, as noted above.
- Avoid dialect and shortened words. Clipped words or dialect can be used in dialogue, but keep them minimal and necessary.

As you edit and rewrite, focusing intently on scenes and dialogue will help you craft your best work possible.

USING PROVEN NEUROSCIENCE TO REVIEW, REFINE, AND REWRITE

A French research team found that action words (kicked, stomped, raced) fired up the motor cortex, which governs how the body moves. Even more specific, describing body parts, such as an arm or leg, activated the part of the brain that controls arm and leg movement. Using evocative language also woke up the hippocampus, which would in turn activate long-term memories and play a significant role in how a reader's mind turned language into meaningful experience. These are the kinds of effects those who write novels, memoirs, screenplays, plays, songs, and so on wish to have on their readers. The primary goal is to establish identification, achieve a textural layering, and evoke emotion.

So how do you use this knowledge? As you review, refine, and rewrite, be sure to accomplish the following:

- **CREATE FULLY ENVISIONED SCENES:** Draw readers into the setting, establishing a mood, and using sensual (sight, smell, sound, taste, touch) descriptions that will engage the sensory and motor processing areas of the reader's brain. If you craft the scene vividly enough, the reader will feel like he's there—and that's what you want to happen.

- **CREATE MEMORABLE CHARACTERS:** Creating characters that are unique (unforgettable) and also familiar (someone your readers might know) increases the appeal of your story because reading about them will stimulate empathy and all the *feel-good* brain chemicals—like oxytocin and dopamine—that come along with feeling sympathetically toward someone else. You want someone your reader will either love or hate, someone they'll root for or against, someone they'd long to be or be thankful they aren't. If you write about someone who is boring (unless you do so cleverly), your reader is likely to lose interest early on and stop reading. Make your characters a lightning rod for positive or negative feelings; someone your reader wants to follow around and can't stop *watching*.

- **GIVE THEM LOTS OF COMPLICATIONS:** To sustain interest, your main characters should be challenged throughout the story. No one wants to read about a character who never does anything interesting. To keep your readers' brains engaged, throw a curveball at your characters every chance you get. Make it a habit to ask: *How can I make this even harder for her?* Make your characters fight for what they want or need, and make the path littered with all sorts of complications. And then make sure the resolution comes from within the protagonist (or antagonist) and never from coincidence (or deus ex machina) or the simple passage of time. Your hero needs to be a conqueror.

- **MAKE DETAILS SPECIFIC:** When describing a character, a setting, or an event, the more specific the details, the more your reader can picture it in her brain. If you just say, "Spain's premier race car driver sped a white Porsche through its paces," it's not likely to awaken a reader's brain the same way the following will: "Spain's premier race car driver throttled a brand-new white Porsche with scary aplomb, at speeds that left it careening around curves, the red and purple stripes blurring, reminding onlookers of his recent near-death experience." See how the use of detail creates a visual for readers and thereby perks up their brains?

- **USE ACTIVE VERBS THAT CREATE VIVID IMAGES:** This is a common writing suggestion, and neuroscience is proving that it's sound advice. Passive writing and nondescript, static verbs put your reader's brain to sleep. If you want your reader's cortex to light up (and you do), use power-packed, precise action verbs. Studies have shown that imagining you are doing something triggers the same neuronal responses that are triggered when you actually do that thing, and the same goes for readers. Give their brains vivid images of events unfolding, as they happen, and their brains will respond in kind.

- **USE SENSUAL WORDS:** Using the five senses, plus variant senses such as hunger, thirst, itch, muscle tension, equilibrium, heat, and pain, draws the reader deeper into the story. As we've discussed, smell is one of the senses writers may not think about as much, but it's one of the most powerful of faculties when it comes to evoking memories and thereby encouraging empathy for your characters.

- **GIVE THEM A SATISFYING ENDING:** Readers want to feel something at the end of a novel (play, screenplay). The ending is the emotional payoff, and whether it's happy or sad or somewhere in between, it should feel satisfying. Contrivances tend to offend readers, while well-thought, appropriate endings tend to lure readers into reading your next book.

Once you've fine-tuned your manuscript and made editing notes for your writing brain to follow, it's time to rewrite.

REWRITE, REWRITE, REWRITE

"Books aren't written—they're rewritten. Including your own. It is one of the hardest things to accept, especially after the seventh rewrite hasn't quite done it," says best-selling author Michael Crichton.

As an author, editor, and a book doctor, I often offer this quote as a reality check for novice writers, many of whom don't see the point in heavily rewriting or rewriting more than once. But writing genius often comes long after the original writer has labored over rewrites and then benefited from the help of a publishing house editor to rewrite again.

Now that you've programmed your brain to become a writing genius, produced a complete manuscript, and mapped out an editing plan for your brain, you are ready to be the first highly skilled editor of your work. All you have to do is put those same methods to work in rewriting—and keep slogging forward until you feel that you've done the best work possible. That's when you solicit agents and editors—not before. In a market in which standards and competition are higher than ever, agents and editors expect writers to submit exceptional work— to be writing geniuses. Once you get through those doors, they will help you refine your manuscript further, but they'll never unlatch the door if you don't offer truly professional, stunning manuscripts. Don't worry, you are fully capable of doing so. Program, nourish, and take full advantage of your brain to develop the writing genius that will get you to the top of an agent's submissions pile.

GEAR UP FOR MARKETING

Now, as you prepare to transition from editing to promoting your book, it can be helpful to utilize everything we've discussed in this book—particularly in regards to this specific work. One way to get absolutely clear that you've written the best version of your story (and to prep for selling and promoting) is to have a conversation with your creative genius.

TRAIN YOUR WRITING BRAIN: INTERVIEW YOURSELF

The New York Times runs a weekly feature called "By the Book." The interview questions are the same each week, and what makes it fascinating is seeing how author personalities and preferences are revealed, how unique and fascinating each author can be, and how much people value the written word. If you're lucky, once your book is published, all sorts of press—from old-fashioned newspapers to modern blogs and vlogs (video blogs)—will clamor to interview you. Often with new writers, this is not the case and you have to generate publicity and solicit those blogs and vlogs on your own. In that case, being prepared to drum up interest really helps.

To further absorb your new status as someone who has *nearly* penned a published manuscript (screenplay, play), take an hour or so to answer questions a sophisticated interviewer might ask, and don't be flip about it—give the exercise its due. What you are doing is training your mind to accept that you are now part of a unique and distinguished group known as published authors (playwrights, screenwriters); and all published authors have to be able to talk intelligently about their work. Consider this exercise preparation for those occasions (and also a great way to spot loose ends, while there's still time to fix them).

TIP: Use a recorder to tape yourself answering questions that a magazine might ask, such as:

- How would you categorize the work? Be global and specific: genre, style, time period, character driven versus plot driven, pessimistic or optimistic, and so on. Is it similar to other novels, a blending of two genres, the antithesis of someone else's work (or your previous work)?
- What is the central theme, dilemma, and plotline of your story? This is widely known as the "elevator pitch"—something you could say in a short elevator ride that would interest an agent or editor (and eventually readers) in your story. Narrowing this down bolsters clarity in regards to discussing your work *and* what you may yet need to accomplish in the rewrite.

- Why this particular subject? What fascinated you enough to write a novel (play, screenplay) about it? Again, you should be well versed on the topic of your story, and capable of explaining why your work is artistic and will hold vast appeal.
- What is the underlying theme or concept? This should be the defining principle of your work—what you most wanted to illustrate.
- What drove you to write this *particular* book?
- What are your protagonist's strengths and weaknesses? What makes her unique and particularly interesting?
- What is the primary journey she embarks upon?
- Who are the other major players in the book, and why are they important?
- What are the five most important scenes in the book? (Note that an interviewer isn't likely to ask these sort of "five" questions, but they are helpful in getting really comfortable talking about the most important elements of your story.)
- What's most important for us to know about your protagonist?
- What are the five things your protagonist has to overcome or master?
- What's most important for us to know about your antagonist?
- What are five ways the antagonist creates mischief or puts your protagonist in peril?
- How does your protagonist grow as a result of her adventures?
- What conclusion can we draw at the end of the book?

Now that you've come up with intelligent answers to these questions, use the answers to make any final adjustments to the manuscript—before you send it to the marketplace.

WRITERS ON CRAFT

"Well, my wife took a look at the first version of something I was doing not long ago and said, 'Goddamn it, Thurber, that's high school stuff.' I have to tell her to wait until the seventh draft, it'll work out all right. I don't know why that should be so, that the first or second draft of everything I write reads as if it was turned out by a charwoman."

—JAMES THURBER

"There is a difference between a book of two hundred pages from the very beginning and a book of two hundred pages which is the result of an original eight hundred pages. The six hundred are there. Only you don't see them."

—ELIE WIESEL

"There are days when the result is so bad that no fewer than five revisions are required. In contrast, when I'm greatly inspired, only four revisions are needed."

—JOHN KENNETH GALBRAITH

"My first draft is always way too long; my books start out with delusions of *War and Peace*—and must be gently disabused. My editor is brilliant at taking me to the point where I do all the necessary cutting on my own. I like to say she's a midwife rather than a surgeon."

—JULIA GLASS

"Artistry is important. Skill, hard work, rewriting, editing, and careful, careful craft: All of these are necessary. These are what separate the beginners from experienced artists."

—SARAH KAY

"It took me fifteen years to discover that I had no talent for writing, but I couldn't give it up because by that time I was too famous."

—ROBERT CHARLES BENCHLEY

APPENDIX

As promised, here's a list of writing books (classics and otherwise) and other resource books that have proven particularly helpful. You can order them digitally online for instant gratification, if you prefer.

Inspirational

Becoming a Writer, Dorothea Brande
Letters to a Young Poet, Rainer Maria Rilke
One Writer's Beginnings, Eudora Welty
The Writing Life, Annie Dillard (Also, *Pilgrim at Tinker Creek*)
Bird by Bird: Some Instructions on Writing and Life, Anne Lamott
      (one of my essentials)
Writing Down the Bones: Freeing the Writer Within, Natalie Goldberg
On Becoming a Novelist, John Gardner
Zen in the Art of Writing: Essays on Creativity, Ray Bradbury
On Writing: 10th Anniversary Edition: A Memoir of the Craft,
      Stephen King

Books on Craft (from Older to More Recent)

Aspects of the Novel, E.M. Forster
The Art of Fiction, Notes on Craft for Young Writers, John Gardner
The Writing of Fiction, Edith Wharton
How Fiction Works, James Wood
How to Write a Damn Good Novel: A Step-by-Step No Nonsense
      Guide to Dramatic Storytelling, James Frey
How to Write a Damn Good Novel II: Advanced Techniques for
      Dramatic Storytelling, James Frey
Telling Lies for Fun & Profit, Lawrence Block
Writing Fiction: A Guide to Narrative Craft (9th Edition),
      Janet Burroway, Elizabeth Stuckey-French, and Ned
      Stuckey-French

Learning to Write from the Masters, Barnaby Conrad (Santa Barbara
    Writers Conference)
*The Complete Handbook of Novel Writing: Everything You Need
    to Know about Creating and Selling Your Work*, Writer's
    Digest Books
*Writing Fiction: The Practical Guide from New York's Acclaimed
    Creative Writing School* (Gotham Writers' Workshop)
The Making of Story: A Norton Guide to Creative Writing
Write Away, One Novelist's Approach to Fiction and the Writing Life,
    Elizabeth George

Specialized Approaches
The Art of the Novel, Milan Kundera
The Art of Dramatic Writing, Lajos Egri
*Stein on Writing: A Master Editor of Some of the Most Successful
Writers of Our Century Shares His Craft Techniques*, Sol Stein
    (an editor's point of view)
The Hero's Journey, Joseph Campbell (a bible for story structure/
    character arcs)
The Writer's Journey: Mythic Structure for Writers, Christopher Vogler
Creating Unforgettable Characters, Linda Seger
The Situation and The Story, Vivian Gornick
Plot Perfect: How to Build Unforgettable Stories Scene by Scene,
    Paula Munier
Writing the Breakout Novel, Donald Maass
13 Ways of Looking at the Novel, Jane Smiley

Nonfiction
*On Writing Well, 30th Anniversary Edition: The Classic Guide to
    Writing Nonfiction*, William Zinsser
*Telling True Stories: A Nonfiction Writers' Guide from the Nieman
    Foundation at Harvard University*, Mark Kramer and
    Wendy Call
Writing About Your Life: A Journey into the Past, William Zinsser
    (Memoir)

The Elements of Narrative Nonfiction: How to Write & Sell the Novel of True Events, Peter Rubie

Playwriting
The Art & Craft of Playwriting, Jeffrey Hatcher
The Playwright's Guidebook: An Insightful Primer on the Art of Dramatic Writing, Stuart Spencer

Screenwriting
Screenplay: The Foundations of Screenwriting, Syd Field
Story: Substance, Structure, Style and the Principles of Screenwriting, Robert McKee
Making a Good Script Great, Linda Seger
On Directing Film, David Mamet

Resources for all Sorts of Things
The Artist's Way, Julia Cameron (Also, *The Vein of Gold*, and others)
The Original Folk and Fairy Tales of Grimm Brothers
The Uses of Enchantment: The Meaning and Importance of Fairy Tales, Bruno Bettelheim
Shadow and Evil in Fairy Tales, Marie-Louise Von Franz
The Maiden King: The Reunion of Masculine and Feminine, Marion Woodman and Robert Bly (Almost anything by Marion Woodman or Robert Bly)
She (or *He* or *We*, or anything written by) Robert Johnson
Meeting the Shadow: The Hidden Power of the Dark Side of Human Nature, Connie Zweig
Gods in Every Man, Jean Shinoda Bolen
Women Who Run with the Wolves, Clarissa Pinkola Estés
The Synonym Finder, J.I. Rodale
A Natural History of the Senses, Diane Ackerman

And finally, here's one of my new favorites, from Jeff VanderMeer, author of *The Steam Punk Bible*, because it's incredibly fresh, unique, and uses imagery in fantastically creative ways: *Wonderbook: The Illustrated Guild to Creating Imaginative Fiction*. It will wake up your senses and rattle your brain!

INDEX

absurdity, 213–14

active sitting, 169–70

affirmations, 34, 42, 111, 203–4

agility, mental, 56

Allende, Isabelle, 90

alone time, 193–94

analysis, 56

Angelou, Maya, 221

antagonist, 102, 103–4, 210

anticipation, 95

anxiety, 195–96

art, 175–77

artist date, 100–101

attention, 92, 183

   selective, 160–62

attention, cognitive, 21

Atwood, Margaret, 29, 239

backstory, 106

Ballard, J. G., 221

Barthelme, Donald, 90

basher style, 56–57

beginning, story, 109–57

Benchley, Robert Charles, 256

Berlin, Isaiah, 52–53

Bettelheim, Bruno, 114

"big picture" elements, 103

biography, writer's, 228–29

blending, conceptual, 68

blogging, 17

Bloom, Harold, 72

bottom brain style, 53–54

Bradbury, Ray, 43, 77–78, 108, 131, 205

brain. *See also* writing brain

   basic facts about, 9–12

   clearing space for writing, 135–36

   executive, 236–56

   health, 23–24

   how it writes, 14–15

   ingenuity of, 91–96

   inspiring, 212–14

   maximizing organizational skills, 120–22

   and music, 147–52

   refreshing, 230–31

   rewarding, 126–27

   sculpting, 29–30

   stimulating, 23

   templates, 87–89

brainstorming, 91–108, 208–9

   tools, 100–101

breaks, 175–77, 200, 218–19

burnout, 196–98

Burns, Gregory, 74

Cameron, Julia, 100–101

causality, bidirectional, 55

celebration. *See* rewards

character arc, 103, 114–15

characters, 102, 103–4, 210, 247–49, 251

   visualizing, 116–18

FIRE UP YOUR WRITING BRAIN

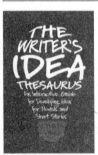